*T*eaching with the Internet:

Lessons from the Classroom

Teaching with the Internet: Lessons from the Classroom

Donald J. Leu, Jr. and Deborah Diadiun Leu
Syracuse University

with the assistance of Katherine R. Leu
George Washington University

Christopher-Gordon Publishers, Inc.
Norwood, Massachusetts

Disclaimer

We have devoted much time and energy to providing accurate and current information in this book. Nevertheless, in an environment as constantly changing as the Internet, it is inevitable that some of the factual information provided here will also change. Information provided at one location may move to another, sometimes without any indication that it has moved. The authors and the publishers assume no responsibility for errors or omissions. Moreover, the authors and publisher assume no liability for any damages resulting from the use of any information identified in this book or from links listed at sites that are described. As we indicate in this book, the best way to protect children from viewing inappropriate sites or receiving inappropriate messages is to implement a sound acceptable use policy and to carefully monitor student use of the Internet in your classroom and at school.

Christopher-Gordon Publishers, Inc.
480 Washington Street
Norwood, MA 02062

Printed in the United States of America

10 9 8 7 6 5 4 3 2 1   02 01 00 99 98 98 97

ISBN: 0-926842-59-5

Credits

Every effort has been made to contact copyright holders for permission to reproduce borrowed material where necessary.
We apologize for any oversights and would be happt to rectify them in future printings.
All electronic mail was reprinted with the permission of the author.

Chapter 1

Virtual Whales Web-Site reprinted with the permission of Fred Sharpe, David Cowperthwaite, Micheal Coyle, and Darius Garncarz.
Weather Here and There Web-Site reprinted with the permission of the National Center for Supercomputing Applications at the University of Illinois.
Pi Mathematics Web-Site reprinted with the permission of Georgette Moore and Betty A. Ganas.

Chapter 2

Netscape Communications, the Netscape Communications logo, Netscape and Netscape Navigator are trademarks of Netscape Communications Corporation.
Arctic Circle Web-Site reprinted with the permission of Norman Chance.

Chapter 4

Teachnet Web-Site reprinted with the permission of Impact II - The Teachers Network.
Interactive Paleontology - PaleoPals Web-Site reprinted with the permission of the University of California Museum of Paleontology and The Regents of The University of California.
Yahooligans is registered trademark used with permission.

Chapter 5

Telecollaborative Learning Around the World Web-Site reprinted with the permission of Nancy K. Schubert.
The Children's Literature Web-Guide reprinted with the permission of David K. Brown.

Chapter 6

The World of Benjamin Franklin Web-Site reprinted with the permission of The Franklin Institute Science Museum, Philadelphia, Pennsylvania.
The Mad Scientist Web-Site used with the permission of Dr. Keith A. McGuinness and The MAD Scientist Network (Washington University Medical School in St. Louis).

Chapter 8

A Fractals Lesson Web-Site reprinted with the permission of Cynthia Lanius.
Brain Teasers on Houghton-Mifflin Education Place. http://www.eduplace.com/math/brain/ © Houghton Mifflin Company.

Chapter 9

Carlos' Coloring Book Web-Site used with the permission of Carlos Pero.
Koala Trouble is an Alex's Scribbles On-Line Production.
The Nanoworld Image Gallery Web-Site reprinted with the permission of The Center for Microscopy and Microanalysis, The University of Queensland.
The Mind's Eye Monster Exchange Project Web-Site designed by Brian Maguire <maguireb@norwich.net>.

Chapter 11

LifeLong Universe - Monster Math Web-Site reprinted with the permission of LifeLong Software at <http://www.lifelong.com/>.

Chapter 12

All classroom web-sites used with permission.

To our parents:
Rose, Anne, Don, and Dan.

Our first teachers, our best teachers

Contents

*P*reface

We wrote this book to give you ideas about how to effectively integrate the Internet into your classroom. The Internet is fundamentally changing the nature of classroom instruction, enhancing children's opportunities to learn about the world around them. We show how this is being done right now by teachers throughout the world.

Several assumptions have guided our work. First, we believe the active role you play in orchestrating experiences with the Internet will determine the extent to which your students gain from this resource. Students left entirely on their own to "surf" the Internet will waste much time and learn little from their experiences. Students who are guided in their explorations of the Internet by a knowledgeable and thoughtful teacher will understand the world in new and powerful ways. We share useful ideas about how to guide students in these explorations.

Second, we assume that understanding an information environment that is as powerful, complex, and constantly changing as the Internet requires us to learn from one another; socially-mediated learning is central to success with the Internet. Our writing is guided by this assumption in several ways. We begin each chapter with a story of a teacher using the Internet in the classroom and then discuss the lessons each of us can learn from this experience. We also include over twenty-five e-mail messages to you from teachers around the world, describing the lessons they have learned from their work with the Internet. Finally, many chapters provide listservs and newsgroups to put you in touch with other teachers facing the same challenges that you face. We all learn from one another in this new electronic environment. We hope to support this learning so that you and your students may benefit.

The classroom episodes that begin each chapter were developed from multiple sources: e-mail messages from teachers using the Internet in their classrooms, descriptions of Internet experiences posted on various listservs, ideas posted by teachers at Internet Project sites, classroom observations, and our own experiences as teachers. Each story represents a fusion from multiple sources; no story represents a single teacher's experiences. We feel, however, that each story faithfully represents the many outstanding classrooms we have encountered in our travels on the Internet.

We could not have completed a complex project like this without the assistance of many individuals. To each, we are indebted. We would like to thank as many of them as possible. Many teachers shared their experiences with the Internet, providing us with important insights that appear in this book. These include teachers from across the United States as well as Argentina, Australia, Canada, Ecuador, Japan, Germany, Great Britain, the Netherlands, and New Zealand. Most are known to us only through their insightful e-mail messages and the descriptions they shared of their classes. We hope someday to have the opportunity to actually meet each teacher and personally express our gratitude for their important contributions. For now, we wish to recognize as many of these outstanding teachers as possible. We apologize for any omissions. We especially wish to thank Carol Allen, Karen Auffhammer, Mary Lou Balcom, Jan Barth, Lisa Brayton, Emily Buchanan, Barb Colson, Gary Cressman, Doug Crosby, Kim Dungey, Ricky Eades, Bill Farrell, Judy Fasanello, Lynn Gatchell, Terrie Gray, Carol Greenwood, Rina Hallock, Kathy Kincheloe, Roxanne Lake, Brian Maguire, Angeles Maitland Heriot, Linda Hubbard, Jeanette Kenyon, Tim Lauer, Richard Love, Gerald Martin, Barbara McInerney, Janet Michalesen, Jodi Moore, Ruth Musgrave, Anne Nguyen, Beverley Powell, Jeff Scanlan, Sandi Sibe, Robert Townsend, and Nicola Yelland. Each is an outstanding educator; each contributes in important ways to our increasingly global community.

Our reviewers also contributed many helpful ideas as we worked through the early stages of this project. They include Phil Loseby of Dzantik'i Heeni Middle School in Juneau, Alaska; Mary Lou

Balcom and Jonathan Dinkin of Edward Smith Elementary School in Syracuse, New York; and Susan Hixson of Tempe Elementary District #3 in Tempe, Arizona. Each of our reviewers is an exemplary teacher and was gracious enough to respond to our ideas with the wisdom gathered from many years of classroom experience.

We are also thankful to the many students and colleagues at Syracuse University who provided us with useful ideas as we shared early drafts with them. Joan Simonetta and Carol Baxter assisted with important aspects of communication and production. Karen Auffhammer and Mary Cunningham provided valuable assistance in checking the accuracy of addresses for each web site.

Dr. Michael Hillinger of LexIcon provided important initial feedback about central ideas in this book. He has also been a valued colleague over the years as we have explored issues in electronic learning together.

Lynne Schueler of OutSide Services assisted in important ways to the final stages of this project. Her work in typesetting and layout can be seen on each page. We greatly appreciate her many contributions.

We especially wish to thank our good friends at Christopher-Gordon Publishers, Inc., without whom this book could not have been completed: Hiram Howard, Susanne Canavan, and Jacob Schulz. Hiram and Susanne shared our enthusiasm for this project at the beginning and gave us the freedom to complete it in the way we envisioned it. They also picked up our spirits at several important points with their kind deeds and words. Jacob managed to obtain all of the many permissions required in this project and assisted in many other aspects of production. The literary allusions in his e-mail messages always kept us smiling. Authors could not ask for a more considerate and helpful publisher.

Finally, a special word of thanks is due our two daughters. Without the assistance of Caity, we could not have completed this book in a timely fashion. She contacted teachers around the world for us and also identified many of the sites on the web that we use in this book. She also made several important suggestions at critical times. We greatly appreciate her many contributions. We also thank Sarah, who was gracious enough to put up with the rest of her family during a very busy and hectic period.

To everyone, our deepest thanks!

Don and Debbie Leu
Manlius, New York

Section I

Welcome to the Internet: Getting Acquainted

Chapter 1
Welcome to the Internet

To: Our readers
From: djleu@sued.syr.edu (Don Leu),
    ddleu@syr.edu (Debbie Leu)
Subject: Welcome!

   Hi! Welcome to the world of teaching and learning with the
Internet! Using the Internet creates many new opportunities to
expand your students' learning. It also presents new opportunities for you as a teacher. This chapter will introduce you to the
Internet and show you some of the wonderful resources available
for you and your students. By thinking carefully about how to use
the Internet in your classroom, your students will be better
prepared for the future that awaits them.
   The approach in this book is to show you how teachers and
students use the Internet in their classrooms and then discuss
the lessons we can learn from these experiences. We believe that
the best teacher is another teacher or another student. Learning
from one another is essential to success on the Internet; this is
a central assumption of this book.
   Throughout the book, we will emphasize effective teaching
practices while limiting the technical discussion of the Internet
to basic essentials. As you use the Internet in your classroom,
drop us an e-mail message and let us know how you and your students are doing! We'd love to hear from you.

Don and Debbie

It's Monday morning. Sarah and Sha'Quann are at their classroom computer, which is linked to the Internet. Ms. Tobias has her fourth-grade class working on a thematic unit about whales. The unit integrates activities in math, science, social studies, reading, writing, speaking, and listening. Sarah and Sha'Quann are working with a group studying humpback whales. The other members of their group are looking over some new books from the library that Ms. Tobias has placed in another corner of her classroom.

This is the first year Ms. Tobias has had an Internet connection in her classroom. One of the first lessons she learned was that students often spend their limited time at the computer just "surfing" for information on the World Wide Web (WWW) of the Internet, moving quickly from site to site trying to find something interesting. Often her students' time at the computer would run out before they had an opportunity to really read and learn anything about their topic. To save time during the whale unit, Ms. Tobias set the computer to open to a thematic unit about whales as soon as they connected to the Internet. This outstanding unit (Whales: A Thematic Web Unit—http://curry.edschool.Virginia.EDU/go/Whales/Contents.HTML) had been developed by a group at the University of Virginia. Here, students could find all kinds of wonderful resources about whales.

Ms. Tobias also learned a second lesson very quickly—her students often taught one another about the Internet faster than she could teach them. After teaching the entire class some basic essentials about the computer and Internet use, Ms. Tobias looked for ways to encourage students to share information. Among other strategies, she set aside a portion of her bulletin board next to the computer for students to post messages about useful sites and to share other information about their work on the World Wide Web. She quickly saw the potential of this activity for building a supportive classroom community and for connecting reading and writing. Some students even used the word processor on the computer to type these notes, so word processing skills were developed, too.

"Cool," said Sarah. She had just located a site on the Internet using an address someone had posted on the bulletin board. The site was called Virtual Whales. (See Figure 1-1). At this location on the Internet, Sarah and Sha'Quann read about the feeding behavior of humpbacks and watched a video of a pack during a feeding lunge (http://fas.sfu.ca/cs/research/projects/Whales/). Then they read about the unique feeding behavior used by humpbacks and watched the simulation of how these whales herded herring into tight schools for feeding. They also heard the sounds used by humpbacks to communicate with each other as they fed. It was a powerful learning experience.

"Look at this!" Sha'Quann pointed to another site (http://unite.ukans.edu/UNITEResource/783750390-447DED81.rsrc) where they could download software containing an extensive set of facts on every known species of great whales.

"That's phat," Sarah said, and they downloaded a copy of this from the Internet onto their classroom computer for their group to use in their research. The other members of their group came over and used this program to find information for their group project. At the end of the session, Sarah and Sha'Quann posted a short note on the bulletin board next to the computer. It said:

> Are you loking for informashon about your whale? We put a grat program on the computer. It is in Whales Unit. It is called Whales of the World. Check it out!

> Sarah and Sha'Quann

Lessons from the Classroom

This short episode illustrates a number of important lessons about using the Internet in your classroom, lessons that will guide us throughout this book. First, it illustrates how resources available to students on the Internet may be used in your classroom to support learning. Reading about the unique feeding behavior of humpbacks and then viewing a short video and animation made this information come alive for Sarah and Sha'Quann. They talked about it all day with other students and even shared this information at home. And, of course, they included this information in their group presentation. Throughout this book you will find other sites on the Internet that are just as powerful for supporting your students' learning.

Figure 1-1.   The Home page of Virtual Whales on the World Wide Web of the Internet
(http://www.sfu.ca/cs/research/projects/Whales/)

The episode also illustrates how an insightful teacher can efficiently direct students to information and help them avoid endless "surfing" to find useful sites. By setting the computer to open to this unit on whales, Ms. Tobias made a number of resources immediately available to students. We will describe additional techniques to help students use their limited time wisely.

In addition, the episode shows how the Internet can be easily integrated into your current classroom activities. We will show you how Internet resources may be used with any of your current teaching practices: writing process activities, author chair experiences, thematic units, cooperative learning groups, response journals, jigsaw grouping, K-W-L, and learning workshops, among others. Many of the examples we use will show you how teachers use Internet resources within an integrated, project-based curriculum. Other instructional models may also be used with Internet resources.

Finally, the episode shows how Ms. Tobias's planning encouraged her students to help one another as they searched for information. Social learning opportunities abound in these rich information resources and Ms. Tobias developed several ways for students to support one another as they worked on the Internet. The bulletin board told others where useful information was located on the WWW. In addition, Sarah and Sha'Quann found a resource others could use and downloaded this onto the class computer, telling others about it on the bulletin board. Ms. Tobias had encouraged all of the students to do this when they came across something they thought others might be able to use. Needless to say, Ms. Tobias's encouragement to assist one another on the Internet also helped to develop a very supportive classroom community, something that carried over into other areas as well. We will show you other ways in which you can assist your students to help one another in this rich environment, an excellent lesson for life.

The Times, They Are A-changin'

This story is not the first you have heard about the Internet. Nearly every day we encounter stories in the press about the Internet and how it is changing our lives; we see ads in magazines and on television with World Wide Web addresses; we hear radio talk-show hosts mention the live "chat-rooms" where listeners can continue their conversations "on-line"; and we hear colleagues talking about all the e-mail they had to answer before going to bed the night before.

You have also seen the changes taking place in your own school. Your classroom may already be connected and you are trying to find time to better understand these new resources for your students. Perhaps your district has recently completed a technology plan and new Internet connections are coming this year for your library/media center, the computer lab, and your classroom. Like many of us, you probably can recall the day when a student first showed you a print-out with Internet information for a class assignment and you began to wonder about the new world all of us are entering. Bob Dylan certainly had it right when he wrote, "The times, they are a-changin'."

Undoubtedly, you have many feelings about these changes. You may be excited, skeptical, nervous, or, like us, you may experience all of these feelings, sometimes at the same time. We get excited when we discover a site like "Whales: A Thematic Web Unit." We become skeptical when we read about politicians who symbolically show their commitment by helping to wire schools, but disappear when it comes time to pay for computers or provide staff development time. We become nervous when we think about the speed of these changes and whether we can ever "know enough." After all, who had even heard of the Internet just a few years ago? And who can tell what new technologies will show up as soon as we begin to understand this one? Yes, the Internet prompts all of these thoughts.

What is the Internet?

If you have only heard examples of what people do on the Internet, it is sometimes hard to figure out what the Internet really is. Sometimes it sounds like a place to buy a car with a computer. Sometimes it appears to be a way of sending e-mail. Sometimes it sounds like a place to read the newspaper. Sometimes it sounds like a way to talk with someone while you view them on your computer screen. It is all of these things, and more. At heart, the Internet is simply a set of computers around the world that are connected to one another. You can go to one computer to check the prices for a car, send e-mail to another computer, and read a newspaper that appears on yet another computer in London, San Francisco, New York, or Moscow. Initially, only large computers at universities were connected to one another. Now, anyone with a desk-top computer and a telephone can get connected and become a part of the Internet. Increasingly, though, schools are moving away from separate phone connections and are beginning to directly wire classrooms to the district's main computer, which is then linked to the Internet. This allows students to go through the district's computer and link up with any other computer, anywhere in the world.

There are many different ways in which you may access information on computers linked to the Internet. You may use an e-mail program to send messages or documents back and forth. Most computers linked to the Internet have this ability because it is relatively simple. Other, richer sources of information are also available on the Internet, including music, video, audio, animation, color graphics, and even software programs. These are located on computers that are a part of the World Wide Web (WWW or, simply, the web). You access the WWW through special software called a web browser. A web browser allows you to read text, listen to music, watch a video clip, observe an animation, and view rich color graphics. The WWW of the Internet is an especially rich source of information for classroom learning.

E-Mail for You

From: Sandi Sibe <slsibe@MAILBOX.SYR.EDU>
Subject: Using the Internet

Hi! Even though I have not yet had the opportunity to apply all that I've learned, I believe that E-mail and the Internet are both going to become even bigger and more important and effective tools for both students and teachers.

The first time I ever came in contact with E-mail was in the Fall of 1995. I must admit, I was a bit nervous about using it. Once I got the hang of it, I was just amazed at the fact that anyone could communicate with anyone anywhere! I also thought it a shame that my friends in France didn't have E-mail. I would so have liked to correspond with them 'electronically'. I realize that there are teachers out there who are hesitant to learn something new like this, mainly because it involves using a computer which, for some, is quite scary. All I can say is that you should give it a whirl and 'get your feet wet'. I think that once you see how easy and efficient E-mail is, and what a great asset it could be to your classroom teaching, you'll be hooked!

As for the Internet and the WWW, I remember that I was also amazed at the tons and tons of information I could obtain from it. I never realized how popular and useful it was. The only thing is that, in my opinion, it can be very overwhelming because in fact there is so much information out there. I can understand how some people may get a bit carried away and spend hours (even days) just 'surfing the Net'. Another very troubling thing that we've been hearing more and more about these days concerns children who have free access to the Internet (at home or at school) and who are tapping into many sites which are not at all appropriate for them. It is imperative that children be supervised when using the Internet either by parents or teachers. In any case, I do believe that the WWW is an excellent resource for teachers and students. When looking for new ideas and new resources to use in their classrooms, the Web is definitely a great place to begin the search.

Sandi Sibe

Figure 1-2 shows you a location on the web developed by teachers for an integrated thematic unit on weather. It includes lesson plans, experiments for students, and links to other weather sites on the WWW, including satellite photos that will soon appear on the evening's news.

Being a part of this large network of computers allows you and your students access to information at any other computer located on the Internet. This is what makes the Internet such a powerful instructional tool for you and your students. There are many, many things you can do when you are connected to the Internet:

- **Send an E-Mail Message to Anyone in the World.** Students in a classroom in New Jersey were each doing an Internet Inquiry Study on a country in Europe. They followed a K-W-L (Know,

Figure 1-2.   An example of a location on the World Wide Web featuring an integrated thematic unit on weather for grades
4–6
(http://www.ncsa.uiuc.edu/edu/RSE/RSEred/LESSONONE.html)

FAQ (Frequently Asked Question)

Who pays when I use my computer to communicate with another computer somewhere else in the
world? We pay for telephone calls. Why don't we pay for the Internet?

?   With a few exceptions, no one really pays for the traffic on the Internet since everyone agrees to let
everyone else travel through their network to get to other, connected networks of computers. The
exceptions are Internet Service Providers such as America On-line and CompuServe, or Local
Service Providers in your community who charge people to connect to their computers in order to
connect to the Internet. While your district may pay a connect fee, the major cost is for purchas-
ing, servicing, and updating your computers and your connections.

Want to Know, and Learn) model developed by Ogle, (1989). During their study, one student discovered a site with e-mail messages from children around the world and shared this location with other class members. Noticing what was taking place, the teacher decided to have each student write to students in their project country, asking them to describe what took place during a typical day. Students followed traditional process writing procedures as they developed their letters: brainstorming, drafting, revising, editing, and publishing (sending). Within a few days everyone was receiving e-mail from Europe describing "typical days." This began a correspondence that lasted throughout the year for many of the students. The collection of "typical day" stories was printed out, included in each student's report, and displayed on a bulletin board for parents to see during the school's Open House. The experience provided a very special window to the cultures of Europe. It was also highly motivating. Students couldn't wait to check their mailboxes each morning to see if they had e-mail from their foreign friends. Many new understandings were developed about life in other cultures.

- **Acquire Information.** You can go to any other computer on the Internet and look for information put there for your use. You can read the complete works of Shakespeare, view a map of the world displaying earthquakes recorded during the past month, take a guided tour of the White House, view videos of different penguin species in the Antarctic, read the news or videos at sites operated by CNN, ESPN, or USA Today, and obtain photos of ancient Egyptian artifacts recently discovered in the Valley of the Dead. The list of information resources available to you and your students is nearly endless because people around the world are adding more each day. Most important, the information on the Internet is almost always more recent than that found in any textbook in your classroom.

- **Communicate with Others Who Share a Similar Interest.** You can join a discussion group and receive messages from others who share a common interest. Are you looking for ideas as you begin to use the Internet in your classroom? Join a discussion group via e-mail with others who are also searching for ways to use this new technology (see Chapter 3.) Are you interested in science/math/music/art/literacy/social studies/ESL/special education? Discussion groups also exist for teachers in each of these areas. In addition to discussion groups, an increasing number of real-time, "chat" locations are appearing on the Internet for teachers. At these locations, teachers can share ideas about instruction with other teachers around the world and immediately read what others think.

- **Acquire New Software.** A new teacher in Olympia, Washington was looking for a better way to keep track of grades in her social studies class. She heard about a free program called Eagle Gradebook that she could download onto her computer and then use to record and average her grades. She went to the site located at Virginia Tech (http://tac.elps.vt.edu/htmldocs/utilities.html) that a friend had located, downloaded the software, and found that it met her needs perfectly. She also noticed programs at the same location for keeping track of attendance, making banners for the classroom, and making calendars. She downloaded these free programs as well and used them during the year.

- **Conduct a Video Conference.** Do you want to have a discussion between your class and a class in a foreign country about a book you have both read or an issue you have both studied? No problem. All you need is the right software and an inexpensive video camera for your computer. The interchange could provide your students with special insights into another culture. Or, conduct a video conference with an expert on the topic your students are studying. This might be a member of Congress, a scientist, a historian, or the author of a book they have recently read. Have your students do their research in advance and prepare their questions for this expert. If you would like to find out more about this technology, visit one of several sites explaining "CU-SeeMe" technology (http://www.indstate.edu/msattler/sci-tech/comp/CU-SeeMe/index.html).

- **Publish a Page on the WWW for Your School and Your Class.** Many teachers are finding the WWW to be a useful location to publish their students' writing and present other information about classroom activities. They find that publishing writing for the entire world to read motivates students to produce exceptional work. They quickly discover that other students, parents, and grandparents visit their classroom page to read their work and learn about classroom activities. Schools and classrooms with web pages also present an image of education that is different from the many unfavorable images portrayed in the press. The importance of this image should not be overlooked as we seek additional funding for education.

These are just a few of the things you can do on the Internet in your classroom. While we will try to present a balanced view of the Internet and not get carried away with the hype that surrounds this new technology, it is easy to see why some people do get a bit excited. The information and communication resources available on the Internet are the beginning of a radical departure in the nature of information available to us and our students. Without trying to hype the technology, it is probably fair to say that the Internet is fundamentally changing the nature of teaching and learning as it enters our classrooms (Kinzer & Leu, in press; Leu, 1996). Our response to these important changes will determine our students' ability to succeed in the world that awaits them. New challenges and new opportunities await us all.

E-Mail for You

```
From: "Emily B. Buchanan" <ebbuchan@MailBox.Syr.Edu>
Subject: Beginning to Use the Internet


    Hi!
    Although I was very excited to start exploring the Internet,
my first few experiences with it were disappointing. The sites I
located were so superficial, I didn't find any worthwhile infor-
mation. It took a long time to locate good sites. I felt I wasted
whole hours on shallow browsing. Then I saw a list of recommended
Websites in "Instructor" magazine. I went to one of them and it
was marvelous! What's more, it was linked to several other fabu-
lous sites, which were in turn linked to other fine sites. I was
hooked.
    I am awestruck at the amount of information that is available
at my fingertips.

Emily Buchanan


P.S. The site is called "Classroom Connect" at http://
www.classroom.net
```

Why Is the Internet So Important to My Students?

The rapidly changing nature of technology affects each of us. More than anyone else, though, these powerful changes affect our students and the opportunities they will have in life. Let's think for a moment about the world our students will enter when they complete their formal education. This is where we should begin our plans for their education. As we think about this, let's make at least one assumption: Let's assume that many of our students will complete four years of education after completing high school, a consideration that is increasingly becoming a requirement for effective employment in a post-industrial society.

To begin our "thought experiment," let's add 17 years to whatever year it is today. This is the time when children who started kindergarten this year will enter the workplace to seek employment. For example, a student beginning kindergarten in 1997 will enter the workplace in 2014. What will it take to be successful in the world of 2014? While we cannot tell with absolute precision, there are several trends that give us a reasonable chance to anticipate the broad outlines for successful entry into society 17 years from now.

First, it is clear that economies around the world will be engaged in a competitive struggle for markets, jobs, and business. We see the beginnings of this now as areas of the world join regional economic groupings, as barriers to trade are lowered, and as companies engage in a global competition for markets. Successful societies will be those who have individuals who can compete successfully in a global economy and educational systems that prepare their citizens for these economic realities.

Second, to succeed in an increasingly competitive global marketplace, organizations will have to change the way they work. In the past decade, many organizations have worked to transform themselves into "high-performance" workplaces. In most cases, this means changing an organization from a centrally planned organization to one that relies increasingly on collaborative teams at all levels of the organization to assume initiative for planning ways to work more efficiently.

There is also a third trend underway. Increasingly, problem-solving skills will be critical to successful performance. As collaborative teams seek more effective ways of working, they will be expected to identify problems that impede performance and seek effective solutions. When students leave school, they will need to be able to identify central problems, find the appropriate information quickly, and then use this information to solve the problems they identify as important.

Fourth, in "high performance" settings, it appears that effective collaboration and communication skills will be central to success. The changes from a centralized to a decentralized workplace will require collaboration and communication skills so that the best decisions get made at every level in an organization and so that changes at one level are clearly communicated to other levels. Our students will need effective collaboration and communication skills when they leave us.

Finally, there is a fifth trend: effective information access and use will be increasingly important to success. Individuals who can access information the fastest and use it effectively to solve important problems will be the ones who will succeed in the challenging times that await our students. This will make informational literacy a crucial determinant of success. We need to prepare our students for the new information technologies that are available now and will become increasingly available as we change from an industrial to an information society.

What does all of this mean for our students? How can we support them to become effective individuals who make important contributions to society? We believe in the truth of the following maxim:

> In the information age in which we all live, the race will be won by individuals, groups, and societies who can access the best information in the shortest time to identify and solve the most important problems and communicate this information to others.

This is why the Internet and other electronic technologies are so important. We need to prepare our students to use these new information and communication technologies because they enable us to identify and solve important problems in the shortest time and communicate our ideas to others. Nothing is more important for the future of our students. This is the challenge we face as educators in the new world we are all entering. This is what we must prepare our students for as we think about their futures.

How Can I Use the Internet to Help My Students?

Throughout this book, we will help you to answer this important question. The Internet is an extensive resource of information and communication, but its effective use in the classroom will ultimately depend upon how *you* take advantage of this resource. Like everything else in education, it is not what the instructional materials are but what you do with them that determines the extent of your students' learning. No packaged set of materials can compete with a teacher who cares about students, understands their unique needs, and responds in effective ways to support their learning. As you begin to consider how to use the

Internet with your students, it may be helpful to see specific examples of what is possible on the WWW of the Internet:

- **Dr. Seuss in Cyberspace.**   After reading *The Cat in the Hat* aloud to your class, have students visit the "Chat with the Cat" site to ask this mischievous character a question (http://www.randomhouse.com/site/seuss2/chatcat.cgi). The Cat in the Hat will answer all e-mail messages directed his way. If a group of students wants to discover more about the life and works of Dr. Seuss, have them visit Cyber Seuss (http://www.afn.org/~afn15301/drseuss.html) and then share what they have found with the rest of the class. Encourage students to make a bulletin board with the addresses and pictures of great Seuss sites on the web. Have students vote for their favorite book by Dr. Seuss and see the continuously updated results of this poll in a bar graph (http://www.iguide.com/kids/drseuss/seusspage.htm). Compare these results with a poll that is taken of students in your school. Invite everyone to test their knowledge of Dr. Seuss's magical world by taking the Dr. Seuss Quizzer (http://www.iguide.com/kids/drseuss/index.htm).

- **Science Learning Network.**   The Science Learning Network is a group of museums and schools devoted to improving science teaching through the Internet. Use the Science Learning Network (http://www.sln.org/) to access descriptions of science units taking place in classrooms around the world based on the National Science Standards and inquiry learning. E-mail teachers who have classes doing the same units as yours to share ideas and resources. Have students use e-mail to discuss their results and compare them with the results from other students. Post science ideas and questions on a bulletin board and receive replies back from other teachers and students. Have your students complete interactive, multimedia units on topics such as the physics of water, storm science, dissecting a frog or a cow's eye, using a scanning electron microscope (students can see the photos of objects they request), and much more.

- **Whales: A Thematic Web Unit.**   This incredibly rich resource described earlier in the chapter (http://curry.edschool.Virginia.EDU/go/Whales/) provides all the resources you will need for a cross-curricular thematic unit using cooperative grouping as your students study whales. Assign small groups to research a particular area and then report back to the whole class. After preliminary reports, decide upon additional questions to explore and develop new groups to explore these issues. Along the way, students can hear the voices of many different species, study the physics of echolocation, track several whales by satellite, and download a software program that provides basic information on all of the major whale species.

- **Activities in Pi Mathematics.**   As students learn about Pi, use this site (http://www.ncsa.uiuc.edu:80/edu/RSE/RSEorange/buttons.html) (see Figure 1-3) to supplement your lessons. Have groups select an activity to complete at this site and then share the results with the class. Some may choose to report on the interesting history of Pi, others may wish to use Pi to determine the best deal at a pizza shop, others may wish to complete an activity to measure Pi using common objects, others may wish to calculate Pi out to one hundred decimal places and then show the class how this can be memorized by singing a popular tune, still others may choose to calculate the circumference of planets and then check their answers at other locations on the Internet. These and other activities are all clearly matched with standards from the National Council of Teachers of Mathematics.

- **Read Newbery Award Winners.**   Are your students looking for a good book to read? Have them visit this site (http://www.psi.net:80/ChapterOne/children/), where they can print out and read the first chapters of 14 Newbery Award winning works, including *The Giver, Missing May, Maniac Magee, Number the Stars,* and many more. This way, they can make a speedy decision about which book to read when they visit the library. If they wish to interview popular authors such as Lois Lowry, Daniel Pinkwater, Jane Yolen, and others, have them visit the "Ask the Authors" site (http://ipl.sils.umich.edu/youth/AskAuthor/) at the Internet Public Library. Ask them to share the results with your class.

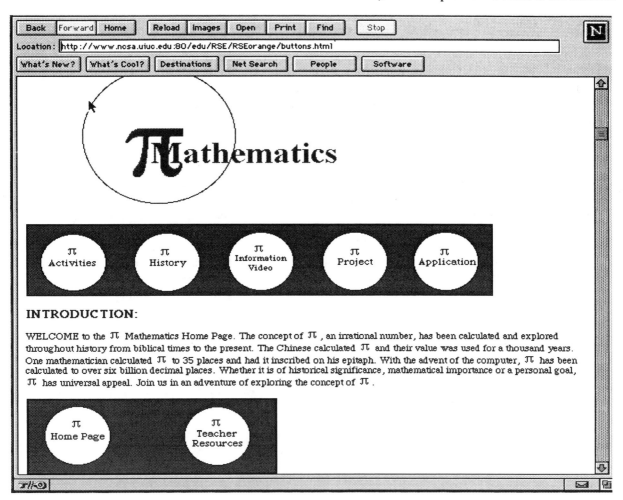

Figure 1-3. Activities in Pi Mathematics: A location on the WWW (http://www.ncsa.uiuc.edu:80/edu/RSE/RSEorange/buttons.html)

Using the Internet Effectively with Your Students

Teaching and learning are being redefined by the communication technologies that are quickly becoming a part of the information age in which we live (Negroponte, 1995; Reinking, 1995). We are experiencing a historic change in the nature of learning as digital, multimedia resources enter our world. The many resources available on the Internet are the beginning of a radical departure in the nature of information available to us and our students. How we respond to these important changes will determine our students' ability to succeed in the world that awaits them.

Internet resources will increase, not decrease, the central role you play in orchestrating learning experiences for your students. Each of us will be challenged to thoughtfully guide students' learning within information environments that are richer and more complex than traditional print media, presenting richer and more complex learning opportunities for both us and our students.

As but one example of how the Internet will make our role even more important, consider recent concerns raised by Birkerts (1995) and Stoll (1995). Birkerts and Stoll worry that electronic information environments like the WWW of the Internet will encourage students to "surf" many unrelated topics on only a superficial level. Left on their own, students may be seduced away from reading and thinking critically about a single topic in depth as they discover intriguing links to more and more locations and move farther and farther away from the initial topic. As a result, students will only skim the surface of many, unrelated, pieces of information, never integrating or thinking deeply about any of them.

We think this scenario is only possible, however, in classrooms where teachers do not actively guide the use of Internet resources and, instead, leave decisions about Internet use entirely to students. When students always determine their own paths through this rich and intriguing information resource there is a powerful tendency to search for what students refer to as "cool," highly interactive and media-rich locations that quickly attract their attention but are unrelated to important learning tasks (Leu, 1996). These often include video, sound, animation, and other elements. As students search for "cool" sites, they are less likely to explore important topics in depth or think critically about the relation of this information to their own lives. Students end up viewing much but learning little.

On the other hand, when students are guided to resources and are provided with important learning tasks to accomplish, they quickly focus on important information related to the issue at hand (Leu, 1996). This is not to say that students should be limited to Internet resources that only you select to complete tasks that only you devise. Clearly, if we wish students to become effective users of the Internet, we want them to develop independent strategies for searching and analyzing information. And, in order to do so, we must provide them with learning experiences which they direct. Still, it does point to the central role you will play regarding this new resource as you support their ability to independently acquire and evaluate information on the web.

Teachers who understand the Internet and thoughtfully integrate its many resources into their classroom curriculum will see students expand their understanding of important concepts and communicate these ideas more effectively. Teachers who simply allow students to explore the Internet on their own after their regular work is completed will see little change in student learning. In fact, this type of Internet experience may actually take students away from thinking critically about important ideas as they search for surface level "cool."

A central assumption of this book is our belief that the role you play in orchestrating experiences with the Internet will determine the extent to which your students gain from this resource. That is why we focus on effective teaching practices while limiting the technical discussion of the Internet to basic essentials.

The Social Nature of Learning with the Internet

It has been common, recently, to point out how learning is best accomplished through social interaction. That is, when students work together, they are often very effective at "scaffolding," or helping, one another on the way to important insights (Meyer, 1993). Theoretical perspectives established by Vygotsky (1978), Bahktin (1981), and others are often used to explain this process. Method frameworks such as cooperative learning (Johnson & Johnson, 1984), peer conferences (Graves, 1983), jigsaw activities (Aaronson, 1978), literature discussion groups (Leu & Kinzer, 1995), text set activities (Short, 1993), and others are thought to be particularly useful because they create situations in which students help one another to learn important concepts.

Socially mediated learning may be especially important for learning within the Internet and other electronic information resources. Because these information resources are powerful, complex, and constantly changing, they often require us to communicate with others in order to make meaning from them. No one person knows everything there is to know about the Internet; each of us has useful information that can help others. I may know something about how to search for information, but you may know a really good location for students who want to publish their work. By sharing our information, we can help one another learn about these rich information resources. Learning about the Internet is best accomplished through social interactions with others, perhaps even more naturally and frequently than in traditional print environments. That is one reason we have asked other teachers to share their insights with you through e-mail.

E-Mail for You

```
From: Barbara McInerney <bmcinern@freeside.scsd.k12.ny.us>
Subject: Using the World Wide Web of the Internet

    Hi!
    I am really excited about the new doors that are opening to
me as a teacher through use of the Internet. However, that ex-
citement is tempered by some reservations and concerns. One of my
biggest concerns is the application of the sources on the
Internet. Will I be able to make the use of the Web integrated
and meaningful to my students? Will I be able to instruct them
correctly and completely in the use of the Web? Will their use of
the Internet add to the completeness of the curriculum or just be
a casual aside? I feel teachers need to be fully trained and
capable in the workings of the Net before attempting to guide
students in its use. We do so many "hit and miss" procedures in
education—but this technology is here to stay and will be an
integral part of their future, so students need to learn its use
completely and correctly to really enhance classroom experiences.
    One of my students, when asked about the feelings they had
about our school becoming hooked up to the Internet and what
possibilities it presented for them, answered in this manner, "I
think it's going to be really cool! I mean, if you are studying,
say China, and you could communicate with students in China to
really see what it is like there, that would be so cool! Or, if
you needed to know some stuff about a topic and all your books
were old, then you could go to the Internet and it could tell you
new stuff."
    Even students with no experience to date on the Internet have
a general idea of what they would like to try to do with it—it
shows they are thinking about the possibilities, as I am.
    I am excited about using this in my class next year!!!!

Barbara McInerney
```

The episode with Sarah and Sha'Quann at the beginning of this chapter illustrates how an insightful teacher can take advantage of knowing how important socially mediated learning is with the Internet. Setting up a bulletin board next to the computer and encouraging students to help one another are simple ways you can support students in these efforts. So is instruction based on cooperation and collaboration. With a little encouragement from you, you will discover students helping one another and discovering new aspects of the Internet to share with still more students. This can make Internet use an effective tool for community building as well as for learning.

The Purpose of This Book

We write this book with three purposes in mind:
- to help you feel comfortable in this new learning environment;
- to minimize the time it takes for you to find useful learning tools for your students; and
- to show you ways the Internet may be used in your classroom to support learning.

To those of us uncomfortable with technology, thinking about using the Internet in a classroom means sweaty palms, a dry throat, and a racing heart as our anxieties about technology start to overwhelm any thoughts of benefits for our students. How can we consider using the Internet when we are unable to set the time on our VCR? We will be sensitive to these concerns. We have had many long discussions about this issue as we planned this book. We will be supportive, inviting, and encouraging as we explain how to use the Internet to assist your students. What we will not do in this book is describe esoteric aspects of the technology unrelated to instruction. We need to keep in mind that we use technology to support teaching; we do not use teaching to support technology. The focus on teaching is what distinguishes this book from others. If we get too far afield, by emphasizing technology and not teaching, send us an e-mail message and let us know. Our learning is socially constructed, too!

A second purpose of this book is to minimize the time you must spend to find useful teaching/learning tools. Classrooms are busy places; teachers do not have much free time to look for locations on the Internet that fit their classroom needs. By identifying the most practical and useful locations on the Internet for teachers, we hope to save you time as you think about how to use this new tool to help your students.

Sharing the best locations on the Internet will assist us in accomplishing our third, and most important, purpose: to show you how the Internet may be used in your classroom to support learning. The best locations on the Internet contain a comprehensive set of integrated learning experiences designed for students at a variety of levels. Looking at these sites will give you immediate insights into how they may be used in your classroom; they often contain clearly written lesson plans and instructional activities. By showing you effective teaching practices, we hope to quickly get your students into the powerful learning tool that is the Internet.

We have organized this book into several sections. The first section will help you to become acquainted with the Internet. In this chapter we want to explain the potential of the Internet to support learning. In the next chapter, we will help you to understand all of the major tools for navigating on the Internet. In the third chapter, we will help you to understand e-mail and communication opportunities available through the Internet.

The second section begins by describing instructional strategies that are useful as you integrate the Internet into your classroom, such as Internet Workshop. Then, it explores specific teaching ideas within each of the major content areas: language arts and literature, social studies, science, and math. It also includes a separate chapter on instructional ideas for young children. Each of these chapters will describe a number of the most useful locations on the Internet for your class and show you how to integrate them into your classroom.

The final section explores three areas that will be important for putting all of this new information together in a busy and diverse classroom. One chapter will describe ways to increase multicultural understanding. A second will explore ways to include all students on the Internet. The final chapter will show you how to develop integrated, project-based units with the Internet by creating a home page on the WWW for your classroom.

Each chapter will contain a description of what we consider to be the most useful Internet sites for that topic. It will also contain the descriptions and addresses for a number of other useful sites on the Internet related to the contents of the chapter. In addition, each chapter will contain several e-mail messages for you from other teachers. These teachers have been kind enough to take time from their busy schedules to welcome you into the Internet and share their experiences with you. You may wish to drop them an e-mail message to thank them and to share your own teaching ideas. Remember, we all learn from one another with these new technologies.

Welcome to the Internet!

References

Aaronson, E. (1978). *The jigsaw classroom.* Beverly Hills, CA: Sage Publications.

Bahktin, M. M. (1981). *The dialogic imagination* (C. Emerson & M. Holquist, Trans.). Austin: University of Texas Press.

Birkerts, S. (1995). *The Gutenberg elegies.* New York: Ballentine Books.

Graves, D. (1983). *Writing: Teachers and children at work.* Portsmouth, NH: Heinemann.

Johnson, D. W. & Johnson, R. (1984). *Circles of learning: Cooperation in the classroom.* Alexandria, VA: Association of Supervision and Curriculum Development.

Kinzer, C. K. & Leu, D. J., Jr. (in press). The challenge of change: Exploring literacy and learning in electronic environments. *Language Arts.*

Leu, D. J., Jr. (1996). Sarah's secret: Social aspects of literacy and learning in a digital, information age. *The Reading Teacher.*

Leu, D. J., Jr. & Kinzer, C. K. (1995). *Effective reading instruction.* Englewood Cliffs, NJ: Prentice-Hall.

Meyer, D. K. (1993). What is scaffolded instruction? Definitions, distinguishing features, and misnomers. In D. J. Leu, Jr. & C. K. Kinzer (Eds.), *Examining central issues in literacy research, theory, and practice.* Forty-second Yearbook of the National Reading Conference. Chicago: National Reading Conference.

Negroponte, N. (1995). *Being digital.* New York: Knopf.

Ogle, D. M. (1989). The know, want to know, learn strategy. In K.D. Muth (Ed.), *Children's comprehension of text* (pp. 205–223). Newark, DE: International Reading Association.

Reinking, D. (1995). Reading and writing with computers: Literacy research in a post-typographic world. In K. A. Hinchman, D. J. Leu, & C. K. Kinzer (Eds.), *Perspectives on literacy research and practice.* Chicago: National Reading Conference, Inc.

Short, K. (1993). Intertextuality: Searching for patterns that connect. In D. J. Leu, Jr. & C. K. Kinzer (Eds.), *Literacy research, theory and practice: Views from many perspectives.* Chicago: National Reading Conference.

Stoll, C. (1995). *Silicon snake oil: Second thoughts on the information highway.* New York: Doubleday.

Vygotsky, L. S. (1978). *Mind in society: The development of higher psychological processes.* (M. Cole, V. John-Steiner, S. Scribner, & E. Souberman, Eds.). Cambridge, MA: Harvard University Press.

Chapter 2
Developing Navigation Strategies with Your Students

```
To:   Our readers
From: djleu@sued.syr.edu (Don Leu),
      ddleu@syr.edu (Debbie Leu)
Subject: The central role of navigation strategies

    Navigation is central to success on the Internet. Knowing how
to find the best information in the shortest time will quickly
advantage certain students over others who have not developed
these skills.
    You already teach navigation strategies in traditional print
materials. Showing students how to use the library reference
system to find a book, to use a book's index to locate informa-
tion, or to use a dictionary to find a correct spelling are all
examples of teaching navigation strategies. As important as navi-
gation is within traditional school tasks, it is even more impor-
tant on the Internet because information is richer and more com-
plexly networked.
    We must seek to understand the navigation knowledge required
on the Internet as we seek ways to support students in developing
this knowledge. At the same time, we should not expect to under-
stand everything about Internet navigation immediately. This type
of knowledge is acquired as we have additional experiences on the
Internet and as we learn new strategies from our students and
from colleagues. As with other aspects of the Internet, we learn
best by sharing our experiences with others. It is likely that
your students will teach you as many things as you teach them
about navigating the Internet.

    Don and Debbie
```

David and Alberto were working together at the computer, completing an Internet tour and scavenger hunt developed by their teacher, Ms. Davidson. This developed navigation strategies on the Internet as it introduced a unit on space exploration during the first week of school. "Look, there is the Apollo XI patch. Print that out. Click the button that says 'Print' . . . Now click on 'Back.' Let's go back and see the other patches."

Ms. Davidson had a computer in her room with the ability to run Netscape Navigator, a program that helps you navigate through the World Wide Web and other resources on the Internet. (See Figure 2-1.) She was teaching her students navigation strategies at the beginning of the year. This seemed to be an important first step. To begin, Ms. Davidson set up a guided tour and scavenger hunt using a feature called bookmarks on Netscape Navigator. Each bookmark took students to a location she wanted them to visit on the World Wide Web. This made navigation very easy since students simply selected bookmarks Ms. Davidson had set and these took them to the correct location on the web. Ms. Davidson was careful to select locations that would be used later in her unit on space exploration. Thus, the activity would teach students navigation strategies at the same time it introduced important elements of the unit.

Figure 2-1.   The page students first saw on the guided tour in Ms. Davidson's class using Netscape Navigator .
(Apollo 11 Mission to the Moon—http://www.nasa.gov/hqpao/apollo_11.html)

Over the summer, the district had developed an appropriate use policy with a committee of parents, students, and teachers. The policy described the Internet, defined the do's and don'ts of Internet use, and defined sanctions for inappropriate use. At the end, it had a place for the student, parent/guardian, and teacher to sign, indicating they had read and understood the policy.

On the first day of class, Ms. Davidson introduced the computer and the Internet. She went over the acceptable use policy with her students, explaining each item. Then she had them sign the form and take it home to obtain the signature of their parent or guardian.

As students returned the forms, she introduced small groups to the fundamentals of navigation using Netscape Navigator, a program used to navigate on the Internet. First, she showed her students how to connect to the Internet using this program. Then she showed them how to go to a site on the Internet by using a preset bookmark on Netscape Navigator. She also showed students how to use the "Back" button (see Figure 2-1) to move back to the previous location they had just visited and the "Forward" button to move ahead. Finally, she introduced the tour and scavenger hunt in Figure 2-2, designed to be completed in pairs. She wanted students to support one another as they developed initial navigation skills. Before they began, she set the home page location on Netscape Navigator to the Apollo 11 home page. This would always be the first page to appear when students connected to the Internet and started their tour and scavenger hunt.

After all students completed the space navigation assignment, Ms. Davidson organized a whole class workshop on the Internet. Students shared additional navigation strategies they had learned as a result of their tour, teaching each other new ways of navigating the World Wide Web. They also shared information they had discovered about space as they completed the scavenger hunt. It was an exciting start to the year and to using the Internet in the classroom.

Lessons from the Classroom

There are a number of important lessons in this episode that you might consider as you think about developing navigation strategies with your students. First, this district had worked carefully with parents, students, and teachers to develop a policy for the appropriate use of the Internet. Developing an appropriate use policy will head off a number of problems, including viewing of inappropriate sites, using inappropriate language on the Internet, and responding inappropriately to e-mail messages from strangers. Moreover, because both students and parents/guardians sign the statement, it informs families about the Internet and how it will be used at school. We will discuss appropriate use policies later in this chapter.

A second lesson is to systematically teach navigation strategies at the beginning of the year. Ms. Davidson realized that navigational strategies were important; students gather more information in a shorter time when they know how to navigate through the Internet. Time was precious in Ms. Davidson's class because there was only one computer connected to the Internet. As a result, she wanted students to know how to use their time efficiently. She developed a thoughtful plan to accomplish this.

Another important lesson is that Ms. Davidson combined two elements: the introduction to the first thematic unit of the year with a guided tour and scavenger hunt to practice navigation strategies. Again, this saved time in a busy classroom; students were learning about outer space at the same time they were developing navigation strategies.

Ms. Davidson saved time, too, by designating a home page location for the space unit. Designating a home page took students immediately to the location she wanted them to visit at the beginning of the activity. There was no time wasted looking for the right page.

There is also a final lesson: how Ms. Davidson used three methods (group introduction, paired learning, whole class workshop) to teach navigation skills. These worked in a complementary fashion to take advantage of social learning opportunities as discussed in Chapter 1. Her initial group presentation explained essential elements for students to practice as they completed the tour in pairs. Working in pairs after the group presentation led to many new learning experiences; students helped one another when they were stuck, discovering new ways of navigating the Internet. Sometimes other students would even stop by the computer to assist a pair that was having difficulty; this saved Ms. Davidson time and allowed

Navigating through Space: Using the World Wide Web of the Internet

Space Traveler: _____ Date: _____

Preparing for Your Mission: Learning from the Apollo Missions to the Moon

1. Start your journey by double clicking on Netscape to connect to the World Wide Web. You should soon see the home page for the Apollo 11 flights to the moon.

2. Click on the picture with the word "History." This will take you to a section on the history of the Apollo flights.

3. Click on the words "Mission Patches." Choose your favorite mission patch and print this out on the printer. You can do this by clicking on the button at the top that says "Print."

4. Find the button at the top that says "Back." Click this until you return to the Apollo 11 home page. (Use the bookmark if you get lost.)

5. Explore other areas of this site. This will get you ready for your flight on the space shuttle as you learn about earlier space programs.

Finding Your Flight on the Space Shuttle

1. Which shuttle flight are you taking? What will your mission be? Open the bookmark menu at the top of the page and choose "Future Shuttle Missions" (http://www.osf.hq.nasa.gov/shuttle/futsts.html).

2. See if you can find the table of future missions at this site. Write down the following information for the next mission (the one you will be taking):

   Orbiter Name: _____ Launch Date: _____

   Crew: _____ Duration: _____

   Mission: _____

3. Explore other areas at this site before continuing. This will get you ready for your flight on the space shuttle.

Look through the Hubble Space Telescope (HST) into Deep Space

1. Ready to take a look at deep space? You may need to make observations of space during your flight. Open the bookmark menu at the top of the page and choose "HST's Greatest Hits 1990–1995 Gallery" (http://www.stsci.edu/pubinfo/BestOfHST95.html#SN1987A)

2. View some of these pictures from the Hubble telescope. Print out your favorite. Write a description of what you can see and attach it to your photo.

View the Earth from a Satellite

1. What will it look like outside your shuttle window? You can get an idea by seeing recent photographs from one of more than a hundred satellites circling our planet. Open the bookmark to "View from a Satellite" (http://www.fourmilab.ch/earthview/satellite.html).

2. Be certain the satellite ACTS is highlighted, or select another satellite if you wish.

3. Click on "View Earth from Satellite." Print out this photo of our Earth. Mark the location of our school on this picture.

Good Work! You are now ready to begin our unit on space exploration. Staple all your space artifacts together and turn them in. You should be certain you have the following:
   • your favorite mission patch from Apollo;
   • your favorite Hubble photograph and a description;
   • your photograph of Earth with our school located on the photograph;
   • this page.

Figure 2-2.   A guided tour and scavenger hunt, used to develop navigation knowledge at the beginning of the year.

her to work with students in other areas of the classroom. Finally, having an Internet workshop at the end of the experience tied everything together for her class, allowing each student to share new navigation strategies they had learned while working in pairs.

The Internet workshop led to many new ideas for navigating the Internet. Someone, for example, had discovered the "Home" button and explained how this worked to take you back to the home page location, the Apollo 11 page. Someone else had discovered how Netscape Navigator saved a list of the locations that were visited during each session. This student took the class to the computer and showed them how they could return to any site that had already been visited, even one without a bookmark, by looking under the menu item labeled "Go." Someone else had noticed that Netscape only required single clicks on the mouse button to activate any link and that double clicking was unnecessary, sometimes causing the program to be confused about what you wanted. All of these new strategies were shared and discussed. It was a very productive session.

It is clear that we can learn many things from Ms. Davidson's classroom. Her lesson contains many lessons for us as we consider how to help students develop navigation skills on the Internet: establishing an appropriate use policy for schools, teaching navigation strategies early in the year, using a tour and scavenger hunt to simultaneously teach navigation strategies and introduce the first unit, designating a home page location to save time, using a combination of methods to teach navigation strategies (group introduction, paired learning, class workshop), and supporting students as they shared navigation strategies with one another.

Netscape Navigator: A Powerful Internet Browser

How, exactly, do we navigate through the Internet? Many books have already been written on this topic (e.g., Giagnocavo, McLain, DiStefano, & Sturm, 1995; Kidder & Harris, 1996; Levine, Baroudi, & Young, 1996; Tretter, 1995) and many more are yet to come. Our discussion will focus on the most important navigation elements for teachers and students in busy classrooms. As you become more adept at using the Internet in your classroom, you may wish to explore this issue in greater detail. We have listed a number of sites on the WWW at the end of this chapter that will provide additional information.

The most important tool for navigating through the Internet is a browser. A browser is a software program that resides on your computer and allows you to connect to locations on the Internet. There are several different browsers (Lynx, Mosaic, Internet Explorer, Netscape Navigator) and each comes in at least two flavors (Windows and Macintosh). Our examples will come from Netscape Navigator for Macintosh. Netscape Navigator for Windows is very similar.

Netscape's browser is arguably the most powerful browser of any currently available because it allows you to access multimedia information (graphics, audio, video, animations) on the WWW at the same time that it allows you to access text-only areas of the Internet outside of the WWW. In addition, it has a number of very powerful features such as e-mail. Figure 2-3 shows the home page for Netscape Navigator. Something like this will appear when you first start the program.

We will assume that you have Netscape Navigator on your computer and that your computer is connected to the Internet. If you have not loaded Navigator onto your computer or you do not know how to obtain Internet access, seek the assistance of a person at your school who can provide technical support. In many schools, this may be a colleague in the room next door who is already connected and beginning to explore the Internet. Sometimes you will be fortunate enough to have a technology specialist for your school.

Launch Netscape Navigator by double clicking on the icon for this program on your computer or follow along by using the illustrations in this chapter. Now, let's take a look at the Internet!

A Few Words at the Beginning

When you connect to Netscape, you will see a screen that looks something like the one in Figure 2-3. Take a close look at this screen and let's talk about several navigation elements that appear there. Starting at the

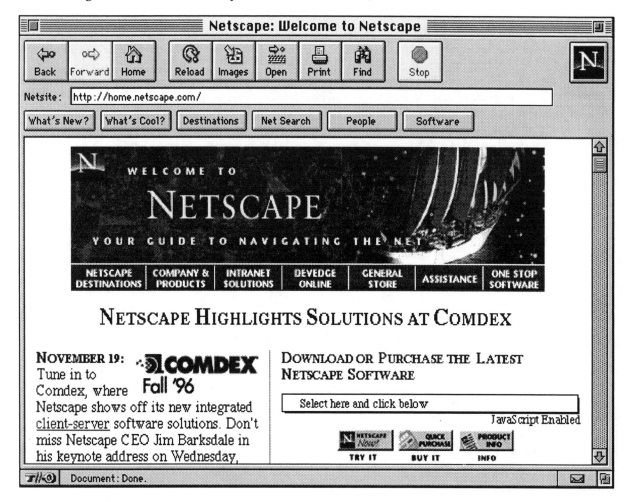

Figure 2-3.   The home page of Netscape Navigator, a powerful WWW browser
(http://home.netscape.com/)

very top, you will see a row of what are called "menu items." These begin with "File" and "Edit" and end with "Window." If you click and hold down your mouse on any of these menu items you will see a number of choices for each item.

Below the menu items you will see a gray bar with the words: "Netscape: Welcome to Netscape." The label on this bar will change as you navigate through the Internet. It will always tell you the title of the page on the WWW that you are looking at. Right now, you are looking at the "Netscape: Welcome to Netscape" page.

Beneath the title bar you will see a toolbar, a row of square boxes with pictures and labels underneath each picture. Items in the toolbar allow you do things with your browser. The toolbar includes items such as Back, Forward, Home, Reload, Images, Open, Print, Find, and Stop. We will explain each below.

Beneath the toolbar is the netsite location window. In this white window, you will see the address for your current location on the Internet. The location showing in Figure 2-3 (http://home.netscape.com/) is the address for Netscape's "Welcome to Netscape" page. No need to know the technical aspects of the language used to mark locations now. Just note that the address of your current location will appear here.

Under the netsite location window, you will see another row of buttons that take you to different locations on the Internet. These directory buttons include What's New? What's Cool? Destinations, Net Search, People, and Software.

E-Mail for You

```
From: Lisa.Brayton@MSB.Mat-Su.k12.ak.us (Lisa Brayton)
Subject: Using the Internet at our school


    Our school, Cottonwood Creek Elementary is located in
Wqsilla, Alaska. We have approximately 500 students in grades
K-5. I teach both kindergarten and fifth grade at Cottonwood. We
are very pleased to have up to three computers in each classroom,
and a fabulous lab set up. The lab consists of 30 MAC computers.
We have a giant overhead set up so that the entire class can
learn how to use the Internet together. Each student visits the
lab at least twice a week for a total of one hour of instruction.
    Using the Internet has become an exciting event for my fifth
grade students. Because our classroom is located across the hall
from the computer lab, we have probably the best access to it! We
have set up a time for students to use the Internet. I send them
in pairs, and let each student have an opportunity to investigate
with the guidance of our computer teacher, Chuck Anderson. The
first experiences on the Internet are exploratory. Many of my
students have gone on their own time to look up information for
reports. I was pleasantly surprised to see this initiative!
    During a unit on whales this past year, I found several in-
teresting web sites. I used the search engines and sat back! We
used these web sites as extensions of the lesson. The Internet
became another station for learning. As the students finished
their work and as space became available in the lab, I sent them
to find something new about whales! The students loved the expe-
rience. Going into the lab also became a reward for students. Mr.
Anderson had passes that he gave out.
    I would really like to see our access improve. What we have
is fabulous, so I can really see the potential if every classroom
was connected. Talk about letting children learn by discovery in
an exciting hands-on way that will promote literacy in a whole
new realm!


    Lisa Brayton
    Kindergarten and 5th grade teacher
    Cottonwood Creek Elementary School
    Wqsilla, Alaska
```

Now look at the viewing window containing the Netscape welcome page just below this final row of buttons. Note how some words are underlined and written in a distinctive color (usually blue). Words that are underlined and/or marked in a distinctive color signal a key navigational feature on the WWW, a hypertext link. If you single click on an underlined and colored word or phrase with your mouse, a hypertext link will take you to the site on the Internet that is linked to that item(s). The same is true for many of the pictures and graphic elements you find on the Internet. If you are at your computer, try clicking (only once) on a hypertext link and notice how a new screen appears with information related to the word(s) or picture you selected. Also note the new address in the location window. You are now at this new location on the Internet and this location probably contains several more hypertext links. You could keep clicking on hypertext links and travel to different locations throughout the Internet, seemingly forever.

The Toolbar

Figure 2-4. The Netscape Navigator Toolbar

Now take a look at items in the toolbar, as shown in Figure 2-4. These tools allow you to do things as you navigate through the WWW. The first button, **Back**, allows you to move back one location from where you are currently. Note that this is only active after you move to a location beyond the first page, the Netscape welcome page. If you haven't already tried moving to another location by clicking on a colored hypertext link, do this now. Then, try clicking on the Back button on the toolbar and note that you return back to the previous location.

The next button, **Forward**, moves you forward one location in your travels through the Internet. Note that this is only active if you have moved back at least one location and can really move forward to places you have visited. Try moving back and forward. You may also wish to try using the hypertext links at some of these pages. As you navigate, note the changes in your current location in the location window.

Home is the next button on the toolbar. This button always takes you back to the location you have designated as the first one to show in your viewing window. Right now, this has been designated at the Welcome to Netscape page. Your home location is an important feature. You may designate another location, such as a thematic unit site, as your home location each time a student begins using Netscape Navigator. This saves time in a busy classroom. More on this later.

The next button, **Reload**, is helpful when you are having problems accessing a popular location on the WWW because everyone else wants to get there, too. When this happens, you will receive a message that says Netscape was unable to connect to your desired location. Press Reload and try again. Sometimes, a screen will not transmit completely to your computer for one reason or another. Press Reload when this happens and you should receive a complete screen.

Images is a button to open up images that have been turned off. Sometimes teachers will turn off Netscape Navigator's ability to send graphics in order to speed up the transmission of text information. (You may do this by selecting the Options menu at the top and unchecking the "Auto Load Images" box.) To see the pictures on any page when they have been turned off, simply press the "Images" button and the graphic images will appear after a short time.

Open is used to travel to a location on the Internet by using its address to take you there. You must know the address of a location to use this feature. Perhaps, for example, you just read an article with the address on the WWW for the American Civil War Information Archive (http://www.access.digex.net/~bdboyle/cw.html). How do you visit this site to see if it will be helpful during a unit on the Civil War? Click on the Open button, type in the address (exactly as it is written), and then press return. This will open any location on the WWW when you know the address in advance. Be careful! A missing period or even the wrong case for a letter (e.g., upper case instead of lower case) will give you an error message. The address must be typed exactly as you find it.

Print does pretty much what it says. You may print out pages on the Internet that appear in your viewing window with this button. This is often helpful in scavenger hunts when students need evidence they have found a location you specified. It also comes in handy in other situations as well. Need a lesson plan for tomorrow? Find a nice collection (http://ericir.syr.edu/Virtual/Lessons/) and print out ones that meet your needs. Note that the Print button will print out all of the pages at a location, not just the single page that appears in your viewing window. You can usually estimate the number of pages by scrolling down through information in the viewing window.

The button **Find** will locate any word you specify in your viewing window. This is not very useful unless you have a very lengthy viewing window. Find does not search throughout the Internet for this word; another button will do this. It only searches the document you have showing in your window.

Stop will abort any transmission to your computer that is in progress. This is helpful when it is taking too long to get into a web site; sometimes too many people want to go to the same place at once. If you don't wish to keep waiting to connect, press Stop. Then move on to another location. Come back in a few minutes and the line may be open.

Location Window

Figure 2-5.   The Location Window

Your current location on the Internet is indicated in the location window. This contains the "Uniform Resource Locator" (URL), or address, of the site that appears in the viewing window. Sometimes these can be quite long. Note, for example, the address for the home page of the Africa History Archives in Figure 2-5.

You may also use the location window to go to a new site as long as you know its address. Simply highlight the current address in the location window with your mouse, type in a new address, and press return.

Directory Buttons

The directory buttons are shown in Figure 2-6.

What's New?	What's Cool?	Destinations	Net Search	People	Software

Figure 2-6.   Directory Buttons in Netscape Navigator

The first item in the row of directory buttons is **What's New?** Clicking on this button will take you to a site containing hypertext links to interesting sites recently added to the Internet. It is a good location for you to begin exploring sites and to practice navigation strategies.

The next item is another popular location to see what is taking place on the WWW, **What's Cool?** Clicking on this button will take you to a list of "cool" sites, often locations richest in multimedia and interesting information.

Sometimes we want to search for information on the Internet by category. The button **Destinations** will take you to a screen showing a number of different categories, including News, Finance, Hardware and Software, Sports, and Travel. Clicking on any of these graphic elements will take you to a set of links to items related to that category.

Often we need to search the Internet for very specific information. The button **Net Search** will take you to a location with "search engines," computers in the Internet that will search for sites containing words or phrases you specify. Are you looking for information about origami for next week's unit on Japan? Click on the Net Search button and then type in the word "origami." Press return (or click the Search button next to "origami") and a list of sites on the WWW will appear, each with information about origami. Often, they will also contain short descriptions of the contents at each location. You may find a great location, Joseph Wu's Origami Page (http://www.dat.co.jp/Origami), with directions for creating many wonderful paper objects as well as information about this Japanese art form. To go to this location, all you need to do is click on the hypertext link that takes you there.

You will notice, after clicking the Net Search button, that there are many different search engines available at this location: Yahoo, InfoSeek, Magellan, Lycos, and others. Each searches in a slightly different fashion. If you develop a preference for one, all you need to do is click on the hypertext link to the search engine you prefer. Or, you may wish to set a bookmark for your favorite search engine.

Notice that most search engines also have a set of categories listed, in case you wish to search by category rather than by a word or phrase. When you click on a category like education, a more specific subdirectory will appear containing additional categories within education. Click on a category such as K–12, for example, and you will find more specific subcategories like science, math, art, or social studies. Continue until you find the types of items you are looking for.

The button **People** is helpful if you wish to search for someone's e-mail address, regular address, or telephone number. Clicking on this button will take you to search engines which specialize in locating people and businesses.

Finally, the **Software** button takes you to a site where you may obtain the most recent version of Netscape Navigator and download recently released "plug-in" modules that allow you to view multimedia features (video, audio, 3-D, and animations) on the Internet. It is useful to check this site periodically, since new versions of Navigator and new "plug-in" modules come out frequently. New software, of course, will require new navigation skills. If you update Navigator, be certain to help students become familiar with its new navigation features. Netscape Navigator is free to educational institutions; you may download new versions without cost.

FAQ (Frequently Asked Question)

Why does my computer sometimes "freeze" when students are using Netscape Navigator? The computer won't respond to commands or the cursor is stuck in one position.

There are always several possibilities when something like this happens. There may be a conflict between different software programs on your computer, for example. This type of problem will usually require technical assistance to resolve. Often, however, we have found a simple cause to the problem: students freeze the cursor because they click the mouse too often and too quickly, trying to get something to happen on the screen, without allowing Netscape Navigator a chance to keep up with their commands. Students are used to the double-click techniques and rapid response typical of most computers. Netscape and much of the Internet only requires a single click to activate a hypertext link. Moreover, it sometimes takes a few moments for a computer in Australia to respond to a student in Michigan. When students use double-click strategies and click quickly on multiple items, it sometimes causes the computer to "freeze" because the computer in Australia can't keep up. We have found that it is important to explain this to students, remind them to click only once on a hypertext link, and encourage them to wait until it says "Done" at the bottom of the Netscape Navigator window before clicking on a new item. Sometimes, you can "unfreeze" Netscape with a little trick. Count to ten and then hold down the Control key, the Option key, and the ⌘ key while you press the Escape key. When a window appears asking you if you wish to quit Netscape Navigator, select "Cancel." This will often unfreeze the cursor.

Using Bookmarks: An Important Navigation Aid for Your Class

Netscape has a special tool that will assist you and your students as you navigate the Internet: the bookmark menu item. This allows you to set a bookmark when you are at a useful location on the WWW. You may then come back to this location quickly at a later time by selecting the bookmark. If you are at your computer and Netscape Navigator is running, look at the top of your screen. (Otherwise, look back to the top of Figure 2-3.) Here you will find a menu item called "Bookmarks." If you open this menu item with your mouse, you will see an item that says "Add Bookmark." Selecting "Add Bookmark" will set a bookmark for your current location. The bookmark will be listed inside the "Bookmarks" menu item. At a later time, if you wish to return to this location on the Internet, all you need to do is to click on the "Bookmarks" menu item and select the bookmark for the location you wish to return to.

Bookmarks are very useful in a classroom. During a unit, you may set bookmarks for sites you wish students to visit and use in their studies. This saves time finding resources and also limits the possibility of extensive "surfing" of sites you do not wish students to visit.

You may manage the organization of your bookmarks in a number of ways. This is accomplished by selecting the menu item labeled "Window" and choosing "Bookmarks." A window will open up on your screen, as in Figure 2-7, listing each of your bookmarks. You may do a number of things once this window is open. You may delete a bookmark by selecting it and then going to the menu item labeled "Edit" and choosing "Delete Bookmark." You may also sort your bookmarks alphabetically by first clicking on the folder with bookmarks you wish to sort and then selecting "Sort Bookmarks" in the menu item at the top that says "Item." You may also move bookmarks around in the list in your bookmark window by dragging them with your mouse and dropping them to another location in your list. Other features and functions may be explored on your own by looking at each of the menu items at the top of your screen when you have the "Bookmarks" window open. When you finish, close the "Bookmarks" window.

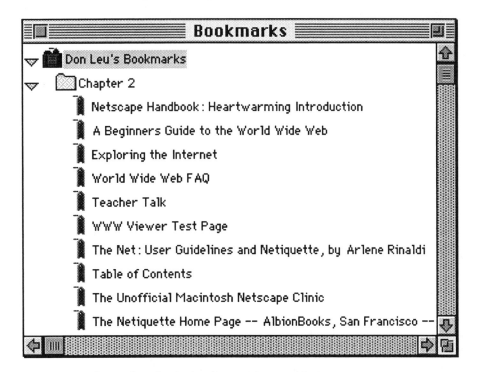

Figure 2-7.   The Bookmark Window box in Netscape Navigator

It is often very useful at the beginning of the year to have an Internet Workshop devoted to the use of bookmarks. At one session, share information about how bookmarks work. Then encourage students to try out some of the additional features described there. At the next workshop session have students share what they have discovered.

Designating a Home Location Page

It is also very useful to designate a home page location on your classroom computer related to content that your class is studying. A home page location is the page that shows up first on your screen each time students connect to the Internet with Netscape Navigator. This, too, saves time in a busy classroom, since students begin immediately with a site containing important content for their work. To change the home location from Netscape's Welcome Page, go to the menu item "Options" and select "General Preference." A window similar to that in Figure 2-8 will appear.

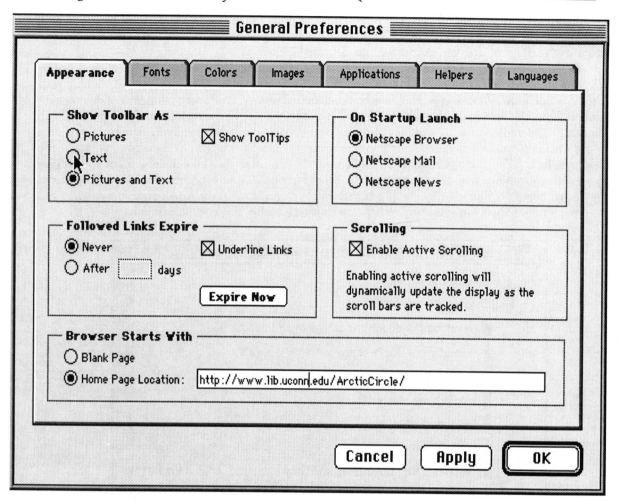

Figure 2-8.   Setting Preferences for a new home location page: The General Preferences Window

At the bottom of this window, type in the address of the location on the Internet you wish to designate as your home page location. In this example, the teacher is designating a site on the Arctic called "Arctic Circle" (http://www.lib.uconn.edu/ArcticCircle/), since his class will begin a unit tomorrow on life in the Arctic. As you can see in Figure 2-9, this location contains many useful resources for students to use in their investigations.

Also note several other options in the General Preferences window in Figure 2-8. Selecting any of the tabs at the top will take you to folders where you may set preferences for fonts, colors, images, applications, helpers, and language. A useful preference in the appearance folder is listed under "Show Toolbar As." If you wish to save a bit of space on your screen, select the button "Show Toolbar as Text." This will eliminate the pictures in the tool bar, take up less room on your screen, and display more information in the viewing window. You may look at Figure 2-9 to see how the toolbar looks with only text and no pictures.

Multimedia Tools for Your Computer: Using All of the Resources on the Internet

OK. You are all set. Your computer is connected to the Internet with Netscape Navigator, you have figured out the essentials for navigating around the world and even visited the Louvre in Paris (http://www.paris.org/Musees/Louvre/) and a wonderful site at the White House where you discovered a special tour for stu-

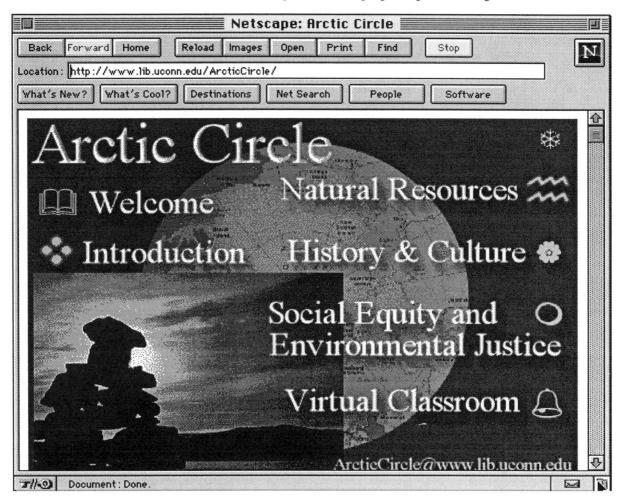

Figure 2-9.   The Arctic Circle Home Page
(http://www.lib.uconn.edu/ArcticCircle/)

dents (http://www.whitehouse.gov/WH/kids/html/kidshome.html). At some locations, you noticed that you can even obtain audio and video in addition to graphics. Sometimes, these came through and sometimes they didn't. Why?

First, a little background. Each location on the Internet may require slightly different tools to read its graphics, audio, and video information. Netscape Navigator has plug-ins and helper tools that let you read many items. Often, though, you reach a site where the person wasn't very thoughtful and used a multimedia tool you do not have. As a result, you discover you cannot hear the audio or view the video or graphic without adding the appropriate tool to Netscape Navigator.

When this happens, a message will usually appear directing you to extend your capabilities by adding a new plug-in tool to your plug-in file. You may be directed to Netscape's central location for plug-in programs and be encouraged to download the appropriate program. Go ahead and follow these directions, restart your computer, and visit the multimedia site you had located earlier. You should then be able to view, read, or listen to the appropriate multimedia element.

Until Netscape Navigator's plug-ins are more widely used by people on the Internet, you may have to tinker a bit to view videos or listen to audio files that require special applications. It is not too hard; it will just take a few moments to add the appropriate helper application. We will try to explain how to add these

E-Mail for You

From: Ruth Musgrave (whaletimes@whaletimes.org)
Subject: Developing Navigation Skills

   Hi! My first bit of advice is, "Play, play, play and play some more, on the Internet first before you do anything." If you're "playing" you'll relax, take all sorts of twists and turns and find many exciting sites (and some you won't visit again!).
   Try the various search engines like Yahoo, Lycos....etc. You'll find that the search engines vary in style and content. Our favorite is "AltaVista"; we've found it to be by far the most comprehensive search engine available. Using key words or phrases, you can find just about anything.
   Now you're ready to allow your students access. Be certain to allow your students time to play, too. If you feel you need to structure the "play" (due to time limitations or other concerns), create a scavenger hunt that encourages students to use the various search engines. Take them all over the world (with a tie-in to geographic studies by pairing with world map). Have them find things like the White House, the IN USA homepage and the Louvre in France. Once they're comfortable traveling via the computer they can begin to use it effectively.
   The biggest challenge is to allow students room to explore without allowing too much freedom. The Internet is this amazing open world. Researchers, web designers, artists....from all over the world allow students to send them questions directly—the minute they think of it. Because of this freedom, we also suggest that you teach your students Internet etiquette (sometimes students take advantage of the anonymity of the computer). Scientists and others who provide e-mail addresses or forms will answer student's letters, but become disenchanted when they begin to receive silly or inappropriate notes. (You may want to read *Net.speak or visit one of the sites on the web that discuss Internet etiquette.) Good luck and enjoy this wonderful tool for classrooms!

   Ruth Musgrave, Director
   WhaleTimes SeaBed
   www.whaletimes.org
   whaletimes@whaletimes.org

   * <u>Net.speak—the internet dictionary</u>, Kelly, Chris; Hayden Books, 1994, ISBN: 1-56830-095-6)

helpers and spare you as many of the technical details as possible. If you are completely uninterested in technical details, skip the remaining portion of this section. You can always come back later if you are interested.

For graphics, you probably have everything you require within Netscape Navigator to read almost anything you will ever encounter. Thus, reading graphics will not be a problem most of the time. More frequently, you may not have a particular program to read an audio or video file and a message will appear on your screen naming the reader you lack. If you require them, the best and most common graphic, audio, and video readers not included as plug-ins are listed in Table 2-1. Just visit the address on the WWW listed for each and download the appropriate programs onto your computer. There is no cost for them. Make a note of where each program was downloaded onto your computer. You will need this information later.

After downloading a helper application you wish to add, select the "Options" menu item at the top of Netscape Navigator and choose "General Preferences." Now click on the tab that says "Helpers." You should see something that looks like Figure 2-10.

Now, we want to tell your helper file where this new application is located. Select the button in Figure 2-10 that says "New." A new window will appear. Find the button that says "Application" and click on this. Then click on the button that says "Browse." Locate the helper application you wish to add to Netscape Navigator (it was probably placed on your hard disk when you downloaded it). After you find this new helper, select it by clicking on it once and then select "Open." Now click on "OK" and return to the Helpers window. You should find this new application in your list of helper applications shown in Figure 2-10.

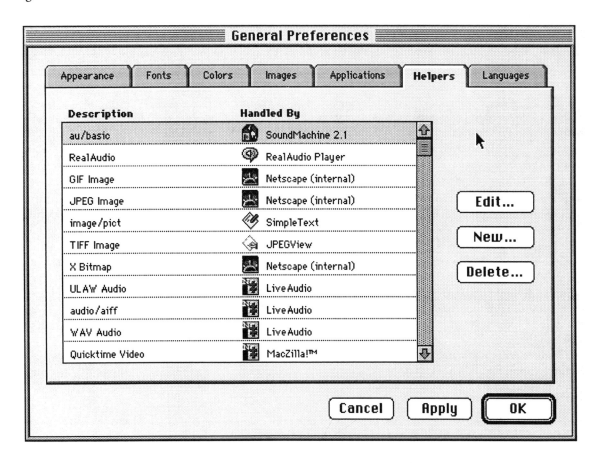

Figure 2-10. Adding multimedia helpers: The helper window in General Preferences

Type of Media Player	Program Name	Available on the WWW at:
Graphic	JPEGView GIFConverter GraphicConverter	http://wwwhost.ots.utexas.edu/mac/pub-mac-graphics.html
Audio	SoundMachine	ftp://ftp.ncsa.uiuc.edu/Mac/Mosaic/Helpers (obtain the file called: sound-machine-21.hqx)
Video	Sparkle	http://wwwhost.ots.utexas.edu/mac/main.html
Real-Time Audio	RealAudio Player	http:www.realaudio.com

Table 2-1.   Useful sites for obtaining graphic, audio, and video players for Macintosh (System 7.5 or higher) that may not be included with your version of Netscape Navigator.

You may wish to test your version of Netscape Navigator to see which multimedia elements it is capable of reading. It is quite easy to do this and to acquire multimedia readers you wish to add to your program. Just visit the WWW Viewer Test Page (http://www-dsed.llnl.gov/documents/WWWtest.html) to test a variety of helpers. Netscape Navigator will play each multimedia element if you have the appropriate application listed in your helpers folder. If not, you will be directed to the appropriate location where you can load it if you wish to do so.

A Word About Some Strange Names You May Encounter on the Internet: FTP, Gopher, Archie, and Veronica

Before the development of the WWW and the rich multimedia resources it includes, the Internet only used the medium of text. You could navigate around to different locations, but you would never see graphics, animation, video, or hear audio. Several different areas of the Internet existed, each using its own structure and its own way of navigating through its sites. There were FTP sites and Gopher sites. To search FTP sites, one used a program called Archie, and to search Gopher sites, one used a program called Veronica. There were also Telnet sites.

With the development of the WWW and powerful browsers such as Netscape Navigator, everything is quickly changing. Now, a single browser can read information at FTP, Gopher, or Telnet sites as well as locations on the WWW where other media sources exist. You no longer need to know special techniques for searching FTP or Gopher locations, nor do you require special software for visiting Telnet sites. All of this, and searching for WWW sites as well, is done for you by powerful browsers such as Netscape Navigator.

Sometimes, for example, you will notice an address in your location window that does not begin with the prefix used for all WWW sites: http://. Instead, you may encounter a Gopher site with a gopher prefix (gopher://) or an FTP site with an ftp address (ftp://). If you come across a Gopher or an FTP site, notice how these include only text information in your viewing window. You will not see other media sources. Most of these older sites from earlier Internet days are quickly being converted to WWW sites. As this happens, it becomes less likely to encounter them on the Internet.

E-Mail for You

From: tgray@pepperdine.edu (Terrie Gray)
Subject: Using the WWW in my classroom

    Hi! My 7th- and 8th-grade students and I are fortunate to
work in a classroom with 15 Macintosh computers and a teaching
workstation all connected to the Internet via an ISDN line, which
means we have fast access. We use Netscape Navigator for our
browser.

    Using the web for research requires navigation skills. When
we first started, two school terms ago, the search engines
weren't as easy to use as they are now, nor were the resources
available to the degree they are currently. Nevertheless, even at
this date, I still find that students of this age tend to become
easily frustrated. Many have not developed skills for selecting
likely sites from a long list. They are not patient readers. Or
they get distracted by something that looks intriguing, but is
off topic.

    Because of this response to my early web projects, I now try
to steer students first to a page I've created which contains
links to sites that will most likely be useful. In the spring I
involve the students in a research project on an animal of their
choice. They are required to search multiple resources, including
the Internet, for information. The page I created for this assignment (the first one I ever made!) is located at:

    http://www.chicojr.chico.k12.ca.us/staff/gray/animals.html

    Since its original creation, students and contacts from all
over the world have contributed links to this collection. 8th
grade students studying the weather were involved in multiple
web-based activities this last year. Our most successful was one
involving lessons and resources located at:

    http://athena.wednet.edu/curric/weather/index.html

    This site contains directions for activities as well as the
links to up-to-date weather maps for collecting data about current conditions. The project we focused on required the students
to choose 3 cities, read and chart the weather for those cities
over a period of a week or two. Then they researched the topology
of the surrounding areas, drew in the nearby land forms and water
bodies on their maps, and tried to figure out what caused the
weather patterns or changes. As students worked through this
project, I moved from group to group asking, "What are you learning from this project?" Most responded that while they had
learned to read weather maps, they were learning much more about
how to use the Internet. That surprised me, but reinforces the
idea that using a tool like the web outside of a content area or
disassociated from real work—like just having kids browse through
"fun" sites—is not as powerful as using it to get what they need
for a complex project.

    Good luck with your own Internet experiences!

Terrie Gray
Science Teacher, Chico Jr. High School
Chico, California

Developing Appropriate Use Policies

Because the Internet is so powerful, it has the potential for great good. At the same time, however, this power may also be abused. Students may travel to sites that are inappropriate for them to view, they may send out an offensive e-mail message, or they may interfere with the running of a computer system.

To respond to the viewing of inappropriate sites, some schools use software filters that deny students access to certain Internet sites, especially in the younger grades. These filters deny access to locations where certain words appear. Teachers and parents may edit the list of words used in the blocking software. You may find out more about these software programs and download evaluation copies for free or view demonstrations at the following locations:

Cyber Patrol—http://www.cyberpatrol.com/

Net Nanny—http://www.netnanny.com/netnanny/home.html

SurfWatch—http://www.surfwatch.com/

Whether your system uses a software filter or not, it is important that your district develop an acceptable use policy as part of a comprehensive program of Internet navigation. An acceptable use policy is a written agreement that is signed by parents/guardians, students, and teachers which specifies the conditions under which students may use the Internet, defines appropriate and inappropriate use, and defines penalties for violating items in the policy. Parents/guardians, teachers, and students all need to be aware of the consequences for misusing the privilege of Internet access. Developing an acceptable use policy and then asking all parties to sign it helps to ensure that everyone understands these important issues.

What does an acceptable use policy look like? Most contain the following elements:

- *An explanation of the Internet and its role in providing information resources to students.* It is important to explain to parents/guardians and students what the Internet is and why it is important. It is also important to explain that students will be taught proper use of the Internet.

- *A description of acceptable and unacceptable behavior which emphasizes student responsibility when using the Internet.* It is important to supervise student use of the Internet, but ultimately each student must take responsibility for his or her own actions. This section describes for everyone what is appropriate and what is inappropriate.

- *A list of penalties for each violation of the policy.* Often this will describe increasing levels of penalties: a warning letter to parents/guardians for a first violation and a suspension of privileges for a repeated violation. A panel may sometimes be established to review cases.

- *A space for all parties to sign the agreement.* After discussing each element carefully with students, the form is usually sent home for parents and students to sign. Teachers will also sign this form before it is carefully filed in an appropriate location.

You may find out more information, print out sample acceptable use policies, and read about other teachers' experiences by visiting the following Internet sites:

Houston Independent School District's Acceptable Use Page

   http://chico.rice.edu/armadillo/acceptable.html

Classroom Connect's Acceptable Use Policy FTP Site:

   ftp://ftp.classroom.net/wentworth/Classroom-Connect/aup-faq.txt

AskERIC's Acceptable Use Gopher Site

   gopher://ericir.syr.edu:70/11/Guides/Agreements

Texas Acceptable Use Gopher Site

   gopher://riceinfo.rice.edu:1170/11/More/Acceptable

Child Safety on the Information Highway. Produced by the National Center for Missing and Exploited Children and Interactive Services Association

http://www.missingkids.org/information_superhighway.html

Global School Network's Guidelines and Policies for Protecting Students

http://www.gsn.org/web/tutorial/issues/index.htm#begin

?

FAQ (Frequently Asked Question)

When I try to go to a location on the WWW, it sometimes gives me a message that the server is not responding. What should I do?

The server (computer) where this web page is located may be down for servicing, someone may have turned it off, or too may people are trying to get in. Our strategy in these cases is to try to get in three times; often you can sneak in, even if it is very busy. If this fails, try again at a later time, especially if it sounds like a good site.

Instructional Strategies for Developing Navigation Skills

If your students are new to the Internet, the weekly structure developed by Ms. Davidson is a useful model. Each week consisted of small group meetings at the beginning to introduce a new navigation strategy, followed by paired work on the Internet to use the strategy as they completed a weekly classroom assignment, and concluded with an Internet Workshop at the end of the week to share experiences.

For a month or two, begin each week with short, small group instruction at the computer on an important navigational strategy such as one of the following:

- the use of search engines
- how to use directories
- using the handbook when you need help
- printing strategies
- how to use graphic elements from the WWW in your writing projects
- using the location window to type in a new address
- using the "Go" menu item
- helping others
- adding new helper programs
- understanding the meaning of addresses on the Internet; and
- strategies for staying on task

During this time, show 5 or 6 students a new aspect to navigating the Internet. Introduce the strategy, show students why it is useful and when it might be used, then give one or two students an opportunity to practice it while others watch. As you move through the year, you may wish to turn this over to the groups themselves. Each week, have a different group be responsible for teaching the other groups.

During the week, students can integrate the new strategy as they complete content work in one of the subject areas or on a thematic unit. While some schools may have sufficient computer resources to allow students to work alone on the Internet during the week, it is actually preferable to have students work together in pairs since this provides more teaching/learning opportunities. Seldom do two students know the same navigation strategies for using the Internet. When students work together, they exchange information and teach each other navigation skills. Rotating partners each week or so ensures that all students have a chance to learn from every other student in the class. This increases opportunities for sharing information about navigation strategies.

At the end of each week, an Internet Workshop will help to consolidate the navigation strategies you introduced at the beginning of the week. It will also raise new navigation issues that you may then explore in subsequent weeks, again in small groups at the beginning of the week, in pairs during the week, and with the whole class at the end of the week.

It is important to note that the time used to develop Internet strategies need not be great. Small group sessions at the beginning of the week should take no more than 5–10 minutes each. The learning that takes place as students work in pairs occurs during regular content learning experiences; this takes little time. Finally, Internet Workshops need not take more than 20–30 minutes as you share navigational experiences and raise questions that came up during the week. You will find that time devoted to developing navigation skills at the beginning of the year pays rich dividends as your students develop confidence and expertise at navigating the Internet on their own.

As your students become more experienced on the Internet, you should think about modifying this initial structure for developing navigation knowledge. Spend a little time observing students working together on the Internet, looking for those students who have not acquired all of the basic navigational strategies. Then, gather these students together in small group sessions at the beginning of each week according to the strategies they need to refine. One group may need additional assistance on using search engines, while a second group may need additional assistance on using the location window to go to a known address. This additional small group work simply ensures that all of your students develop the essential skills of navigation. It probably won't take more than a week or two to accomplish this. During this time, students may continue to work in pairs on classroom assignments, helping one another.

As students develop the ability to navigate on their own, you will find yourself devoting less time to this area and spending more time on content projects. Questions during Internet Workshop, for example, will gradually and naturally move from questions about how to navigate to discussions of content locations that students have discovered on the Internet for classroom work. As you move through the year, you will find less and less time devoted to navigation and more and more time devoted to how to use the information students have found on the Internet in effective ways.

E-Mail for You

From: Richard Love <rlove@standrews.sa.edu.au>
Subject: "Help! I have 900,000 hits for my search!!"

What would you do if one of your students said this when they
entered 'whales' or 'Egypt' as the keyword for their search on
the Internet? Using information and communications technologies
for research requires skills—and in many ways these skills are
generic to the different technologies. That is, searching for
information on a Library's computer network, or on an encyclopedia on CD-ROM such as Encarta or Grolier requires students to
know how to enter a keyword for their search, how to refine their
search, how to access the information, how to use the information, etc. These skills are much the same when searching on the
Internet.

Let me provide an example! Shortly after the 1996 Atlanta
Olympic Games, Alexandra in Grade 4 wanted to find a list of the
world records for the 100m and 200m sprints. Her initial keyword
search (using Alta Vista) was running. The search request returned 500000 matches!! Most of them were concerned with running
businesses, computer programs, etc! As a class, we discussed how
we could use more sophisticated techniques for the research. We
thought we should use the term "world record" in our search, but
knew we could not use the word "metre" because it is spelt differently around the world. Our final search request was the following: "world record" +100m. We very quickly found a list of
men's and women's 100m and 200m world record times from the beginning of the modern Olympics up to and including the 1996 Olympic Games.

This knowledge transformed our use of the Internet for
search. Students became far more efficient and effective when
using the Internet for research. In addition, they are now 'better' researchers on CD-ROMs and the Library!

Richard Love

Navigation Resources on the Internet

A Beginners Guide to the WWW—http://www.cs.unc.edu/~bedi/report.html

This is just what it says it is. Clearly written, this document explains the basics of the WWW and navigation. A good beginning point for new users. This might be a useful location to direct your class to at the beginning of the year.

Adam Rosen's Quick Guide to Viewing the World Wide Web—http://www.cgicafe.com/~ajrosen/guide.html

Have you been working hard trying to figure out how to navigate in the WWW and are in need of a little humor? Visit this (very) quick guide to viewing the WWW and enjoy the joke. Cute.

AskERIC Virtual Library: Educational Questions—http://ericir.syr.edu/Qa/userform.html

At this location you may ask any question regarding educational research or practice and receive a personalized response back via e-mail within 48 hours. The "Educational Questions" site is a part of the Educational Resources Information Center (ERIC), federally funded national information system. Many other useful resources are also located here.

Entering the World Wide Web: A Guide to Cyberspace—http://www.eit.com/web/www.guide/

Though it is becoming a little dated, this book provides the clearest explanation of the WWW we have found. It is also the most comprehensive. A nice introduction to the world of the Internet with many useful examples and graphics. Because it was written in 1994, it has little useful information about Netscape Navigator. Still, an excellent location to begin reading about how the Internet and the WWW work.

Life on the Internet—http://www.screen.com/understand/exploring.html

If you are just beginning your travels on the Internet, this is a good location to assist you with information about navigation issues. In addition to an easy-to-read style, it includes many useful links to locations that will be useful to you as a new user. This might also be a useful location to direct your class to at the beginning of the year.

Frequently Asked Questions About Acceptable Use Policies—ftp://ftp.classroom.net/wentworth/Classroom-Connect/aup-faq.txt

This location, sponsored by Classroom Connect, provides a very useful discussion of what acceptable use policies are, why they are important, and how to go about developing one for your school. A sample acceptable use policy is provided so that you can copy and edit it for your school's use.

Online Support Center—(http://www.onlinesupport.com/)

Need help navigating the Internet? Here is the place for you. This site provides free on-line support and will answer any questions you have about navigation or other aspects of the WWW and the Internet.

Netscape Navigator Handbook—http://home.netscape.com/eng/mozilla/2.0/handbook/

This is the location for the official handbook of Netscape Navigator. It is the most accurate information resource for using Netscape to navigate the Internet that you can find.

Teacher Talk—http://www.mightymedia.com/talk/working.htm

A useful discussion area for teachers to talk about issues of instruction and technology. If you have a question, post it here and you will receive answers from other teachers. You will be asked for your name and a password to enter. Do not use your e-mail password or another password you use on a computer. Use a different one to prevent anyone from accessing your accounts.

The Net: User Guidelines and Netiquette—http://www.fau.edu/rinaldi/netiquette/index.html

This Internet book provides a useful discussion about socially responsible ways of using the Internet. It would provide useful background information before developing an acceptable use policy. It would also be useful as required reading for older students at the beginning of the year. Included is a list of Ten Commandments for Computer Ethics from the Computer Ethics Institute. This might be printed out and posted next to each computer in your classroom.

World Wide Web FAQ (Frequently Asked Questions)—http://www.boutell.com/faq/#intro

This site contains much detailed information about the WWW. It is organized in a question–answer format and includes information about a number of topics: the World Wide Web, obtaining and using web browsers, establishing and using web servers, authoring web pages, using images and scripts. The site is most useful for someone who is already somewhat familiar with the WWW.

WWW Viewer Test Page—http://www-dsed.llnl.gov/documents/WWWtest.html

At this location you may test many common helper applications to see if they are in your Helpers folder. If they are not, this location will connect you to a location on the WWW where you may download them onto your computer.

References

Giagnocavo, G., McLain, T., DiStefano, V., & Sturm, C. (1995). *Educator's Internet companion.* Lancaster, PA: Wentworth Worldwide Media.

Kidder, G. & Harris, S. (1996). *Netscape Navigator quick tour,* 2nd edition. Research Triangle Park, NC: Ventana.

Levine, J., Baroudi, C., & Young, M. (1996). *The Internet for dummies,* 3rd edition. Foster City, CA: IDG Books Worldwide, Inc.

Tretter, M. (1995). *How to use the Internet,* 2nd edition. Emeryville, CA: Ziff-Davis Press.

Chapter 3
The Power of Communication: E-mail, Mailing Lists, and Newsgroups

```
To:    Our readers
From:  djleu@sued.syr.edu (Don Leu),
       ddleu@syr.edu (Debbie Leu)
Subject: Communicating on the Internet
```

The Internet is clearly a powerful tool for linking and locating information. Equally important is its ability to link people. In fact, electronic communication is one of the net's most popular uses.

Compared to other modes of communication such as using the telephone and writing letters, communication on the Internet is often quicker, cheaper, and more efficient. It also lends itself to a variety of purposes and activities for teachers as well as students. Some activities may appear to be just updates of previous techniques; for example, penpals become "keypals." But Internet versions often expand the scope of older lessons and move students toward more independent learning. Students often feel freer to express themselves and ask questions via e-mail, too. The most important advantage of electronic communication is that it exposes students to a wide range of viewpoints and people from around the world. Integrating these diverse (and even contrary) ideas with their own experiences will help students develop analytical and critical thinking skills.

E-mail is not only another way to get information; it also gives us the opportunity to share what we know through the power of communication.

Don and Debbie

?

FAQ (Frequently Asked Question)

What exactly is e-mail? What are mailing lists?

E-mail is electronic mail, messages sent electronically from one computer to another. Special software programs allow any person who has an e-mail address to send and receive messages to any other individual who has an e-mail address. You can also send and receive messages to specific groups of people by subscribing to a mailing list (also known as discussion lists and listservs). Both e-mail and mailing list messages are sent directly to your electronic mailbox.

Mr. Diaz was especially excited about the upcoming school year. The first major unit in social studies was the Middle East. He and the other seventh grade teachers were working together so that the students could study various aspects of Middle Eastern culture in all of their classes. As in the past, Mr. Diaz was using the Internet to find information related to the unit, but this summer he was also trying to improve his e-mail skills. As a result, he began using electronic communication more often, and was surprised to realize what a powerful tool it could be.

He had started rather casually by asking for suggestions from Ms. Walker, the leader of a recent in-service for his district. Although she lived in another city, e-mail made it easy for him to contact her. He didn't need to call at a certain time, or leave messages on her answering machine. And he felt more comfortable asking for help since e-mailing didn't interrupt her routine the way telephoning would have. She suggested that he check out some keypal sites on the net and encouraged him to ask for advice from other teachers on SCHOOL-L, a mailing list they both subscribed to.

He thought international keypals would be great. The students could ask questions, conduct interviews, and perhaps exchange photos. They could learn a lot about another culture. When he searched for keypals, Mr. Diaz was pleased to find that not only could his students look for individual keypals, but also he could request a partner class. He did this by subscribing to a mailing list at Intercultural E-mail Classroom Connections (http://www.stolaf.edu/network/iecc/), where he posted a message introducing himself and his class and asking if there were any classes from Middle Eastern countries that might want to partner with his class. It might be good to have keypals that were all from one class and a co-teacher to share ideas with.

Although Mr. Diaz had subscribed to SCHOOL-L for some time, he had never sent a message. The list always had good information, though, so he submitted a message asking for suggestions about sites and resources on the Middle East. Within a day, he had several responses. One teacher suggested working on an in-depth project with a partner class, and mentioned that he could find really helpful information on designing collaborative projects at a site called NickNacks (http://www1.minn.net:80/~schubert/EdHelpers.html#anchor590458).

Mr. Diaz hadn't done many collaborative projects, so he sent another message asking for help on projects, and was pleased to get a return message suggesting the Project Approach site (http://www.ualberta.ca/~schard/projects.htm), which included information on teaching with projects, project assessment, and a link to a projects discussion group. This might work out well if he could find a partner class.

Mr. Diaz noted ideas from both sites and began thinking about the kind of projects that would be worthwhile and enjoyable for the students. He wanted to make good use of e-mail's capabilities. Just exchanging facts that could easily be found in an encyclopedia wouldn't be very effective. Perhaps he could get two partner classes from different countries. Then, the students could get information on specific topics and compare the different viewpoints. Maybe they could even do some sort of analysis in math class. He kept notes on index cards about several ideas so that he could share them with the students and get their input before they made a final decision.

After reading another message from a teacher who had just returned from the Middle East, Mr. Diaz also started wondering how his class should present their ideas to a partner class. This message focused on cultural differences and ended with a suggestion to have some discussions about diversity and courtesy on the Internet.

In addition to thinking about content, Mr. Diaz had been working with the other teachers to develop a plan to expand the students' computer skills and manage their time on the computer. Each classroom had only one computer, but this year students would have their own e-mail accounts; this would be a big change from last year when they had sent their messages from their teacher's account. Last year's teacher had kept an electronic folder for each student in her account, so she could easily monitor what they wrote. Mr. Diaz would have to use a different system. He didn't really want to print out all their messages, but he wouldn't have time to read each one as it was sent, either. Perhaps they could have a discussion about manners on the net, relating to themselves as well as to their keypals. He could even do a workshop and maybe some role plays about how they would feel if they received a mean message. He was looking forward to the new year, but there was still a lot to do.

Lessons from the Classroom

This scenario illustrates several lessons for using electronic communication effectively. First, as a teacher, Mr. Diaz used mailing lists and newsgroups to get suggestions from other teachers. This is one of the most powerful ways for teachers to expand their knowledge and learn from others' experiences. Many lists have hundreds of members, and newsgroups may have a thousand readers; together, their composite expertise covers almost every topic and point of view. Having e-mail is almost like having access to an "individualized" in-service program anytime you need it.

Second, Mr. Diaz had clear goals and purposes. He didn't see the Internet as an end in itself but as a tool whose use could be incorporated into the curriculum to help students develop certain skills and meet desired objectives. In this case, electronic communication would help increase understanding of other cultures, provide practice in collaborative teamwork, develop critical thinking, and encourage tolerance and respect for others.

Third, his students' ages and previous computer experience played a large role in Mr. Diaz's planning. He chose age-appropriate activities that included student participation in project choices. This would expand their e-mail skills and foster better decision making, both of which would help prepare them to use electronic communication more independently in the future.

Fourth, by planning lessons and projects that involved not only obtaining information, but also analyzing and synthesizing it, Mr. Diaz was helping his students develop their critical thinking skills.

Finally, Mr. Diaz planned lessons on "netiquette." As an e-mail user himself, he knew the importance of good "net manners." With a younger group of students, he would have posted a list of rules. However, because he recognized his seventh graders' developing ability to understand the need for order and safety, he would have them participate in discussions to formulate their own netiquette guidelines.

Using E-mail on Netscape Navigator

In order to use electronic communication effectively, you need to integrate Internet knowledge and skills with your own teaching practices. You will want to reflect on how it fits in with your approach to education, as well as consider which uses seem more suitable for students and which are better for teachers. The best place to begin your exploration of electronic communication is with e-mail. The basics of e-mail are quite straightforward, but if you haven't used it before, you should allow yourself some extra practice time to become proficient before using it in the classroom. The more proficient you are, the easier it will be to anticipate your students' needs and develop effective teaching/learning strategies.

You need only two things to begin using e-mail: an e-mail account and an e-mail software program.

Your E-mail Account

The first step is to request an e-mail account from your service provider, who will then give you an e-mail address and an e-mail password. E-mail addresses follow a standard, three-part format:

userid@host.domain

1. The <u>userid</u> (pronounced *user I.D.*) is the name or identifying number of the account user.
2. @ is the <u>"at" sign.</u>
3. The <u>host.domain</u> is the name and location of the computer that handles the account user's mail.

Here is an example: ddleu@syr.edu

The last part of the domain (<u>edu</u>) is a sub-domain category that refers to the type of group which hosts the account. For example, <u>edu</u> means the host is an educational institution; *com* means commercial; <u>gov</u> means government; and <u>net</u> means network.

Your e-mail password will be a number, word, or some combination of these. It is known only to you, somewhat like a PIN number for your bank account. Most programs allow you to change your password, but do not choose an easily guessed word or number because your password provides security for your account. For this reason, you should memorize it and keep it secret. Never let anyone else use your password.

It's also a good idea to shut down your computer, or at least sign off your account, when you leave the terminal, even for a short time. That way, no unauthorized person can read your files or use your account. If your students will send e-mail through your account rather than have their own individual accounts, it is a good idea to spend some time talking about security and privacy issues.

E-mail Software

Your second step is getting an e-mail software progam. There are several different programs, so check with your technical resource person for information about which programs your service provider supports. If you are already using e-mail and like the program you have, you may want to continue with it. On the other hand, Netscape Navigator Mail is easy to use, and because its functions are integrated into the web browser, it has the added convenience of allowing you to open any web location directly from your e-mail screen rather than having to switch back and forth to other applications. You may wish to try it out before deciding.

We will explain e-mail using examples of Netscape Navigator 3.0, but don't be concerned if you have a different version of Netscape or another kind of software. The various programs perform the same functions, require basically the same user information, and use similar terminology. As a result, you should be able to follow the procedures quite easily.

FAQ (Frequently Asked Question)

There are so many different e-mail programs and hosts. Do I need different kinds of software to communicate with everyone?

No, any e-mail software will allow you to communicate with anyone else who has an e-mail address, regardless of their location or software program.

Setting up Mail Preferences

Before you actually communicate via e-mail, you must let your software program know who you are and where to get your mail. This is done by "setting preferences." Netscape Navigator offers many options, but only a few must be set before you begin sending and receiving messages. You will need the information below to set your preferences. Contact your resource person or service provider for any information you are not sure of. You may wish to write it down for easy reference.

Your name: _____

Your e-mail address: _____

Your reply-to address: _____

Your organization: _____

Your outgoing mail server: _____

Your incoming mail server: _____
(usually the same as the outgoing server)

Your POP ID: _____
(usually your userid)

To begin setting your preferences, open Netscape Navigator. Locate the menu bar at the top of the main window. Move the cursor to the Options heading. Depress the mouse button, move it down to Mail and News Preferences, and release the button. Then click on the Identity tab. This will open the Identity preferences panel as in Figure 3-l.

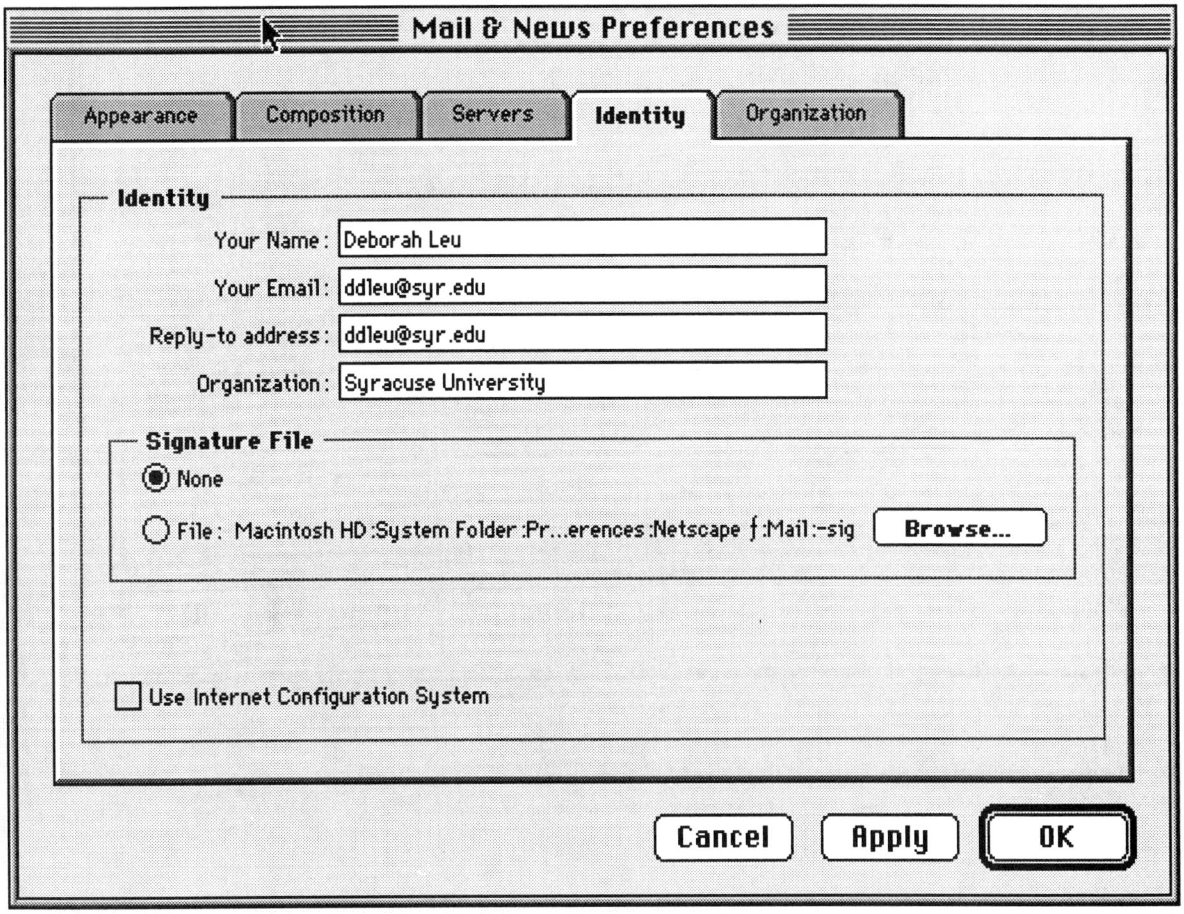

Figure 3-1.   This is an example of the Identity Tab of the Mail and News Preferences Panel.

Enter your name, e-mail address, reply-to address, and organization in the appropriate boxes. An example is provide in Figure 3-l above.

Now, click on the Servers tab. Enter your outgoing and incoming servers (these are usually the same) and your POP ID (which is usually your userid). An example is provided in Figure 3-2 below. Click on OK, which closes the Mail and News Preferences panel. These are the only preferences that must be specified to use e-mail. You may wish to explore General Preferences or Mail and News Preferences under the Options heading of the main menu in order to customize your mail service. You can also get help from your technical support person.

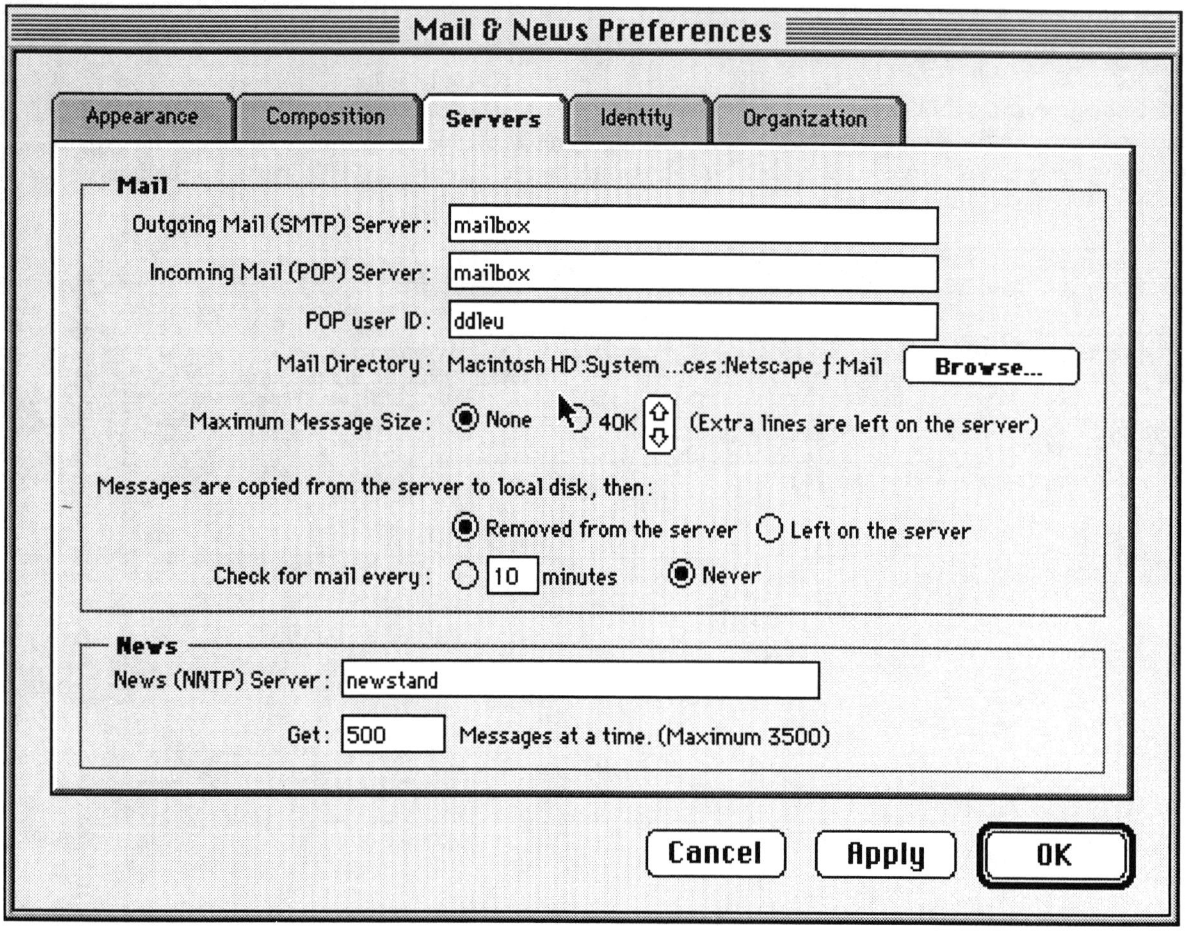

Figure 3-2.   This is an example of the Servers Tab of the Mail and News Preferences Panel.

The Mail Window

Now you are ready to use e-mail. Open the Mail Window by clicking on the mail icon, the small envelope in the lower right corner of the main Netscape screen. (See Figure 3.3)

Figure 3-3.   Note the mail icon in the lower right hand corner. Clicking on this will open your e-mail window.

When you first open the Mail Window, Netscape Navigator will attempt to check with the mail server to see if you have any new mail. Before it retrieves the mail, however, it will ask for your e-mail password. (See Figure 3-4.)

Figure 3-4.   This is the Password Request Box. Type your password in the box and click on OK to access your mail.

Type your password in the dialog box and click OK. The Mail Window (Figure 3.5) will be displayed on the screen. Notice that it is divided into three panes.

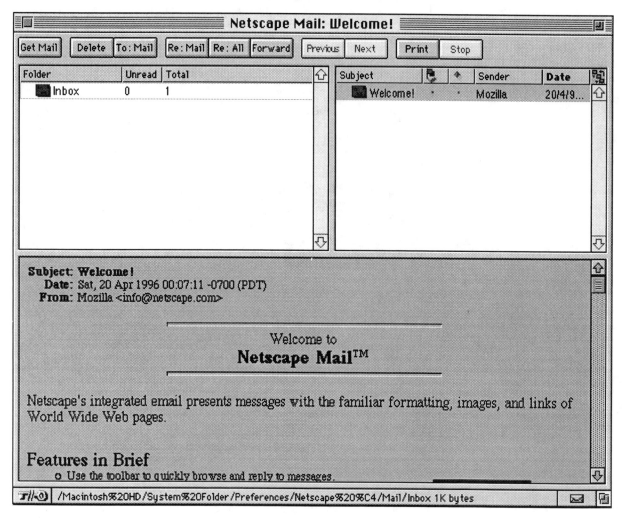

Figure 3-5.   The Mail Window. Note the Inbox folder in the left pane and message file icon in the right pane.

The top left pane shows your mail folders. If this is the first time you have used Netscape Navigator Mail, only an Inbox folder will appear. To the right are two columns displaying the number of Unread and the number of Total messages.

The top right pane shows the message files in the currently open folder. If this is the first time you have used Netscape Navigator Mail, there will be a message waiting for you from Netscape. If someone else has already sent you a message, it will also appear in this pane; if you have no messages, the pane will be empty. In the middle of this pane are two columns, one headed by a red flag and the other by a green diamond. The red flag is for marking a message for further attention. To make use of this reminder, just click on the gray dot next to the message and a red flag will appear. A green diamond next to a message means that it hasn't been read yet. You can control either feature by clicking it on and off. The three columns on the right of this pane indicate each message's subject, sender, and date. The bottom pane displays the current message.

Receiving and Reading Your E-mail

Netscape Navigator will automatically check for new messages the first time in each session that you open the Mail Window. If you want to read your messages at that time, enter your password when the dialog box appears. If you want to read them later, click Cancel. You may get your mail at any time during a session by clicking on Get Mail.

If you have new mail, the messages will be sent to your Inbox and their file icons will appear in the pane to the right. To read a message, click on its message file icon, and it will appear in the bottom pane for you to read. To read additional messages, continue clicking on each succeeding message icon, or click on the Next and Previous buttons in the tool bar at the top of the Mail Window.

Replying to a Message

In many cases, you will want to respond after reading a message. You can do this by using either the Re: Mail (reply to mail) button or the Re: All (reply to all) button. If the message you want to reply to was sent by one person and has only one address on the From: line, click on Re: Mail while the message is in the mail window. If the message contains multiple addresses, and if you want to reply to all of the senders, click on the Re: All button. Clicking either button will open the Message Composition Window (Figure 3-6).

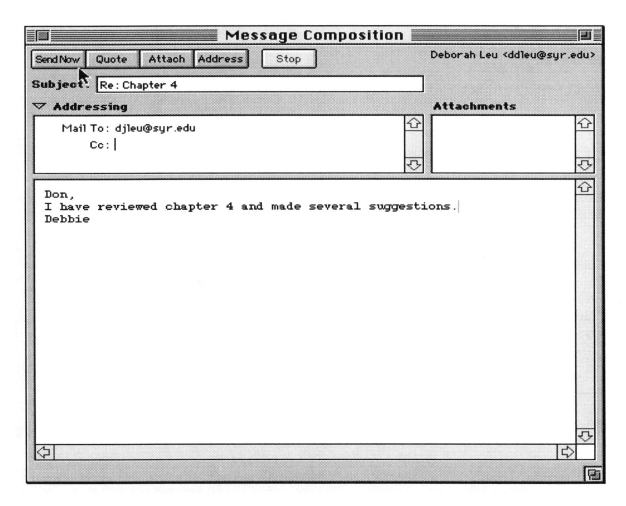

Figure 3-6.   The Message Composition Window with the Subject and Mail: To lines already entered.

Notice that the subject and address(es) are already entered. However, you may edit any entry by moving the cursor to the appropriate box and deleting or adding information. Next, move the cursor to the bottom pane of the Message Composition Window and type your message. When you are sure your message is ready to be sent, read it over one last time, confirming both the contents and the recipient. Then click on the Send Now button. Once you have clicked this button, it is impossible to stop or retrieve your message.

The Quote Button

When you reply to a message, you may choose to include the original message within your message by using the Quote button. Clicking the Quote button adds the original message to your message. (See Figure 3-7). Each line of the original message will begin with an angle bracket (>) to identify it as a quote. You may edit the quote by moving the cursor and adding and deleting information.

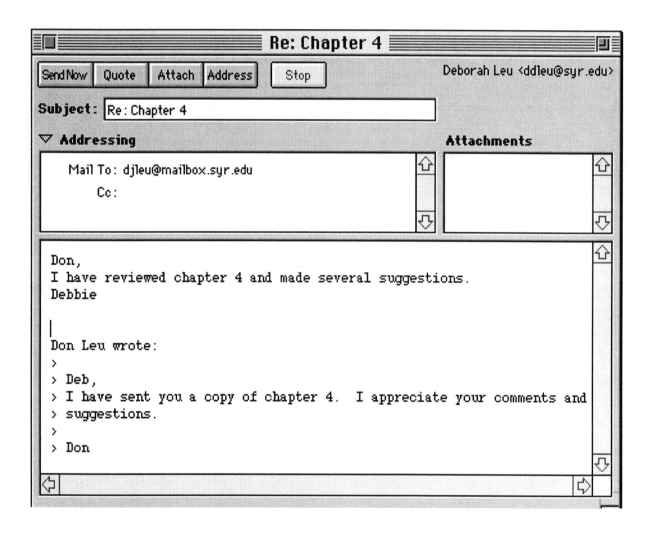

Figure 3-7. This Message Composition Window shows an included original message. Note the angle brackets that identify the quoted message.

Composing and Sending a New E-mail

Composing a new message is basically the same as replying, but you need to begin by clicking on the To:Mail button in the tool bar. This will open the Message Composition window, but the subject and addressing boxes will be empty. You must enter the e-mail address of the person to whom you are sending the e-mail. It is also a good idea to type in a subject. This isn't required, but it's helpful for a receiver with a long list of messages to be able to prioritize them by skimming their subjects. Next, type your message in the bottom pane. When you finish, and you are sure your message is ready, click the Send Now button.

Managing Your Mail

Now that you understand the basics of e-mail: (reading, replying to, and composing messages), let's move on to some additional functions that will help you mangage your mail more effectively. The most necessary of these are creating folders, saving messages, and deleting files and folders. Other useful functions are printing, forwarding, copying, and attaching.

Creating Folders

After you read a message, it remains in your Inbox folder unless you move it. As a result, your Inbox becomes crowded and disorganized, and when it gets too full, you can't receive any new messages. Moreover, if you want to refer back to a message, it can be difficult to find it in a long list. Therefore, it is a good idea to get in the habit of moving messages out of your Inbox and into another folder as you read them. If you want to keep a message, you need to save it in a folder. At this point, you have only your Inbox folder, so you need to create a Saved Messages folder.

It's easy to create a new folder by going to the menu at the top of the main screen. Move the cursor to **File.** Depress the mouse button, move the mouse down to New Folder, and release the button. When you release it, a dialog box will appear (Figure 3-8). Type the name of your new folder (in this case, Saved Messages) in the dialog box and click OK. The new folder will then appear below the Inbox folder in the left pane of the Mail Window. As you accumulate more messages, you can create additional folders to further organize your mail.

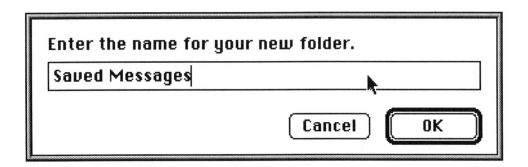

Figure 3-8.   This is the New Folder Dialog Box. Type the name of your new folder and click OK.

If you have younger students, or only one computer in your classroom, it is quite likely that your students will be using your e-mail account. Creating a folder labeled with each student's name is a good way to manage their e-mail. You can keep track of their messages and monitor their correspondence if you wish, or teach them how to save and delete messages (see the next section) for themselves. You may also want to discuss privacy issues and remind students to use only their own folders.

Saving Received Messages

Saving a received message is easy once you have a Saved Messages folder. Just click on the file icon for the message you want to save (in the right pane of the Mail Window). Then, while depressing the mouse button, drag (move) the icon over to the left pane and drop it into the desired folder by releasing the button on the appropriate folder icon.

Saving Sent Messages

Many people like to keep copies of the messages they send. If you would like to do this, you need to set a preference. Move the cursor to the Options heading of the main menu. Depress the mouse button and release it on Mail and News Preferences. Click on the Composition tab. (See Figure 3-9.) This will open the Composition panel. Go to the "By default, copy outgoing messages" section. Click the mouse button

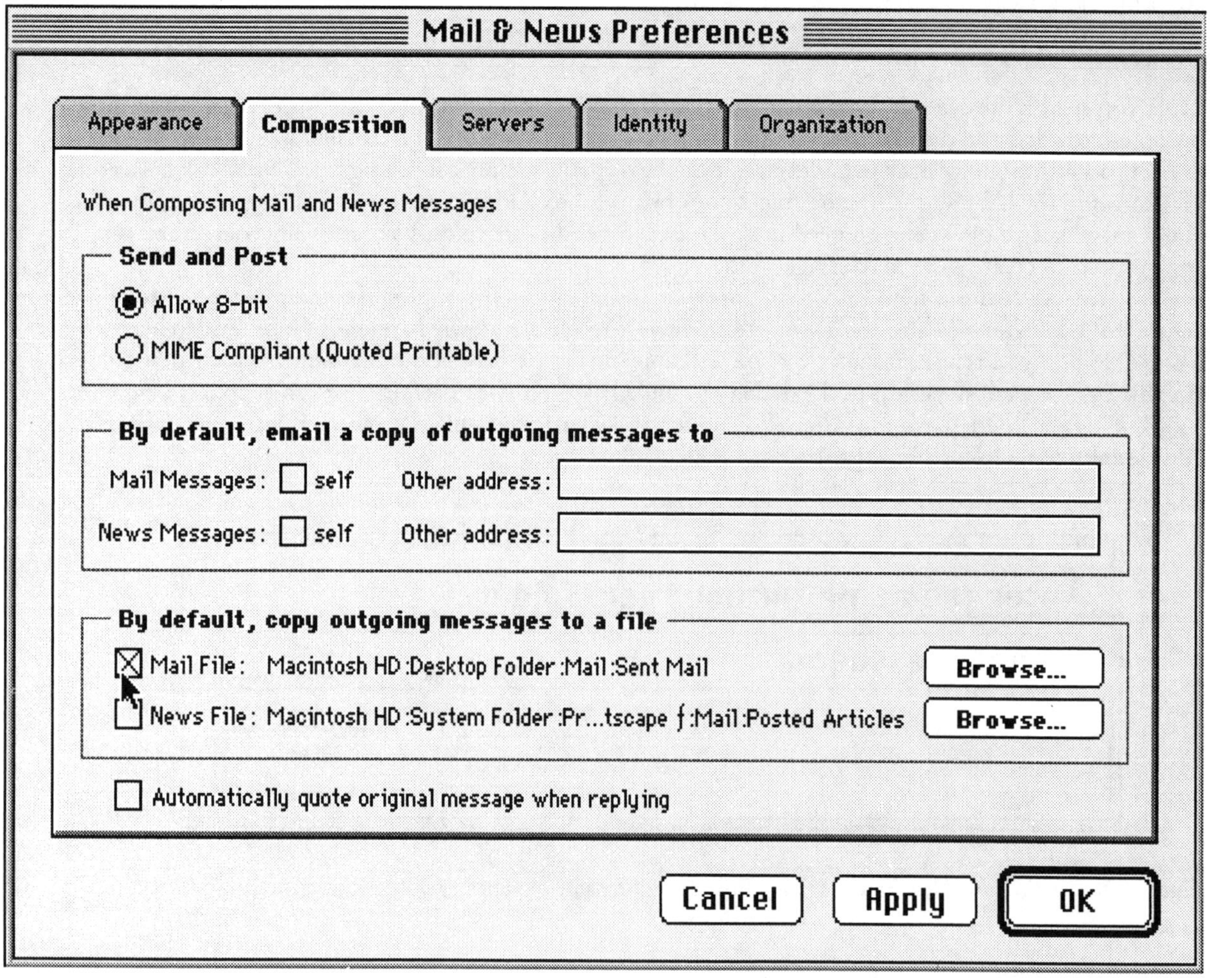

Figure 3-9. This is the Composition Tab of the Mail and News Preferences Panel. Note the "X" in the Mail File Box.

on the Mail File box. Then click OK. This preference setting will place a Saved Messages folder in the left pane of the Mail Window and automatically copy all messages you write into that folder. If you want to further organize your sent mail, you can create additional folders. Label them accordingly, by month or subject, for example, and then move the appropriate messages to the desired folder.

Deleting Message Files

Deleting messages is also easy. First, highlight the message you want to delete by clicking on its message file icon in the right pane of the Mail Window. Then, simply click the Delete button in the Mail Window tool bar. If you have several messages to delete, you can "block delete" them as a group by highlighting each message file icon while holding down the shift key. Then click Delete and they will be removed as a group.

The Trash Folder

At this point, although you have deleted your messages, they are not really gone from your mail service. They are in the left pane of the Mail Window in a Trash Folder, which Netscape Navigator created when you deleted your first message. This can be a convenient feature if you have accidentally deleted a message that you need. Just click on the Trash Folder and retrieve the message by dragging it to another folder.

In order to really get rid of your deletions, you must complete a second step, emptying the Trash Folder. You can do this by moving the cursor to the main menu and selecting File. Depress the mouse button, move it down to Empty Trash Folder, and release the button.

Deleting Folders

Only empty folders can be deleted, so the first step is to delete all of the messages in the folder you want to get rid of. Remember, you can block delete messages by clicking on each message file icon while holding down the shift key, and then clicking Delete. When the folder is empty, go to the menu at the top of the main window and select Edit. While depressing the mouse button, move down to Delete Folder, and click on it. This deletes the folder.

Reading about e-mail can become tedious, and, like swimming, you don't really know how to send e-mail until you try it. So take some time for hands-on practice. Try one or two things at first and work at your own pace. You may wish to work with a partner. If your school doesn't have a media specialist or technology coordinator, try to find someone a bit more experienced who can help out. Remember, no one knows it all, and everyone was a beginner once.

E-Mail for You

```
From: Doug Crosby <cherry@digisys.net >
      Cherry Valley School
      Polson, MT
Subject: E-mail

Dear fellow educator,
    Once we were hooked up to e-mail and the Internet in our
school library, it didn't take long for us to realize that we
were no longer an isolated school but rather part of a much wider
community. To help illustrate this for our school community we
put up a US and world map above our computer and started running
pieces of yarn from our location to all the places we had re-
ceived e-mail from. What a lesson in geography! At present we
have yarn running to most of the continents in the world and well
over half the states in our nation. Teachers and students now
communicate freely with colleagues, friends and family all across
the globe.
      Doug Crosby
      First Grade Teacher
      Cherry Valley School
      Polson, Montana
```

Additional E-mail Features

Now you are familiar with the most important features of e-mail. This next section introduces some additional features that you may find useful.

Printing

Printing a message is one of the easiest features. Just click on the Print button in the tool bar while the message you want to print is displayed in the Mail Window. You can use this feature to print out e-mail messages for posting on a bulletin board. It's also nice to print out some of a student's messages to share with parents at home or at an open house.

Forwarding Mail

Sometimes you receive messages that are really great or that you know would be useful for colleagues. It's easy to share these messages by using the Forward button on the Mail Window tool bar. Just click the Forward button while the message you want to forward is in the Mail Window. This will bring up the Message Composition window; the subject box will be filled in, and the forwarded message will be in the attachments window. All you need to do is enter the Mail To: address and type your own message in the lower pane of the window. Then when you are sure your message is ready, click on Send Now.

Sending a Copy

If you want to send your message to more than one person, type the additional e-mail address on the Cc: (carbon copy) line. You can send copies to as many people as you wish by separating their e-mail addresses with commas or spaces as illustrated in Figure 3-10.

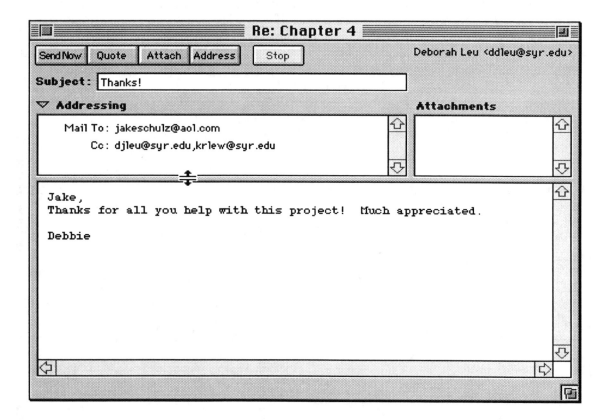

Figure 3-10.   Note that the multiple addresses on the Cc: line are separated by commas.

Attaching Documents

Another useful option that Netscape Navigator facilitates is attaching documents and sending them by e-mail. To attach a document that you have on your computer (for example, a paper that a student has written in Microsoft Word), begin by clicking on the To: Mail button in the Mail Window. This will bring up the Message Composition window, which indicates where you should type in the address, the subject, and your message. Next, click on the Attach button in the tool bar. An Attachments dialog box will appear, as shown in Figure 3-11.

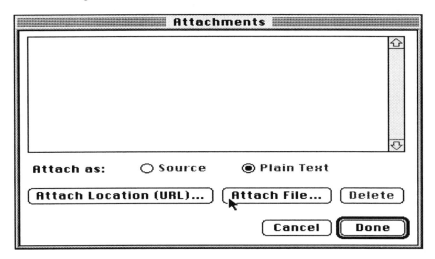

Figure 3-11.   Click on the Attach File Box when attaching a document. Then click on Done.

Click on the box that says Attach File. This will open another small window which contains a list of the documents on your computer. Search the list of documents and click on the one you want to attach. Then click Open, which will bring the document name into the Attachments window. Click Done. This will return you to the Message Composition window and place the document in the Attachments pane. You may attach more than one document by repeating this procedure. Make sure your message is ready. Then click on Send Now. The document(s) will be sent along with your message.

Attaching World Wide Web Locations

In addition to attaching your own documents, you can also attach web locations in a similar way. Click the Mail To: button which will bring up the Message Composition window. Enter the e-mail address, the subject, and type your message. Then, click the Attach button. As before, this will bring up the Attachments dialog box as in Figure 3-11. This time, click on the Attach Location box. If a site is currently displayed on the computer screen, its web location (URL) will appear in the Attachments window as in Figure 3-12. If this is the location you want to attach, click OK.

```
╔═══════════════ Attach Location ═══════════════╗
║ Please specify a location to attach:          ║
║                                               ║
║ Location (URL): │http://www.kidlink.org/home-std.html│ ║
║                                               ║
║                        [ Cancel ]  [▶ OK ]    ║
╚═══════════════════════════════════════════════╝
```

Figure 3-12.   Check the location in the Attachment Box. Then click OK.

Or, if you want to attach a different site, type its location address in the Attachments window and then click OK. After you have clicked OK (in either situation), click Done. This will return you to the Message Composition window and place the web location in the Attachments pane. You may attach more than one location by repeating this procedure. Make sure your message is ready. Then click Send Now. A fully interactive version of the web location(s) will be sent along with your message. Note, however, that the receiver must also use Netscape Navigator (Version 2.0 or later) in order to receive the web location you send.

When you feel comfortable with most of the above features, you can customize your mail service further by choosing options such as an automatic signature, a personal address book, deferred sending, and different window configurations. All of these can be found by exploring the menu at the top of the main Netscape Navigator window, or you can seek help from your local resource person.

Using E-mail in the Classroom

Learning how to use e-mail does take some time, but it is well worth the effort when you think of the many ways you can use it. Perhaps the most common way is for communication with people you already know—just like a letter. Other ways, especially for students, include writing to keypals, getting information from experts, and working on projects.

Keypals

Writing to penpals has traditionally been an exciting and educational activity for students. The Internet equivalent is corresponding electronically with a keypal. Because of the speed of e-mail, students can do much more than correspond once or twice a month. They can get almost any kind of information by asking questions and conducting interviews in their own country or internationally; they can practice a second language; they can share cool web sites; they can work on joint projects; they can even help each other with homework.

There are numerous sites for locating keypals and partner classes. The sites included below are ones that we have found to be especially useful; nevertheless, it is best to think of them, and of all our recommendations, as just starting points for your own explorations. The Internet changes quickly and often; some of these sites may disappear; certainly new ones will come online. Most importantly, you know best which sites meet your and your students' needs. Therefore, we encourage you to move on from our sites and find your own list of favorites.

The first two sites below require (free) subscription to mailing lists which will then send you messages from teachers and students looking for keypals and partner classrooms. The third and fourth sites let you search their databases directly at their web sites. You can add your message or your class's message at all four sites.

Pitsco's Launch to Keypals—(http://www.keypals.com/p/keypals.html)

This is one of the best keypal sites, containing a master list of mailing lists from different organizations. There are lists that link teachers to teachers, students to students, and classes to classes. On most lists you can post your own as well as read others' requests. You can subscribe directly from their web locations.

Intercultural E-mail Classroom Connections—(http://www.stolaf.edu/network/iecc)

This is another good source, especially for linking with partners from different countries. IECC is their mailing list for K-12 teachers who are looking for partner classrooms. They also have a mailing list for discussing the applications of intercultural e-mail communications, IECC-DISCUSSION. You can subscribe directly from their web page.

Rigby/Heinemann Global Keypals—(http:www.reedbooks.com.au/heinemann/global/global1.html)

This site is located in Australia and updates its offerings every week. Both teachers and students can make contacts and enter their own messages for students in the following age groups: 5–10, 11–13, and 14–18. This site also includes its own Netiquette Guide for Keypals.

E-mail Classroom Exchange—(http://www.iglou.com/xchange/ece/ecesearch.cgi)

This is a site for partner classes where you can search by category: school name, location, language, or grade level.

If you want to do your own search for keypals sites, Lycos works very well. Use their "customizing your search" feature and type in "keypals." We found hundreds of matches.

Expert Advice

In addition to communicating with other students, classes can communicate with experts in almost any field. If your class knows an expert, chances are they can e-mail that person directly. If you don't know an expert in the area you are studying, try Pitsco's "Ask an Expert" (http://www.pitsco.com/p/ask.html). This is by far the most comprehensive site—you can contact an expert in almost any field, as they say, from "Amish to Zookeeper." Most of the sites included in this list have a form that you can fill out on-screen if you are using Netscape or another graphical browser that supports forms. (Otherwise, you can copy the e-mail address and send a message from your own e-mail account.)

Projects

Once students have contacted their keypals or partner class, they can develop collaborative projects; for example, they might work on a newspaper, compile biographies of famous scientists from each of their countries, or do a presentation on commerce between their two states. Again, there are numerous sites to choose from.

NickNacks's Online Resources for Telecollaborating—(http://www1.minn.net:80/~schubert/ EdHelpers.html#anchor590458)

This is a great all-around site. They have a getting started section, information on free and for-fee projects, lists of other web locations for finding projects, and templates for developing your own collaborative projects.

Kid Projects—(http://www.kidlink.org:80/KIDPROJ/)

This site from KidLink is a good source of projects to join. It can also be used to announce your own project. Geared to ages 10–15.

Global SchoolNet Foundation Projects Registry—(http://www.gsn.org/gsn/proj/index.html)

One of the largest and best sites for projects. In addition to the registry, this non-profit group also sponsors newsgroups and mailing lists. This is a very safe site—they screen projects and moderate their lists.

As with keypals sites, you are encouraged to do your own search. Lycos also worked well for this topic; just enter "K12 projects."

The activities above represent only a few of the ways you can use e-mail. We hope you are getting excited about its potential for your classroom. You may be wondering, though, how to get started, especially if you and your students have never used electronic communication before. Perhaps the following e-mail message will help.

E-Mail for You

From: Jeanette Kenyon (jkenyon@ahoynet.com)
      jkenyon@pen.k12.va.us)
      Moncure Elementary School
      Stafford, Virginia
Subject: Using E-Mail in Third Grade

Dear Colleague,

    One of the first skills I taught to my 3rd grade children
after becoming connected to the Internet was e-mail. This seems a
logical starting point for teachers as well as students. We began
by sending e-mail to the class next door to us. Even though my
students have many friends in that class and they see each other
daily, the e-mail they exchanged during our Computer lab time
became a weekly "event." We composed collective messages where we
chatted about what was going on in our room, interesting units we
were working on, and general greetings to individuals from their
friends. We often included the latest "knock knock" jokes and
sometimes posed difficult math problems for the other class to
solve. As the students became more skillful at sending e-mail we
moved beyond our own school and began sending messages to family
and friends. Parents love to receive messages at work from their
children and far away relatives are thrilled to hear from their
young family members. After becoming comfortable with the workings and etiquette of e-mail, the students were confident about
sending messages to various people on the World Wide Web. They
found that there were experts in almost any field who would
gladly answer their questions, and they corresponded with a variety of students around the world whom they had located on the
WWW. Many eight and nine year olds are reluctant letter writers
but it is amazing how long they will sit at a keyboard painstak-
ingly composing an e-mail message.This is also a great incentive
and opportunity to improve keyboarding skills which are also an
integral part of our curriculum.

    Jeanette Kenyon
    Moncure Elementary School
    Stafford, Virginia

    Jeanette Kenyon's message might almost serve as a guide for introducing e-mail, beginning simply within the classroom and gradually expanding its scope to include the world. Depending on the age and experience of your students, you might want to start out with a message composed jointly by the students, but entered by the teacher. The message and any responses could be printed out and kept in a binder or put up on a bulletin board near the computer. Later students could work in pairs or small groups to send their own messages to other students in their school. Then they could move into their community by e-mailing questions to local businesses and organizations. Finally, they might each have their own international keypal.

Keyboarding and Netiquette

Jeanette's message also brings up two issues that become more important as students begin to use e-mail more independently and extensively: keyboarding and Internet etiquette, or "netiquette" as it is called. Should students learn keyboarding at a young age to prevent the development of bad habits, or is it beyond their small-motor coordination? How should it be taught? Is it worth the time, or will it bore them so much at any age that they will lose interest? Such questions are made more difficult to answer given the limited resources of many schools. Your school district may already have a policy on keyboarding and its place in the curriculum; if not, it is an area that will probably need to be discussed.

The second issue, netiquette, is especially important in the area of e-mail communication. With e-mail communication, we are unable to share facial expressions, voice tone, and body language. As a result, the Internet is especially prone to miscommunication. Thus, it is important to help students develop good Internet manners. We are not referring here to actions that are dangerous or illegal, but to politeness and courtesy. Because the Internet is not run by any single group or government, there are no official rules to teach, nor is there a single source of information about what constitutes acceptable behavior. Nevertheless, we can help our students realize that the Internet, as a place of social interaction, has its own traditions and customs. We can discuss Internet use as a privilege, not a right, and together with our students develop guidelines that encourage a tolerant attitude toward the diversity of people, languages, and viewpoints that exists on the net.

People often talk about netiquette in terms of "common sense," but common sense varies depending on factors such as age, culture, and experience. Therefore, before you discuss this issue with your students, you may want to get some background information from the following sites.

Netiquette Homepage by Arlene H. Rinaldi—(http://www.fau.edu/rinaldi/net)

This is the most comprehensive site we found. It's fairly detailed and gives nettiquette advice on e-mail, lists, newsgroups, and other areas of the net. It includes a question and answer section as well as a bibliography. Depending on the level of your students, you might choose appropriate sections for them to read and discuss. For example, "The Ten Commandments for Computer Ethics" is a straightforward list of "thou-shalt-nots" which would probably be effective with all but the youngest students (http://www.fau.edu/rinaldi/net/ten.html).

Patrick Crispen's Roadmap 96—(http://www.brandonu.ca/~ennsnr/Resources/Roadmap/map07.html)

This is another informative general site which features a humorous article from his online tutorial. While it is a little less comprehensive, it contains most of the important information.

You can also find more focused netiquette advice for specific areas of the Internet. For example, mailing lists usually include suggestions for new members in their Welcome Message and many newsgroups have FAQs that answer questions about expectations for new users. Real-time conversation areas usually include rules in their entrance directions as well.

Mailing Lists

In addition to using e-mail for one-to-one communication between individuals, an e-mail address also allows you to participate in one-to-many communicaton by joining mailing lists. You can think of mailing lists, also called discussion groups and listservs, as "group e-mail," where a message sent to one address is automatically forwarded to a whole group rather than to an individual.

This is accomplished by a special computer program which maintains a list of people, the subscribers, who have joined a particular list in order to discuss a specific interest area. Subscribers participate by sending and receiving e-mail messages which come directly to their electronic mailboxes. Some lists are moderated by the owner or another person who screens and selects the messages that are sent out.

There are thousands of mailing lists covering almost every interest area. Most are intended for a specific audience, but are open so that anyone can subscribe. There are some closed lists, however. Some lists have thousands of members and are very active. Others are quite small and generate only a few messages a month.

Given these characteristics, mailing lists are very useful in education. As was the case for Mr. Diaz, they are great places to ask questions, get information, locate resources, and share information. Some care is necessary, however, when deciding how to use lists in the classroom because there is no way to know in advance what will appear in the list. If a list is moderated, obvious problems such as bad language will be avoided, but there may still be topics or viewpoints that are not desireable for everyone.

There are lists especially for kids and other education-oriented lists where kids can participate with interested adults. Still, almost anyone can subscribe to an unmoderated list, and even moderated lists may not be able to screen with 100 percent effectiveness. So it is possible that even an "appropriate" list might ocassionally contain inappropriate material for some students. Nevertheless, lists are great resources for teachers, and many teachers do use them with their students. It is probably best for you to participate in a mailing list or lists before deciding how to use them in your situation and with your students.

A message from a teacher who has used mailing lists in several different ways follows on the next page.

Finding a List

The first step is to find the name and e-mail address of a list you want to join. There are thousands of lists, so you might begin by checking with colleagues and professional organizations or looking through journals. Thankfully, there are also many Internet sites that contain master lists of mailing lists. You may want to check back at these list sites occasionally because mailing lists are continually being added and discontinued.

Liszt Select—(http://www.liszt.com)

This is the most comprehensive site. It contains over 50,000 lists, including some managed by listserv, listproc, and majordomo, as well as some independently managed lists (other master lists usually contain only listserv). You can either do a search for lists in your interest area, or click the Liszt Select box, for a much smaller, annotated list of sites picked by Liszt.

TileNet—(http://www.tile.net/tile/listserv/index.html)

This is another comprehensive list (but it contains only listserv lists). You can search for lists alphabetically by name, host country, sponsoring organization, most popular, or subject categories.

Pitsco's Launch to Lists—(http://www.pitsco.com/p/listservs.html)

This site doesn't have search capabilities, but the list is focused on education.

EdWeb—(http://k12.cnidr.org:90/lists.html)

This is a somewhat smaller but useful list that focuses on K-12 issues, educational technology, and education reform. It also has a little background on mailing lists and an example for subscribing.

Subscribing

In order to subscribe to a mailing list, you need to send an e-mail message to the server that manages the list. It is very important to send your request to the correct address. Mailing lists have two addresses, one for administration, which begins with the name of the server that manages the list; and another for "posting" (sending contributions to the list members), which usually begins with the name of the list. Make sure you subscribe to the administration address. Most of these begin with "listserv@...", the most common server. However, some addresses begin with "listproc@..." or "majordomo@...", or less frequently with some other server.

To subscribe, type the administrative e-mail address of the list in the addressing box of the Message Composition window. Leave the subject line blank. Then type a subscribe message in the first line of the

E-Mail for You

From: Rina Hallock (rhallock@micron.net)
     K-5 Resource Teacher and IBM TLC Network System Operator
     Washington Elementary School
     Caldwell, ID
Subject: Listservs and Projects

   We had fun "getting our feet wet" on the internet this past
year. My students and students from other classrooms enjoyed
having the opportunity to participate in projects. We began with
some apprehensions, and some false starts; but by the end of the
year, we had a positive feeling about our small beginnings!

   I think all of the projects actually started as a result of
getting on some listservs. Some are like a newsletter, and some
are like a bulletin board to post questions and answers. NOVAE, a
listserv that is monitored by Art Galus, piqued our curiosity
[majordomo@uidaho.edu].

   To do the activities we did, all you really need is an e-mail
account. Our first major project involved Global School Net Foundation [http://www.gsn.org]. It was a Santa project—elementary
classrooms would be matched with classrooms of older children.
The older children would be "Santa" and the younger children
would write letters to Santa. The letters came back just before
Christmas and the kids were absolutely thrilled. Another nice
feature of this project is that it was very well organized. There
were lesson plans for both teachers. The Santas were instructed
on what to say and what not to say (e.g., don't *promise* to
bring anything). There were units mailed out to teachers covering
both sets of expectations.

   Another project we did was with some of my older resource
room students. I had subscribed to another listserv[iecc-
request@stolaf.edu]. This site allows a teacher to post a request
for keypals...My students enjoyed receiving mail regularly. It
was a great motivation for getting reluctant writers to write.
And they sometimes opened up in amazing ways. There were draw-
backs, of course. Time is always limited, and I wound up entering
most of the letters that the students had written. But I made
sure that the students at least witnessed the entry and sending
of a letter as well as the reception of their mail.

   We did some other small projects in response to requests from
the listserv at Classroom Connect [crc-request@classroom.net].
It's a relatively simple thing to do, it's safe—we didn't give
out student last names or home addresses, and it's meaningful to
the students.

     Rina Hallock
     Caldwell, ID 83605
     rhallock@micron.net

     "Our task is to provide an education for the kinds of kids
     we have, not the kinds of kids we used to have, or want
     to have, or the kids that exist in our dreams."
                                             —K.P. Gerlack

message pane. Usually case is not significant, but people often type the name of the list in capitals. Your message should look like this, but with your name, and without the brackets:

subscribe [list name] [your first name] [your last name]

For example, if I wanted to subscribe to the SCHOOL-L list, it would look like this:

subscribe SCHOOL-L Deborah Leu

Don't put any other information, such as an automatic signature for example, in the message pane. Any extra information is rejected by the server and invalidates the request. Rarely a list may have a different procedure, but this is usually indicated on the master list or on the list's web page.

The Welcome Message

Shortly you should receive a return message that welcomes you to the group and details its procedures Save this message! It contains important information about expectations for members, how to get help and, most important, how to get off the list.

Usually you can leave a list by sending a message similar to your subscription request. Some lists do have special procedures, though. Generally, to leave a list type "unsubscribe" or "signoff" instead of "subcribe." For example:

unsubscribe SCHOOL-L

Also, remember to send this message to the administrative address, not the posting address.

Netiquette

Nettiquette is especially important for mailing list subscribers because their messages may be read by hundreds of people from all around the world. In addition, a list is a bit like a club where you may run into other members at any time—you don't want to offend someone that you know you will be "meeting" (electronically) several times a week.

In order to get a feel for the culture and "personality" of the list, it is strongly recommended that you "lurk" for a week or two, that is, just read the list for awhile before posting any messages. This will give you a chance to see how the group operates and find out answers to some of your initial questions. Most group members are tolerant and helpful to beginners. However, the introduction of an inappropriate topic or the tenth repetition of a basic question sometimes receives a nasty response.

Posting a Message

When you feel ready to make a contribution to the discussion, you should send your message to the posting address which usually (but not always) begins with the name of the mailing list. Posting information is also included in the welcome message—another reason to save it. If your message is a response to an individual's question, it is usually better to send your reply to him/her rather than to the whole list. This is easy to do because most e-mail progams give you the option of addressing your reply to either an individual or to the group. (Netscape Navigator has the Re: Mail button for an individual and the Re: All button to reply to the group.)

Privacy

The issue of privacy is often overlooked by newcomers to the Internet. Perhaps because we often use e-mail in private, we believe it is private. Actually it may be even less private than regular mail. Just as in the regular mail system, electronic communications occasionally get missent or lost. In addition, virtually all e-mail is archived somewhere, "indefinitely" as we have been told. It is most likely kept in an out-of-the-way file, known only to a system administrator, so it is unlikely that anyone would search through thousands of messages to see what you have written, but it is possible.

Postings from mailing lists, however, are more accessible. Many lists are archived in relatively accessible places. Some lists keep their own archives, which are available only to members, but that could be a number in the hundreds. Some education lists are archived at ERIC and are easily accessible through a net search. Other lists are posted to Usenet newsgroups, which may be read by thousands of people around the world.

This information is not meant to alarm you, but only to caution you to think about what you write. We have heard that you should never write anything that would embarrass you if it happened to be announced at your next town meeting. We think this is sound advice.

Useful Lists

It's difficult to recommend mailing lists because everyone's needs and expectations are different, but we found the following lists to be especially useful while writing this book.

KIDSPHERE—(kidsphere@vms.cis.pitt.edu).

This active list provides an opportunity for kids, parents, teachers, and administrators and other interested people to discuss anything related to education. People post news items, share good books, ask for help and give suggestions, and discuss the advantages and disadvantages of various educational practices.

SCHOOL-L—(listserv@listserv.hea.ie)

Another active site that is really useful for primary and secondary school discussion. Most subscribers seem to be teachers and technology coordinators. Teachers request and share all kinds of information. There are often postings about other good sites and useful resources.

MIDDLE-L—(listserv@postoffice.cso.uiuc.edu)

Sponsored by ERIC, this list is for classroom teachers, administrators, parents, and anyone else interested in middle schools and middle school students. People share ideas, resources, advice, and problems.

WWWEDU—(listproc@educom.unc.edu)

This is a moderated list whose stated purpose is ". . . to offer educators, webmasters and policy makers a continuous discussion on the potential of World-Wide Web use in education. WWWEDU is targeted for use by educators, as well as webmasters and web providers, but anyone with a keen interest in the use of Web methodology in education is welcome to join." This list seems a bit more focused and has fewer postings of individual requests for resources than the ones above.

EDTECH—(listserv@msu.edu)

This is a very active list about the use of technology in education. It's not for everyone because it is quite technical, but there seemed to be quick and friendly responses for set-up and equipment problems.

NOVAE—(majordomo@uidaho.edu) Your subscription message should read: subscribe novae [your full e-mail address]. This list cannot mail to BITNET addresses.

This is a mailing list that "provides timely news articles to classroom teachers who really don't have time to drive the Information highway." They send weekly postings from other teachers on the Internet as well as information about Funding, Elementary and Middle School Projects and Keypals, and Secondary Projects.

HILITES—(majordomo@gsn.org)

This is a moderated list by the Global SchoolNet Foundation limited to K–12 teachers. They send announcements of carefully screened projects that meet their criteria. They cross-post with other lists and also have an archive of previous projects to help you get ideas.

Usenet Newsgroups

One of the most popular uses of e-mail is reading the postings in Usenet newsgroups. Usenet is a world-wide network of distributed discussions. It consists of thousands of newsgroups that are organized hierarchically by category and topic. Like mailing lists, newsgroups are a one-to-many type of e-mail-based communication. However, they differ from mailing lists in several important ways.

First, access is different. While mailing lists are limited to individual subscribers, newsgroups are available to almost everyone. Earlier we compared mailing lists to group e-mail, like copies of a letter being sent to each person on a list. Usenet is more similar to a bulletin board where anyone who is in the vicinity can read whatever is posted over a period of days or weeks. The length of posting time varies by newsgroup, but many groups also archive their messages. This allows you to browse a large number of messages quickly and read at your convenience rather than having to check your mail every day.

A second difference is that messages are not sent to individual mailboxes. They are sent and stored on computers at Usenet sites around the world, where they can be accessed by other computers. In a way, you can think of your service provider as a kind of subscriber in that providers select the newsgroups which they will access and make available on their servers. This means you have access to hundreds of messages without worrying about your mailbox becoming too full.

Finally, there is a difference in the users. Many more people from all around the world participate in newsgroups than in mailing lists. In addition, unlike mailing list subscribers, newsgroup readers are not necessarily posting to their major interest groups; they may just be browsing when they find a group they want to contribute to. This, together with the fact that very few newsgroups are moderated, results in an incredible variety of topics and viewpoints.

Reading News With Netscape Navigator

We will explain Usenet newsgroups using examples of Netscape Navigator 3.0. Don't be concerned if you have a different software program. The basic processes are similar for most programs.

It will be easy for you to use Netscape Navigator News since it is very similar to Netscape Navigator Mail. Just as with Mail, you must set preferences before you can use News. The only new information you will need is the name of your news server. If you don't know it, check with your service provider or technical support person. You may wish to write your news server here: _____.

Setting Preferences

To begin, open Netscape Navigator. Then go to the Options heading of the main menu, and select Mail and News Preferences. This will open a preferences panel like the one in Figure 3-13.

Click on the Servers tab. Go down to the News section of the panel and enter the name of your news server in the appropriate box. Click OK, which will close the panel and return you to the main Netscape window.

The News Window

Now you are ready to use News. Go to the main menu and click on the Window heading. While depressing the mouse button, move the cursor down to Netscape News and release the button. This will bring up the News Window, which looks very similar to the Mail Window. (See Figure 3-14.)

Notice that there are three panes. The left pane lists the newsgroups. It also has a subscribe column indicated by a blue check and columns for Unread and Total messages. The right pane lists the messages that are posted to the group. Just as in the Mail window, it also has a red flag column in which to mark

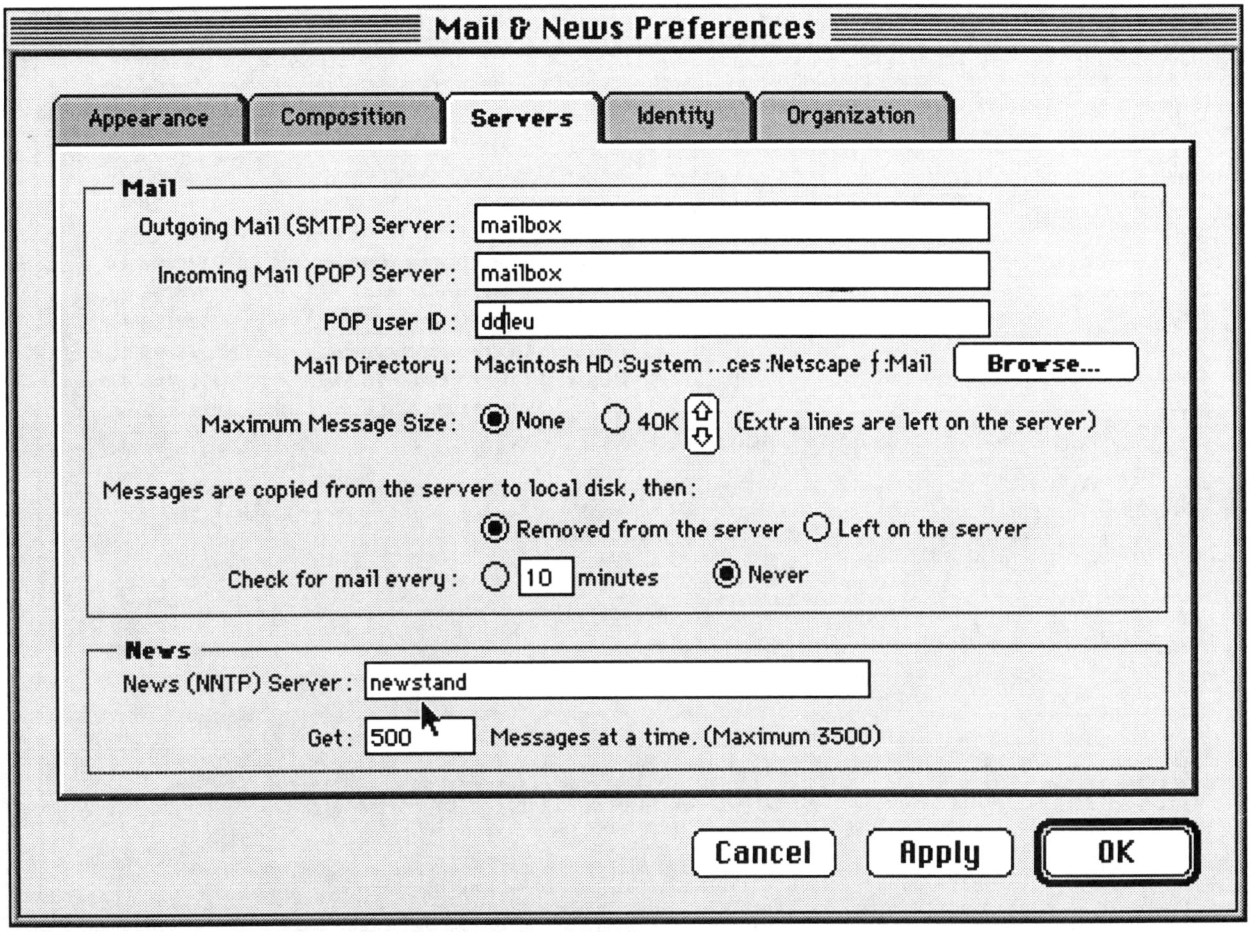

```
▦▦▦▦▦▦▦▦▦▦▦▦▦▦═ Mail & News Preferences ═▦▦▦▦▦▦▦▦▦▦▦▦

  ┌─────────┐┌───────────┐┌─────────┐┌─────────┐┌──────────────┐
  │Appearance││Composition││ Servers  ││ Identity ││ Organization │
  └─────────┘└───────────┘└─────────┘└─────────┘└──────────────┘

  ┌─ Mail ──────────────────────────────────────────────────────┐
  │      Outgoing Mail (SMTP) Server :  [mailbox            ]    │
  │      Incoming Mail (POP) Server :   [mailbox            ]    │
  │              POP user ID :          [ddleu              ]    │
  │          Mail Directory :  Macintosh HD :System ...ces :Netscape ƒ :Mail   [ Browse... ] │
  │     Maximum Message Size :  ◉ None   ○ 40K [⇕]  (Extra lines are left on the server) │
  │                                                              │
  │   Messages are copied from the server to local disk, then :  │
  │                  ◉ Removed from the server   ○ Left on the server │
  │       Check for mail every :  ○ [10] minutes   ◉ Never       │
  └──────────────────────────────────────────────────────────────┘

  ┌─ News ──────────────────────────────────────────────────────┐
  │      News (NNTP) Server :  [newstand          ]             │
  │               Get : [500]  Messages at a time. (Maximum 3500) │
  └──────────────────────────────────────────────────────────────┘

                          ( Cancel )  ( Apply )  (( OK ))
```

Figure 3-13. This is an example of the Servers Tab of the Mail and News Preferences Panel with the name of the news server entered.

important messages, and a green diamond column to indicate read and unread messages. It also shows the sender and the time sent. The bottom pane is used to display the current message. Each pane scrolls independently.

If this is the first time you have used Netscape Navigator News, Netscape will create a newsreading file for you and subscribe you to three groups for newcomers (shown in the left pane of Figure 3-14 on the next page). The groups are:

- news.announce.newusers
- news.newusers.questions
- news.answers

As you have time, you should look over the postings in these three groups because they contain helpful information about participating in newsgroups and also answer frequently asked questions. Many of the messages in these groups are reposted on a regular basis so that they are always available to newcomers and others for reference.

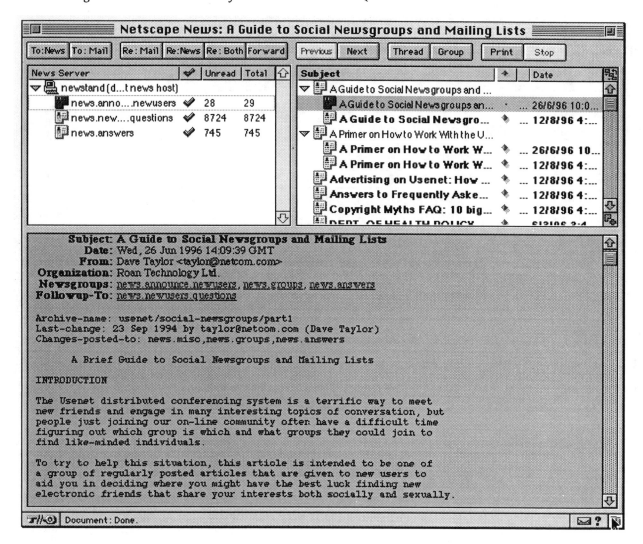

Figure 3-14. The News Window has three panes. Note the three newsgroups in the left pane.

Newsgroup Names and Hierarchies

Take a moment to look at the format of the names of the newsgroups on the previous page. Newsgroup names consist of hierarchical categories and topics. They are always written in lower-case letters with periods between the words. Examples of common Usenet hierarchies include:

alt	alternative (just about any topic)
bit	bitnet (a network)
biz	business
comp	computers
k12	primary and secondary education
misc	miscellaneous
news	Internet news
sci	science research
soc	social issues and world cultures
talk	discussion of controversial issues

It is usually easy to figure out the topic of any group by reading its name from left to right as in the following examples:

<u>news.announce.newusers</u>

This group is in the "news" hierarchy and its topic is "announcements" for "newusers."

<u>k12.ed.comp.literacy</u>

This group is in the "education" hierarchy and its topic is "computer literacy."

Choosing Newsgroups

In addition to the newcomer newsgroups above, you will want to read and subscribe to others that are in your areas of interest. There are tens of thousands of newsgroups to choose from, but not all of them will be carried by your service provider. Therefore, the next step is to find out which groups are available to you.

You can view all the newsgroups offered by your provider by going to the Options heading of the main menu and selecting Show All Newsgroups. This will download the list of the groups that your server receives and display them in the left News Window pane. This may take some time, since many servers subscribe to several thousand groups. The finished list will look similar to Figure 3-15 below.

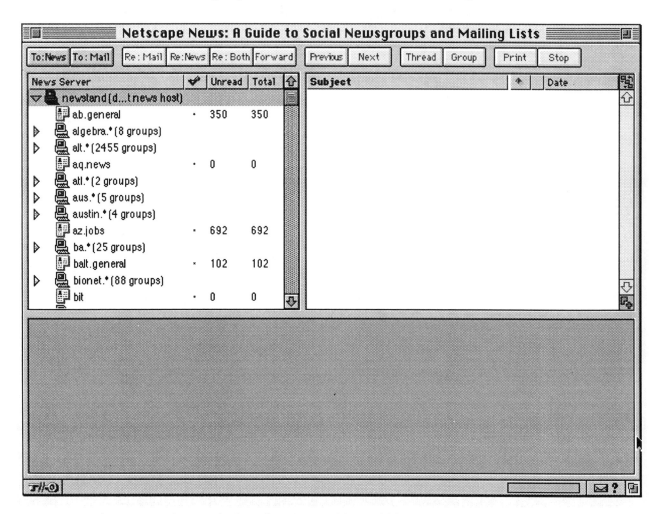

Figure 3-15. The News Window can display only a portion of the available newsgroups at any one time.

Triangle Icons

Notice that some of the newsgroups displayed in Figure 3-15 have a small triangle to the left of their icon. When the triangle points to the right, it indicates that there are sub-groups of that heading nested inside. If you want to see the sub-groups, click on the triangle so that it points down. This will spread out the list so that you can read it.

Reconfiguring the Window Panes

Sometimes a window pane does not display the whole name of a group or message listing. If you want to see more, you can reconfigure the panes by adjusting their borders. To do this, click and hold down the mouse button on the border you want to move. The cursor will appear as two short parallel lines and arrows to show that it is located at a moveable border. When you see this icon, drag it to the desired location and release the mouse button. In this way, you can adjust the size of almost any pane or column in the News Window. Figure 3-16 shows the subject column of the right pane as it is about to be moved.

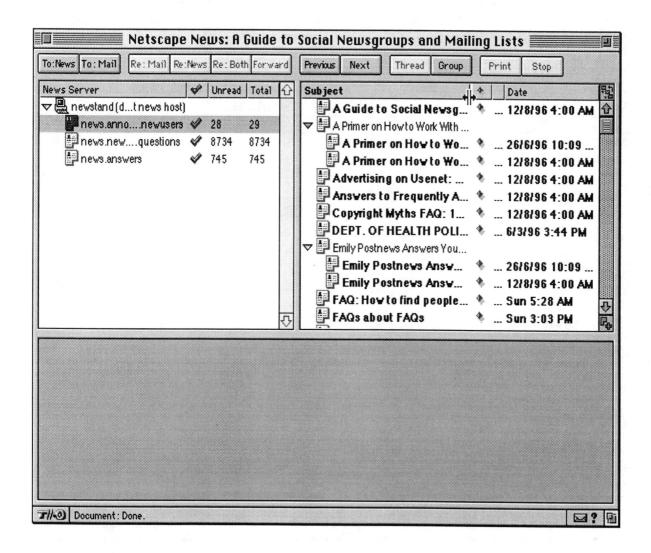

Figure 3-16.   The subject column in the right pane is about to be reconfigured. Note the parallel line icon.

Reading Messages

The next step is to scroll down the list until you find something interesting. When you find a promising topic, click on its icon. This will open the newsgroup and display the list of posted messages in the top right pane. If you see a message you would like to read, click on its icon and the message will be displayed in the bottom pane. Netscape News will automatically mark it as read and remove the green diamond icon. You can continue reading messages by clicking on them or by using the Next and Previous buttons in the tool bar.

Threaded Messages

Netscape Navigator News displays "threaded" messages. This means that messages with the same topic are linked together, and all replies to a previous message are automatically given the same subject line. As a result, you can "view" a discussion and see which message is a reply to which other message by looking at its stucture. Figure 3-17 shows a thread from the k12.chat.teacher group, which you can recognize by its nested icons.

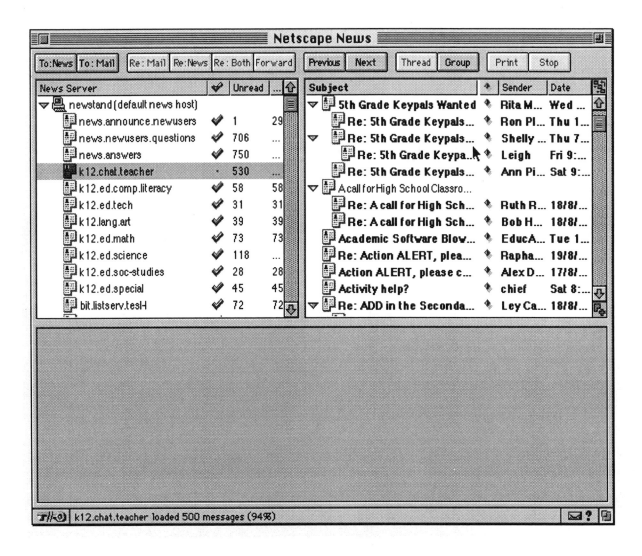

Figure 3-17. A Message Thread from the k12.chat.teacher newsgroup. Note the indented message icons.

The Thread and Group Buttons

The Thread button allows you to mark all of the messages in a thread as already read. This is useful when you have no interest in a particular topic. Rather than clicking the Next button several times or scrolling, you can save time by clicking the Thread button. The news reader will then skip over the rest of that thread to the next unread message. In addition, the messages marked as read with the thread button (like the messages you actually read) will not be displayed the next time you open the News window. This really saves time if you read several newsgoups.

The Group button is similar but it marks the entire group of messages as already read. You might use this feature if you have been away on vacation and don't want to take time to catch up on a group. By using the Group button, all of the older messages would be marked as already read, and you could read a more manageable and current list of messages.

Subscribing and Unsubscribing to a Newsgroup

After previewing a newsgroup, you may decide you want to subscribe to it. To do that, just click on the gray dot in the subscribe column (headed by a blue check) next to the newsgroup's name. A blue check will appear, indicating that you are subscribed.

If you want to unsubscribe from a newsgroup, click on the blue check next to its name, and it will change to a gray dot, indicating that you are not subscribed. You may subscribe and unsubscribe at any time by clicking in this column. Figure 3-18 shows both subscribed and unsubscribed newsgroups. Note the checks and the dots.

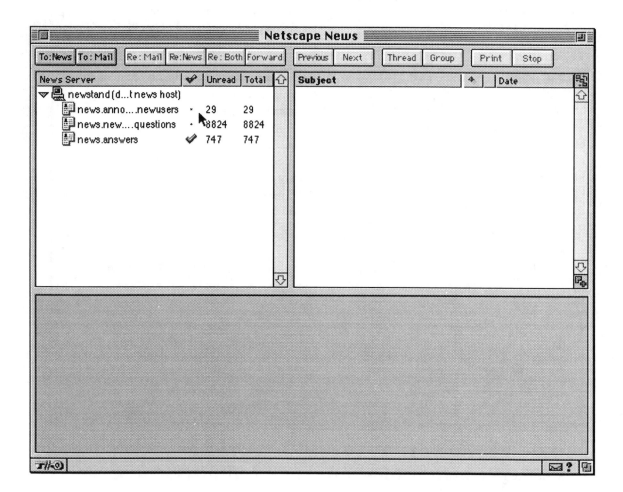

Figure 3-18.   The left pane of the News Window indicates the subscribed newsgroups with a check.

Of course, you are not actually subscribing and unsubscribing; instead, you are indicating which of your server's available groups you want to read on a regular basis. Netscape News will keep track of your preferences and display them in the left window pane (if they contain any unread messages) every time you open the News window. This saves time by allowing you to receive only those newsgroups that you want.

Replying to Messages

Replying to messages in News is nearly the same as replying in Mail. You may reply to any newsgroup message while it is in the bottom pane. If you want to reply directly to the author, click on the Re: Mail button, which brings up a message composition window just like the one in Mail with the sender's address and the subject already entered.

If you want to reply to the whole newsgroup, click on the Re: All button. This again brings up the Message Composition window with the address and subject already entered, but the addressee will be the newsgroup.

You can reply to both the original sender and the newsgroup by clicking on the Re: Both button. The subject and both addresses will already be entered. When you have checked your message and are sure it is ready, using any of the above options, click on Send Now.

Composing and Sending New Messages

To send a new message, click on the To: News button. This also brings up Message Composition window, but it will be headed with the name of a newsgroup if you have selected one. If you haven't already selected a newsgroup, enter the address of the group you want. Be sure to add an explanatory subject. Remember, readers will be looking for messages in their interest area. There are so many messages on Usenet that many readers just ignore non-descriptive topics such as "help." Type your message and, when you are sure it is ready, click on Send Now.

Additional Buttons

The other buttons in the tool bar work the same way whether you are using Netscape Navigator Mail or News. This means you can use the Quote button to copy the original message into your message, and use the Attach button to attach documents and web locations. The Print button will print any message that is in the bottom pane of the News window. You may also forward a message to someone else using the Forward button.

Netiquette

In general, newsgroup netiquette is similar to that for e-mail and mailing lists. You can get more specific information, however, by reading the postings in the news hierarchies for newusers. Another good place to look is at Usenet FAQs (http://www.cis.ohio-state.edu/hypertext/faq/usenet/). This site lists all of the FAQs that are in news.answers. They are alphabetized by topic. Finally, it is always helpful to lurk (just read) for awhile until you have a sense of the culture of the new group.

Using Usenet Newsgroups in the Classroom

The wide open readership and diversity of views found in newsgroups makes them an excellent source of information and a great way to broaden horizons. These same characteristics, however, can cause concern in the classroom since there are sure to be some topics, language use, and discussions that are unsuitable for students. Moreover, several of the newsgroup "alternate" categories contain explicit discussions of sex-related topics. Many of these areas may not present problems for you, however, depending on your service provider. If your provider is your school district or a state network, for example, chances are they will not carry controversial newsgroups.

On the other hand, even the inavailability of certain groups cannot totally guarantee appropriateness, because it is still possible for almost anyone to post anything to any group. Perhaps the only way to completely avoid these kinds of problems is for the service provider to join a moderated newsgroup service, which will screen both the partipants and the messages to ensure a safe and educational newsgroup environment. The Global SCHLnet Newsgroup Service (http://www.gsn.org/gsn/schl/index.html) does an excellent job, providing a large number of its own newsgroups as well as seeking out the best project postings from around the net. In addition, they post the discussions of several educational listservs. There is a fee, but it is based on the size of the network and the number of adult users. They also offer a free trial subscription. You may wish to discuss this option with your service provider or technical resource person.

Even though the number of obviously unsuitable (at least for students and schools) newsgroups is relatively small compared to the total, many teachers have reservations about using Usenet with their students. Others teachers, however, point out that having students compare the diverse viewpoints it presents can be very helpful in improving critical thinking skills, as long as there is guidance and supervision from the teacher.

In short, opinions on Usenet vary. Therefore, we strongly encourage you to try out newsgroups for yourself before deciding whether to use them or not. As always, you are the best judge of what suits your situation and meets the needs of you and your students.

Internet Resources for Newsgroups

As we pointed out earlier, the newsgroups that are available to you depend on your service provider. Since you can find that list using Netscape Navigator News, it is not really necessary to search the web. However, if you want to see a more complete list, you can check the following sources. If you do find an interesting site, you can always ask your provider to consider adding it.

Liszt Select—(http://www.liszt.com/cgi-bin/news.cgi)
This site allows you to search its huge database by topic.

TileNet—(http://www.tile.net/news)
This site has an alphabetical index and also lets you search by description or by hierarchy.

Real-time Interactions

E-mail, mailing lists, and newsgroups are non-synchronous forms of electronic communication. There are, in addition, several types of real-time, live communication available such as Real Audio (for listening to radio programs), MOOs (text-based "virtual rooms" where you can "move around" along with other participants), IRC (Internet Relay Chat, which allows you to "converse" on various topics with people around the world by reading and writing simultaneous messages), and audio and video conferencing. These areas of the net are changing rapidly, require different types of software and access and can be confusing to use at first, especially for newcomers. As a result, you may want to seek help from a more experienced user or your technical resource person when exploring them.

On a positive note, real-time interaction is getting easier as various sites offer step-by-step instructions or clik-on capabilities. You may wish to check out the following sites.

- The University of Oregon's Babel, for definitions (http://babel.uoregon.edu/yamada/interact.html)
- The Teacher's Network, for discussions with other teachers (http://www.teachenet.org/).
- Teachers Helping Teachers Caht Area (http://www.pacificnt.net/~mandel/ircinfor.html)

Section II

Teaching in Content Areas with Internet Resources

Chapter 4

Teaching With The Internet: Effective Instructional Strategies

```
To:      Our readers
From:    djleu@sued.syr.edu (Don Leu),
         ddleu@syr.edu (Debbie Leu)

Subject: Effective Instructional Strategies

    A second grade student once described the Internet as a big
encyclopedia with a telephone: "It's like an encyclopedia because
it has all kinds of information and it's like a phone because you
can talk to anybody about what you find." This student had it
pretty close to the mark; the Internet is just another informa-
tion and communication resource to use with your class.
    As a result, developing effective instructional strategies
with the Internet is really not as difficult as it might seem.
There are only a few major issues to consider. Once you consider
these issues, Internet resources may be easily integrated with
nearly all of the instructional practices you already use in your
classroom.
    On the other hand, the Internet will increase, not decrease,
your central role in orchestrating learning experiences. You will
be challenged to thoughtfully guide students' learning within
information environments that are richer and more complex, pre-
senting richer and more complex learning opportunities. Teachers
who abdicate this responsibility will frequently find students
"surfing" quickly from one location to another, not reading or
thinking critically about information they find. Time spent will
largely be time wasted. However, teachers who have thoughtfully
considered how to weave Internet experiences into the curriculum
will provide important learning opportunities for their students,
opportunities their students would not be able to have otherwise.
Moreover, they will have provided students with a better under-
standing of our increasingly interdependent and global community.

    Don and Debbie
```

Mr. Erickson said good-by to the last few students as they left for their buses. He went around the room straightening things up a bit, checking the hamsters, and writing the schedule for tomorrow on the chalk board. It was the end of the day and his thoughts turned to tomorrow's activities and plans for the next few weeks.

He remembered that he needed to pull things together for the dinosaur unit he was planning for his third grade class. It would start soon. He was gathering resources and ideas from a number of sources: his folder from last year's unit, the school library, and the Internet. He went to his classroom computer to see what he could find.

First, he checked his e-mail. He had been using several search engines to locate information and he had found a few things on dinosaurs. What he really wanted, though, was to see what other teachers had done with this topic. Yesterday he posted requests for instructional ideas about dinosaurs at several locations:

- the "Let's Talk" section of IMPACT II—The Teachers Network (http://www.teachnet.org/)—this is a location for teachers to post and respond to messages about teaching ideas (see Figure 4-1); and
- the guest book of the web page for "Teachers Helping Teachers" (http://www.pacificnet.net/~mandel/) —this is a location to post messages for other teachers about Internet activities in the classroom.
- The School-L Listserv—this is a listserv/mailing list for teachers using technology in their classroom. Earlier Mr. Erickson had subscribed to this support group by sending a subscription message (subscribe SCHOOL-L Mark Erickson) to listserve@listserv.hea.ie

Now it was time to see if his inquiries had brought in any useful ideas.

Figure 4-1.   The home page of Impact II—The Teachers Network (http://www.teachnet.org/)

He had several e-mail messages in his mailbox. Teachers had responded from California, Oklahoma, Arizona, Alberta, Manitoba, Florida, Washington, and Great Britain. They shared a number of great ideas about dinosaur units on the WWW:

- Have students take a guided tour of a paleontology museum. As students follow the tour, have them make entries in a "Digging for Dinosaurs" journal, writing down interesting information about dinosaurs and indicating where it was obtained. Several locations for tours were included with teachers' e-mail messages:

  — the University of California's Museum of Paleontology (http://www.ucmp.berkeley.edu/exhibit/ exhibits.html);
  — the Field Museum in Chicago (http://www.bvis.uic.edu:80/museum/Home.html);
  — and a master page with hyperlinks to these and other paleontology locations around the world, Virtual Tours of Dinosaur Sites (http://www.comet.net/dinosaur/docs/tours.htm).

- Conduct a "Reading About Dinosaurs" session with students reading and sharing the information they gathered during the week in their journals using the "author's chair" in the class.
- Print out a list of books for children on dinosaurs, a dinosaur crossword puzzle, a word search puzzle, a dinosaur flip book, and blackline masters for drawing full-scale outlines of several dinosaurs provided by the Field Museum in Chicago at their website (http://www.bvis.uic.edu:80/museum/ education/LOTguide1.html).
- Have students view animations of dinosaurs and play several interactive games (http:// rs6000.bvis.uic.edu/museum/exhibits/lot_media/Media1.html)
- Provide time for students' independent exploration of the WWW, but direct this exploration by setting a bookmark to Yahooligans, a web guide with information screened for children (http:// www.yahooligans.com/). Have students share their search strategies.
- Have students create an image of their own dinosaur at the web page for Create-a-saurus (http:// www.adventure.com:80/science_lab/3d_dino/createasaurus/). Then have students paste the picture into their word processor and either write a story about it or use the picture in a report about that species.
- Request the excellent classroom packs for dinosaur study provided by the Field Museum (http:// www.bvis.uic.edu:80/museum/education/LOTguide1.html). These are available for short-term loans to schools and teachers.
- Help students become what a teacher from Texas called "healthy skeptics." Require them to cross reference claims from several sources before accepting them as accurate. She noted that anyone can publish information on the Internet and one is never certain about the accuracy of information found there.
- Ask a real paleontologist questions about dinosaurs. Have students visit a site called PaleoPals at the University of California at Berkeley (http://www.ucmp.berkeley.edu/museum/pals.html) (see Figure 4-2) and send a question via e-mail. It will be answered by a paleontologist at the museum.

As he read these ideas, Mr. Erickson went to his web browser, found each location, and quickly reviewed the contents, determining whether it would fit his goals for the unit. He made a bookmark for the Virtual Tours of Dinosaur sites and decided to use the journal activity, "Digging for Dinosaurs." He also made a bookmark for the PaleoPals and the Create-a-saurus sites; he would have students use these sites, too. He also set a bookmark for Yahooligans to provide independent exploration time in an area of the web for kids. He printed out the lists of children's books on dinosaurs and decided to ask the school librarian to send these books down to his class. Then, he printed out the activity pages he found at the Field Museum. He would also use these during the unit. He especially liked the flip book and the idea of drawing full-size patterns of several dinosaurs. Since he lived in Chicago, he called to order the classroom packs from the Field Museum. These would come in handy during his unit. Things were coming together nicely.

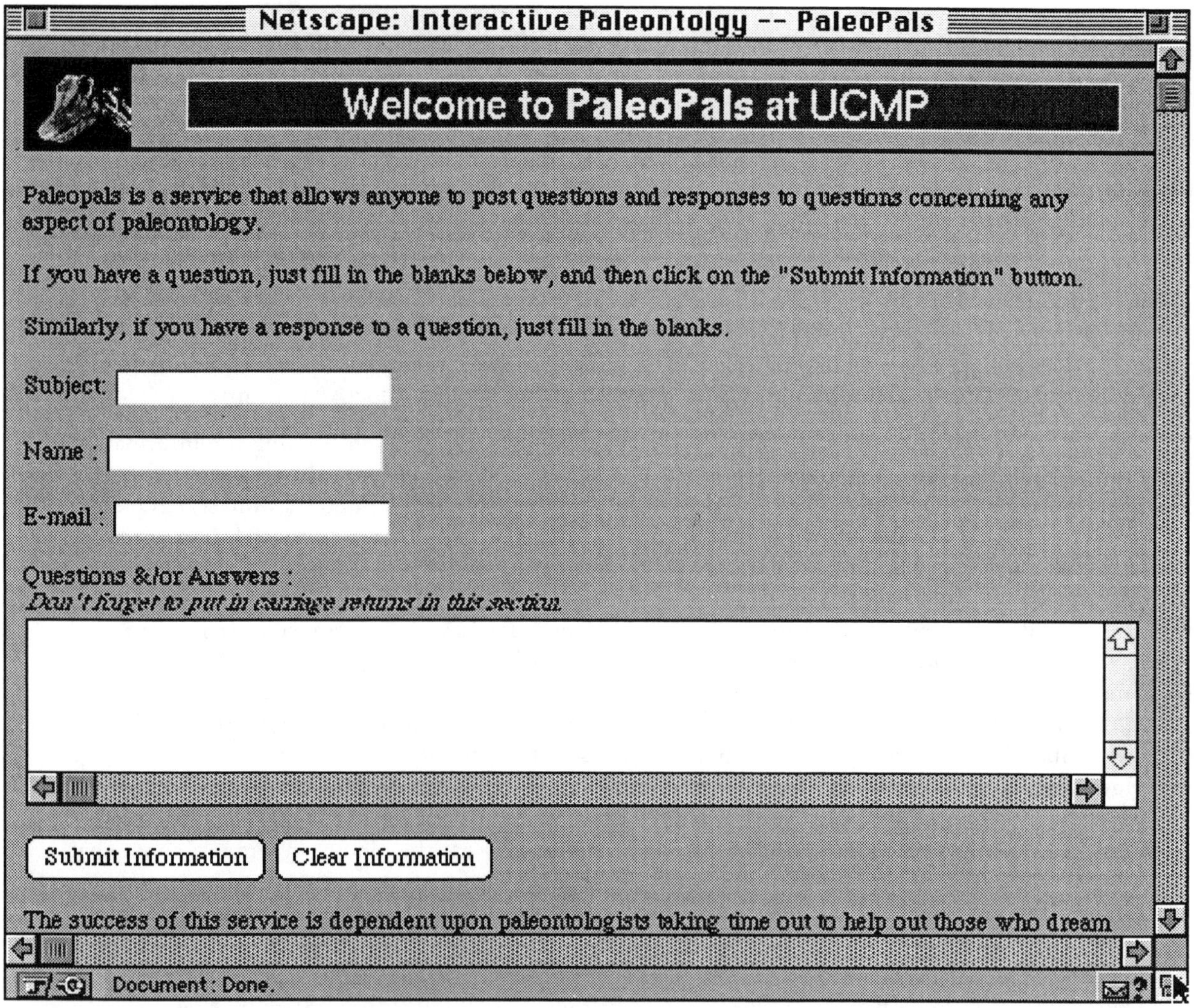

Figure 4-2.   The WWW site of PaleoPals from the University of California, Berkeley
(http://www.ucmp.berkeley.edu/museum/pals.html)

Earlier in the year, Mr. Erickson had developed a schedule for students to use with the single computer he had that was linked to the Internet. This schedule provided equal access for each student. Each week, every student received a half-hour alone on the computer and a half-hour on the computer with a partner. If students needed more than an hour of Internet access, they would sometimes go down to the media center and use the connection there. While he always wished he had more time on the Internet for his students, Mr. Erickson noted that students quickly learned to use their Internet time efficiently. This appeared to help them develop useful strategies for navigation. You can see his schedule in Figure 4-3.

His schedule had worked well in other units, so he planned to continue its use. However, he was going to rearrange partner pairs. He wanted each student to have an opportunity to work with different peers during the year.

During the first two weeks of the unit, he would have students take tours and keep journal entries for each session. Later, students would do an Internet inquiry project about a dinosaur species or another issue of paleontology they had selected.

He also liked the idea of having a "Reading About Dinosaurs" session for 30 minutes each week to share information students had acquired and the new locations they had found. He would do this on Fridays.

	Monday	*Tuesday*	*Wednesday*	*Thursday*	*Friday*
8:30–9:00	Michelle	Michelle/ Becky	Chris/Emily Cara	Shannon/Cara Jennifer	Cynthia/
9:00–9:30	Chris	John/Peter	Jeremy/Dave	Kati	Patti
9:30–10:00	**Internet Workshop**	Ben	Aaron	Lisa	Julia
10:00–10:30	Shannon	**PE**	Paul	**PE**	Andy
10:30–11:00	**Library**	Mike	Scott	Faith	Melissa
11:00–11:30	Cynthia	Eric	James	Linda	Sara
11:30–12:30	**Lunch**	**Lunch**	**Lunch**	**Lunch**	**Lunch**
2:30–1:00	Jennifer	Dave	Peter	Cara	Emily
1:00–1:30	Becky	Jeremy	Ben/Sara	Mike/Linda	John
1:30–2:00	Eric/James	Aaron/ Melissa	**Music**	Paul/Scott	**Class Meeting**
2:00–2:30	Kati/Lisa		Faith/Andy	Patti/Julia	

Figure 4-3.   Mr. Erickson's computer schedule posted next to his Internet computer

Yes, the unit was coming together. Now, if he could find another class on the Internet that would like to do a collaborative activity on dinosaurs, maybe they could share the results of their Inquiry projects. This would help his students develop written communication skills. He decided to see if any other teachers were on the live chat area at Impact II—The Teacher's Network (http://www.teachnet.org/) or at "Teachers Helping Teachers" (http://www.pacificnet.net/~mandel/). Yes, the chat sessions were going strong. They were always active after school. He located a third grade teacher in Detroit who was interested in doing something together. They agreed to think about joint projects tonight and share ideas later via e-mail. It was time to get off the computer and prepare a few things for tomorrow.

Lessons From The Classroom

The episode with Mr. Erickson provides us with a number of important lessons as we consider effective instructional strategies using the Internet. First, it is clear that developing a weekly schedule for Internet use in single computer classrooms helps to ensure that all students receive access to this important resource. Sometimes, certain students will tend to dominate access to the Internet and other students will have their time curtailed. It is important to guarantee that all students have time to access resources on the Internet.

Second, the use of a workshop each week helps to share important information students have discovered during their work. We have already mentioned the use of this procedure for developing navigation skills; it is also highly effective for sharing content information.

It may also be useful to help students evaluate the accuracy of information they find on the Internet. Since anyone can publish nearly any information they wish on the Internet, it is hard to be certain the information you find is accurate. We need to help students become "healthy skeptics" if we wish them to become effective consumers of information.

It is also important to note the special opportunities on the Internet for developing cooperative learning projects with classrooms in other parts of the country. This turns academic projects into important learning opportunities as information is shared and new questions are developed. Cooperative learning projects require advance planning between teachers, but the rewards are often well worth the additional time it takes to do the planning.

Note, too, how Mr. Erickson provided opportunities for his students to search for information on their own. After students have developed initial navigation strategies, it is important to provide opportunities for independent navigation through the Internet and discover even more useful strategies. Providing opportunities for independent research on the Internet, as Mr. Erickson did with his Internet Inquiry Project, accomplished this.

It is also important to realize that Internet use may be easily integrated with other instructional practices with which you are already familiar. Mr. Erickson's use of a journal while students took a dinosaur tour is but one example of this. He also wove in a practice found in many classrooms, the use of an "author's chair." Here, students could read their selected dinosaur entries to the class. Nearly every instructional activity you currently use in your classroom may also be used with the Internet.

Finally, while the Internet is a tool to support students' learning, it is also a powerful resource for planning instructional activities. In a short session after school, Mr. Erickson quickly gathered resources and ideas for an extensive thematic unit. As you become more familiar with the Internet, you will also develop efficient strategies for using the Internet to plan activities. After a short time, you will wonder how you ever taught without having this resource available.

Integrating The Internet Into Your Classroom

It is essential that you thoughtfully plan how to integrate Internet experiences into your classroom curriculum. Teachers sometimes abdicate this responsibility when they make Internet experiences available only after students' regular classroom work is completed and provide little direction for what should be done. Using the Internet in this way makes it one of several "free choice" activities in the classroom. There are several problems with this approach.

Equity is one of the problems. Making the Internet available only when regular work has been completed ultimately results in more advanced students having greater Internet access. This leads to a case of "the rich getting richer," because advanced students become more proficient in their ability to access and analyze information on the Internet, while weaker students are denied the same kind of opportunities to improve their abilities.

Another problem is that teachers often report extensive surfing when students do not have a clear purpose for their Internet use. When the Internet is used without direction and guidance, students will often be diverted from thoughtful integration and analysis of information and engage instead in random, unconnected surfing experiences. You will see this pattern, too, in your classroom unless students have a clear purpose each time they sit down to use the Internet. Internet experiences should always have a purpose; they should always be an integral part of your instructional program. This requires that you thoughtfully plan how this integration will take place.

How can you integrate the Internet into your classroom to avoid these problems? Developing effective instructional strategies with the Internet is not difficult. Most of your current practices work well with the Internet. In addition to the child safety issues discussed in Chapters 2 and 3, there are only a few issues you will need to consider:

E-Mail for You

```
From: Linda Hubbard (lhubbard@mail.tempe3.k12.az.us)
Organization: Tempe School District No.3
Subject: Classroom Activities on the World Wide Web

     In my fifth grade classroom we combine the use of NASA web
sites and NASA satellite TV. During each shuttle mission, while
school is in session, we watch the shuttle launch, live, if pos-
sible. Then we access the various WWW sites which provide us with
background and real-time information about the particular mis-
sion. We have the chance to "log in" as visitors to the shuttle,
learn about the crew, monitor the progress of any science experi-
ments, and watch the tracking map for the orbits. The URL address
for the NASA Shuttle Web, covering current shuttle missions, is
http://shuttle.nasa.gov/index.html. For information on the
shuttle crew currently in space, we use http://
liftoff.msfc.nasa.gov/spacelab/lms/realtime/crew_tl/minute.html.
One of the class favorites is the web site which displays the
global tracking map of the shuttle flight (http://
shuttle.nasa.gov/sts-69/demos/).
     All of these activities give us opportunities to relate our
curriculum in all areas to real-world space exploration. We also
use the flight schedule information from the web sites to find
out when the astronauts will be working in the open payload bay
or making a space walk. We tune in to NASA TV to watch those live
when we can. The web sites also give us a chance to see photos
taken during the mission. Finally, our interest in current mis-
sions has led us to explore NASA web sites with historical infor-
mation from the start of the space program. APOLLO Manned Mis-
sions is very interesting (http://ceps.nasm.edu:2020/APOLLO/
Apollo.html). Exploring the Universe with NASA'S Astro-2 (http://
astro-2.msfc.nasa.gov/) is also an interesting site covering a
variety of topics including the Marshall Space Flight Center and
JPL's space calendar of up-coming missions.
     With each shuttle mission we monitor, we discover more web
sites to explore. All of which makes our science unit on explor-
ing space much more meaningful for all of us.


     Linda Hubbard
     5th grade teacher
     Carminati Elementary School
     Tempe, Arizona
```

- scheduling computer time appropriately;
- using Internet Workshop;
- planning Internet projects;
- helping students become healthy skeptics about information accuracy; and
- developing independent search strategies while being sensitive to child safety concerns.

Once you consider these issues, Internet resources may be easily integrated with nearly all of the instructional practices you already use in your classroom.

Scheduling Computer Time Appropriately

There are many different ways in which Internet access is provided to schools. In some cases, Internet computers will be available for the entire school to use in the library or media center. In other cases, a lab or cluster will exist with many Internet computers in a single room. In still other cases, each classroom will have at least one computer connected to the Internet. In very unusual cases, five or more computers will be linked to the Internet in each classroom.

We will not discuss Internet scheduling for situations where Internet access is limited to one or two computers at a school, often in the library or media center. This situation usually makes Internet access too limited for systematic integration within each classroom; it often becomes more of a novelty item than a focal point of the school curriculum. Some schools, however, have a teacher willing to take the time to use a software program such as Webwhacker which downloads useful web sites onto a disk. This information is then transferred to other computers in the school where students may use it. We will also not discuss scheduling issues if you have a large number of Internet computers in your classroom or in a computer lab down the hall. If you are fortunate enough to enjoy access to many Internet computers, time management issues are easier to handle.

Many of us, though, have a single Internet computer in our classroom and seek ways to maximize its use within a limited amount of time. This presents a special challenge. We are required to modify our classroom procedures to fully integrate this resource into instruction and provide equal opportunities for all students to benefit from its use.

One of the best solutions to this situation is the one developed by Mr. Erickson. You will recall that he devised a schedule so that each of his 28 students had a half-hour on the Internet with a partner and a half-hour on the Internet by themselves. Each student had a minimum of one hour per week to use the Internet for class projects. While not ideal, this is the best solution we have seen for providing equity in classrooms with only a single Internet connection. It will, however, usually require you to adjust your organizational patterns slightly to optimize Internet use. You will need to be sufficiently flexible so that at any time during the day, one student or student pair will miss regular, on-going instruction. That is, students will need to leave the regularly scheduled class or group activity to work on the Internet during their assigned time. In most cases, this is a minor matter; both teachers and students adjust to the situation remarkably well.

There are, however, a few issues you should consider. First, be certain that you periodically rotate the assigned times on the computer schedule so that the same students do not miss their time because of regular conflicts with the school's special functions (for example, regularly scheduled school assemblies, student council meetings, or special activity meetings). It would be unfair, for example, to have a student miss her Internet time on Monday of each week because she had to attend a leadership meeting.

Second, rotate partners regularly at the computer so that all of your students have an opportunity to work with many different individuals in your class. This increases opportunities for improving social skills while at the same time increasing opportunities to learn new things from other students about Internet navigation.

Finally, if you organize your schedule around traditional subject areas, consider scheduling students who are strong at math during math time, students who are strong in language arts during language arts time, and so forth. This prevents the situation where a student misses subject area instruction who really needs every moment in that area.

Developing a regular schedule for Internet use will help you to manage equity issues in your classroom. In the future, this problem will be resolved as additional connections are made to school classrooms. For now, we need to develop adequate sceduling strategies to accommodate our students' learning needs.

Using Internet Workshop In Your Classroom

A second addition you may wish to consider is the use of Internet Workshop once a week in your class. Internet Workshop is used to support students' ability to acquire information from the Internet and to think critically about the information they obtain.

The nature of Internet Workshop activities differs depending on the teacher and the students who use it. Often, however, it shares several common characteristics. First, it takes place during a regular time period, usually at the beginning or the end of the week—a regularly scheduled time period allows all members to anticipate the session and prepare for it. Second, Internet Workshop provides opportunities for both the teacher and students to share navigation strategies as well as content information. Internet Workshop provides an important opportunity for all members to learn from one another about the Internet and the information they find.

Teachers usually direct the first few sessions of Internet Workshop to model what they wish to take place. After students understand the process, teachers usually turn over responsibility for the session to students. When you are modeling the first few sessions, Internet Workshop consists of two steps:

1. The teacher shares something new he/she recently learned about the Internet and encourages others to respond.

2. The teacher shares something he/she is still trying to figure out about the Internet and encourages others to respond.

During the second step, share with your students something you discovered while working on the Internet. This might be a navigational issue such as how to contact an expert in colonial history to answer a question you have about the Boston Massacre. It might also be a content issue such as what you found out about the Boston Massacre. After you share what you have recently learned, allow students an opportunity to ask questions or share their experiences related to your item. They might, for example, be interested in locations where they can contact an expert in the area they are studying. Or, they might share the experiences they had in contacting experts. It is important during this step that students understand that they need to stay on task and only share items that are related to the topic under discussion. This will be a special challenge for younger students.

During the second step, share something about the Internet (either navigation or content) that you want to learn but haven't quite figured out. After you share what it is you wish to learn, allow others to respond and see if anyone knows how to do this. If a student does, encourage him/her to share the information. This will allow others to try it out after the workshop session to see if it works.

Sometimes, the solution will not work as the student described it. When this happens, encourage students to bring their experiences to the next workshop to see if the problem can be solved by others or if the solution was misinterpreted. In either case, the discussion that occurs during the second step is often a time when some of the most productive learning about the Internet will take place in your classroom.

After one or two sessions in which you direct the Internet Workshop, encourage students to follow the same procedures that you have modeled: share something they learned about the Internet and allow others to respond; share something they want to learn about the Internet and allow others to respond. Gradually, encourage students to assume ownership of Internet Workshop so that the class is always focused on items which students find most helpful in their work. You should, though, always come to Internet Workshop prepared to share your items if students do not have something they wish to share. After you begin the use of Internet Workshop, this will seldom happen.

Often teachers will add a rule for everyone to follow during Internet Workshop: each student may only respond twice until everyone else has had a chance to contribute a response. This rule prevents individuals from dominating the conversation and will encourage quieter students to contribute.

It is important to recognize that both navigation issues (e.g., "How do I set a bookmark so I can come back to a location?") as well as content issues (e.g., "Has anyone found information about volcanoes?") are appropriate topics for Internet Workshop. Initially, you will find students more interested in navigation issues. As the year progresses, however, and they become more skilled in navigating the Internet, content issues will dominate.

Internet Workshop does much more than teach students how to use the Internet. You will also find that it is a prime vehicle for developing oral language and problem-solving skills. Through their experiences, students will develop the ability to clearly define complex problems and accurately communicate solutions for complex issues. They will also develop the ability to listen carefully to explanations since the information is often very useful to them. These interchanges can be a central part of your oral language program, a curricular area that often does not receive the attention it deserves.

E-Mail for You

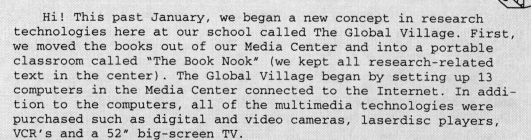

From: Judy Fasanello (fasanell@pinellas.k12.fl.us)
Subject: An alternative way to organize Internet use

Hi! This past January, we began a new concept in research
technologies here at our school called The Global Village. First,
we moved the books out of our Media Center and into a portable
classroom called "The Book Nook" (we kept all research-related
text in the center). The Global Village began by setting up 13
computers in the Media Center connected to the Internet. In addition to the computers, all of the multimedia technologies were
purchased such as digital and video cameras, laserdisc players,
VCR's and a 52" big-screen TV.

The "Village" works like this: A student, group of students,
or whole class decides they want to know more about a topic. They
come to the "village" and search the Internet, our CD-ROM collection, or laserdisc collection for information. The Media specialist pre-searches the topics in advance so that students have
sites already bookmarked, which keeps them out of trouble. Once
the information is gathered, they return to their class and begin
assembling the information into a logical, sequential, meaningful
presentation on 5" by 8" index cards (storyboarding). The third
step is a return visit or two to create a multimedia presentation
using Hyperstudio software and their storyboarded index cards.
Finally, the entire class and invited parents come to the Global
Village to see the multimedia presentation on the big-screen
television.

The units that have been done quite successfully since January are: Famous African Americans, Native American Cultures,
Rainforests, Jamaica, the 1996 Olympics, and Ocean Life. This
concept has not only been wonderful for teaching students computer skills and information skills, but has improved writing,
reading and speaking skills while peaking student interest and
motivation. Teachers learn with their students in the village,
and parents are thrilled.

If you would like further information on the setup or opera-
tion of the Global Village, a section can be found on our
school's website at: http://www.clearview.pinellas.k12.fl.us or
by e-mailing your questions to: fasanell@pinellas.k12.fl.us.

Judy Fasanello
Network Manager/Technology Specialist
Clearview Elementary School
Clearview, Florida

Planning Internet Projects

As you use the Internet in your class, there will come a time when you feel confident enough to explore cooperative learning possibilities with others at locations around the world. Internet projects take place as you work with another class on a common project, with students and teachers communicating extensively about the topic both classes are exploring. Internet projects also take place when classes contribute data to a common site and then, after the data are analyzed, see how their data compare with others. Often there will also be discussion between participating classes about the results and even opportunities to use the data set for further analyses. Each leads to rich learning opportunities.

Communicating with others around the world on a common classroom project provides special opportunities for your students, opportunities they will not experience without the Internet. You should seek out these opportunities for your students and integrate them into your curriculum for several reasons. First, communicating with students from a culture other than their own helps your students to develop a greater appreciation for the diversity that characterizes our world. Understanding diversity leads children to respect differences, a value that is becoming increasingly important in a global community. Moreover, writing takes on a very different meaning as students learn that their messages must be perfectly clear for others to understand what they mean. Communication in writing requires meaning to be very explicit; children come to learn this through misunderstandings from poorly written e-mail messages. It serves to help them learn important lessons about correct spelling, sentence structure, and organization since each may get in the way of effective communication. In addition, reading information from other places on our planet becomes an exciting way to learn. In fact, all of your curriculum will suddenly come to life when you are able to share work with students in another location who have similar interests. These special opportunities for communicating and learning from others comprise an important advantage of Internet use. You should seek them out as often as you can.

How do you make connections with another class or participate in a joint project with other schools? While locations for linking up with another class on the WWW are constantly changing, four sites that provide a wide range of cooperative opportunities and are not likely to soon disappear from the WWW are listed below.

Global SchoolNet's Internet Project Registry—(http://www.gsn.org/gsn/proj/index.html)

If you only want to visit one site for Internet Projects, this might be your best choice. It contains an extensive listing of registered projects and allows you to list your own project so that others might find it. An excellent resource for Internet Project ideas and contacts.

Using the Internet in Your Classroom—(http://bvsd.k12.co.us/docs/apple.html)

This site, located within the WWW site for the Boulder Valley School District in Colorado, contains an extensive set of links to cooperative sites, including NASA school projects, a monster drawing project for young children around the world, several global competitions for students, links to mentoring sites, links to Keypals (e-mail pen pals) and many other great projects.

Classroom Connect's Teacher Contact Database—(http://www.classroom.net/contact/)

This is a nice data base to review possible connections with teachers doing similar projects. It also allows you to register your project so that others might find you.

Kidsphere Message Archives—(gopher://ericir.syr.edu:70/11/Listservs/KIDSPHERE-List)

This is a gopher archive of messages appearing on Kidsphere, a discussion group made up of teachers from around the world. It is a good place to link up with teachers interested in Internet Projects.

Helping Students Become Healthy Skeptics About Information Accuracy

While the Internet makes more information available to more classrooms, it also presents new challenges to both students and teachers. One of the important challenges we face is that we are never certain about the accuracy of the information we find on the web. Traditional forces that guarantee some degree of control over the accuracy of information in published books generally do not affect the Internet, where anyone may publish anything. As a result, searches for information may sometimes turn up web pages created by people who have political, religious, or philosophical stances that influence the nature of the information they present to others. Or, sometimes a person simply gets the facts wrong on a web page.

As a result, we need to help our students become healthy skeptics so that they can evaluate the nature of any information they find on the web and be confident about its reliability. Such skill has not always been necessary in classrooms where the textbook has always been assumed to be correct.

There are a number of strategies that may be used to help students become healthy skeptics, including:

- Ask students to provide at least two references for major claims they make in their written or oral reports. While citation style rules for Internet sources are still evolving, a useful location with examples for citing sources may be found at http://www.wentworth.com/classroom/ CitingNetResources.htm

- Keep a bulletin board entitled "Discrepant facts: Who is right?" Encourage students to post copies of material they find containing contradictory information. These may come from the Internet or from printed material. You will be surprised how quickly students will find different spellings, different dates for events, different birth dates for famous individuals, and other information that differs between two sources.

- Discuss this issue in your Internet Workshop sessions and see if students can come up with strategies for evaluating the accuracy of information. Strategies might include looking to see if document references are provided, the reputation of the source (an individual you do not know versus a source with a commercial reputation that they want to protect) or biases the author may display.

FAQ (Frequently Asked Question)

I like variety. How can I vary the structure of Internet Workshop for my students so it doesn't become boring?

There are probably as many ways to do Internet Workshop as there are teachers with creative ideas. One way to increase social learning opportunities in your class is to have small groups of students (or computer pairs) identify something new they learned and something they want to learn. Then, have one small group teach another small group what they have learned. Afterwards, have them exchange roles. Finally, have each group share what it is they want to learn in order to initiate a discussion about possible solutions. This technique breaks down the larger, whole class approach to Internet Workshop and encourages advance preparation and planning by each small group. As you circle around, listening to the discussions, you will hear many new ideas being learned as students share their Internet experiences with one another.

Developing Independent Search Strategies While Being Sensitive To Child Safety Concerns

There is an inherent tension between child safety on the Internet and helping children to develop the independent search strategies necessary for effective Internet use. If we protect children by restricting their access to the Internet, they fail to develop comprehensive search strategies and do not learn how to use the full power of Internet resources. Many districts are beginning to resolve this tension by developing a graduated access policy; older students are provided with greater access while younger students are restricted in what they may access on the Internet. Some districts purchase commercial solutions with built-in graduated access to the Internet that may be set by teachers or administrators. Most districts are also developing acceptable use policies and requiring teacher supervision of Internet use.

It is impossible to completely protect children from viewing sites they should not see. The best policy, in the long run, is to educate children, parents, and guardians about how to use the Internet safely, develop an acceptable use policy, and always supervise student use of the Internet. This is your best insurance for all child safety issues.

One way that teachers often guide very young children's Internet experiences is to bookmark safe items and limit children's Internet use to these items. This makes it less likely that young students will view sites that are inappropriate for their age.

In addition, some teachers, especially in the primary grades, limit viewing to certain areas in the WWW that have been selected with some attention to a younger audience . There are a few sites on the WWW that attempt to do this. None, however, are able to guarantee that children will not be able to view inappropriate sites since links within sites change on a daily basis. Moreover, the nature of the WWW is such that sites are linked to sites, which are linked to still other sites, and on and on. No one can guarantee the appropriateness of third level links or greater. Still, if you wish to limit the resources your students view but still allow them to develop independent search strategies, you may wish to designate certain areas as appropriate for your younger children to explore. The best site we have found is Yahooligans (http://www.yahooligans.com/). (See Figure 4-4.) This is a special area with a vast set of information resources for students and a search engine that allows them to search sites approved for children's use. You may wish to make a bookmark for this location or designate it as your home page location (see Chapter 2).

As children become older and more aware of child safety issues, you will want them to view more of the Internet and begin to use search engines for finding information. After all, as students grow older, we want them to develop effective strategies for finding information efficiently. You will need to make this decision or, perhaps, it may be specified in your school's acceptable use policy.

Adapting your current instructional strategies to the Internet

Once you consider these issues, most of your current instructional practices may be easily integrated with Internet resources. Instructional practices such as thematic unit activities, cooperative learning groups, inquiry projects, K-W-L, journal activities, self-selected vocabulary and spelling lists, discussion groups, and many others may be used in conjunction with the Internet. In many ways, the Internet is simply another information resource for your classroom, much like a very powerful encyclopedia. Certainly it also has special potentials, especially in the area of communicating with distant locations or with experts in the area you are studying. But, by and large, the Internet is just another information resource for your students to exploit as they engage in classroom learning activities.

Using The Internet To Plan Instruction

General Planning Resources

As you have seen from the example with Mr. Erickson, the Internet can be an important tool for planning instructional activities and units for your class. You may contact other teachers, read about projects other schools have used, find useful sites for instructional activities, collaborate with another teacher at a distant location, and read professional articles. All of these will provide important assistance as you plan for instruction. You may wish to visit some of these general resource sites to see how the Internet may assist you as you plan activities for your students:

Classroom Connect Jump Station—(http://www.classroom.net/classroom/edulinks.html)
This location provides links to many useful planning resources, including chat rooms, instructional resources, a teacher contact data base, and many others.

Teachers Helping Teachers—(http://www.pacificnet.net/~mandel/)
The goals of this site include: to provide basic teaching tips to inexperienced teachers; to provide new ideas in teaching methodologies for all teachers; and to provide a forum for experienced teachers to share their expertise and tips with colleagues around the world. It achieves each of these goals very well.

The Staff Room of Canada's SchoolNet—(http://www.coreplus.calstate.edu/KALEIDO/Nav2.html)
This is one section of a rich teaching resource. It contains links to lesson plans and teaching resources as well as other areas. Especially valuable for teachers in Canada or for teachers who wish to link up with Canadian schools, though all teachers will find these resources useful.

Figure 4-4.   The Yahooligans Home Page on the WWW
(http://www.yahooligans.com/)

K-12 Kaleidoscope—(http://www.schoolnet.ca/adm/staff/)

The curriculum page of this rich resource is organized around major curricular areas. Developed in California, it contains an extensive set of links to support busy teachers looking for instructional ideas and resources.

Global SchoolNet Foundation Home Page—(http://www.gsn.org/)

This non-profit organization has connected teachers and students around the world in many important projects. An especially useful location for developing Internet Projects.

The Boulder Valley School District Home Page—(http://bvsd.k12.co.us/)

This is an excellent example of a district home page with many useful planning ideas for teachers. See, especially, the links to educational resources for teachers and resources for students.

Lesson Plan Locations

Sometimes it is helpful to see the lesson plans developed by other teachers for classroom projects. These sites will give you many useful ideas:

Teacher Talk Forum: Lesson Plans—(http://education.indiana.edu/cas/ttforum/lesson.html)

Teachnet.com—(http://www.teachnet.com/lesson.html)

Mustang List of Lesson Plans—(http://mustang.coled.umn.edu/lessons/lessons.html)

Locations for communicating with other teachers

Finally, there are times when it is very helpful to be able to talk to another teacher. Other teachers, of course, are often the best source of information, especially about Internet use in the classroom. These locations allow you to read and post comments on bulletin boards from other teachers or engage in chat sessions:

The Teacher's Network—(http://www.teachnet.org/)
The "Let's Talk" area at this site contains both bulletin boards for teachers as well as a live chat area.

Classroom Connect's Virtual Auditorium—(http://www.classroom.net/conference/welcome.html)
This area of Classroom Connect contains a live chat area for teachers on topics that are announced in advance.

Teachers Helping Teachers Chat Area—(http://www.pacificnet.net/~mandel/ircinfo.html)
At this location you may download Internet Relay Chat software by following directions and then participate in chat sessions with other teachers around the world.

A Final Word

We said earlier that it is not the information on the Internet, though this is considerable, that makes the difference for your students. Instead, it is what you decide to do with this information that makes the difference. As you begin to incorporate the Internet into your classroom, making it an integral part of teaching and learning, you will develop new ideas and new ways of teaching. We want to encourage you to share these ideas with other teachers who are also learning about this new resource for education. Though we have no evidence, we suspect that the Internet will have its greatest impact on teaching and learning through the new ideas that teachers share with one another and the new connections that are formed between teachers and students around the world. For too long, teachers have spent much of their time isolated from other teachers within the walls of their classroom. The Internet allows us to transcend these walls and learn from one another about best instructional practices. We want to encourage you to take the time to support others and to learn from others as you begin your journey.

Instructional Resources On The Internet

Bartlett's Familiar Passages, Phrases, and Proverbs—(http://www.cc.columbia.edu/acis/bartleby/bartlett/)
The classic reference for quotations. This is the complete work available through Columbia University's Project Bartleby, which also includes many other classic works in their entirety from Paine to Melville to Sandburg.

Blue Dog Math—(http://kao.ini.cmu.edu:5550/bdf.html)
Blue dog answers all your basic math problems by barking the answers. A fun site and especially useful in the primary grades for developing basic math skills.

Children's Literature Web Guide—(http://www.ucalgary.ca/~dkbrown/)
This is the most comprehensive location on the web for links to children and young adult's literature. A great resource for teachers and students.

Civil War Photograph Collection—(http://rs6.loc.gov/cwphome.html)
This site contains over 1,000 photographs from the Civil War, many by Mathew Brady. Viewing these images makes you feel the national conflict and struggle during this period.

Classroom Connect—(http://www.classroom.net/classroom/default2.html)

One of the better on-line resources for teachers. Includes the "Classroom Web" (a database of school Web sites); "Conference Web" (educational conference listings from around the world); "Products" (books, videos, software, seminars, etc.); and a "Jump Station" (links archive).

Eisenhower National Clearinghouse—(http://www.enc.org/)

If you are looking for WWW resources in science and math, this is probably the best place to look. Lesson plans, resource sites, a math/science search engine, publications, answers to questions—this site has it all. Sponsored by the U.S. Department of Education.

NASA Aerospace Education Services Program—(http://www.okstate.edu/aesp/AESP.html)

Designed to increase students' awareness of science, technology and space. Great science, literature, math, language, astronomy and writing resources, as well as museums and exhibits, cross-curricular projects and more.

SchoolNet Ocean Site—(http://schoolnet2.carleton.ca/english/manuals/virtualprod/ocean/)

Developing a unit on the oceans? Here is the site for you. It contains links to many lesson plans, teaching activities, information resources, and thematic units on a wide variety of ocean-related topics.

Teaching and Technology—(http://pathfinder.com/@@rppq4AYATv7NSGLu/time/teach/index.html)

This electronic journal for teachers by Time, Inc., provides useful background information and articles about teachers using technology in classrooms.

The Exploratorium—(http://www.exploratorium.edu/)

A palace that houses hands-on science learning in San Francisco, this site makes many of its outstanding interactive adventures in science available to the world. A great location for science, fun, and learning.

The Nine Planets Tour—(http://seds.lpl.arizona.edu/billa/tnp/)

This is the best tour through the solar system that exists. At each stop, beautiful photographs of each planetary object are displayed along with information about the object. Short sound clips and videos are also available. Many links take you to related sites. A wonderful journey!

The Tele-Garden—(http://www.usc.edu/dept/garden/)

If this site doesn't get too popular, your students can view and interact with a remote garden filled with living plants. Members can plant, water, and monitor the progress of seedlings via an industrial robot arm.

The United Nations Electronic Field Trip—(http://www.pbs.org/tal/un/)

It used to be that only students in New York City could take a field trip to the United Nations. No longer. Many classroom activities.

VolcanoWorld—(http://volcano.und.nodak.edu)

Study volcanoes around the world, talk to a vulcanologist, obtain real-time data on active volcanoes, and many more fun activities for kids and adults.

Listservs/Mailing Lists for General Teaching Issues

K12–AUP—(k12-aup-request@merit.edu) Only write the word "subscribe" in the body of your message. A discussion of acceptable use policies

K12ASSESS-L—(mailserv@lists.cua.edu)

A forum focusing on issues related to educational assessment, grades K–12.

L-ACLRNG—(listserv@psuvm.psu.edu)

A discussion of active and collaborative learning

Usenet Newsgroups for General Teaching Issues

K–12 Math Education—(k12.ed.math)

disscusses issues of mathematics curriculum in K-12 education.

K–12 Science Education—(k12.ed.science)

Discusses issues of science curriculum in K-12 education.

K–12 Social Studies Education—(k12.ed.soc-studies)

Discusses issues of social studies curriculum in K–12 education.

Chapter 5

*U*sing the Internet for Language Arts and Literature

```
To:    Our readers
From: djleu@sued.syr.edu (Don Leu),
       ddleu@syr.edu (Debbie Leu)
Subject: A computer isn't the same as reading a good book


    It certainly isn't! On-line literary experiences and a liter-
ary experience with a book are two very different things. And, we
probably should not tell you this, but....we tend to prefer our
literary experiences with books. This may change in the future as
richer and faster multimedia become possible on the Internet,
providing students with new types of literary experiences which
take full advantage of mutimedia and communication resources. For
the moment, however, a richly illustrated book propped up on a
tummy, as a child snuggles into a bean bag chair in the reading
corner of a classroom, contains richer literary potentials than
any current story on the Internet. Imagining worlds through a
good book contains richer potentials for evocative, critical, and
emotional response.
    Having said this, we also believe the Internet can make a
literary experience with a book even richer, more meaningful, and
more "authentic" in a world of global electronic links between
individuals around the world. In addition, using the Internet to
connect reading and writing provides powerful support for the
language arts. Most important, though, literary experiences and
the language arts can be supported through a project-based ap-
proach to learning on the Internet.


    Don and Debbie
```

Ms. Meyer had developed a cross-curricular thematic unit about diversity. Her goal was to increase students' understanding and respect for diversity as they studied math, science, social studies, reading, writing, speaking, and listening. In math, she planned experiences for students to explore number systems from other civilizations, including a study of systems using bases other than 10. In science, she was going to use the unit on biodiversity she had developed in a summer workshop at the university last year. In social studies, she developed experiences for students to better understand the cultures of Native Americans as well as immigrants who had arrived in North America. Finally, in language arts, she was planning experiences around "pourquoi tales," explanatory myths that appear in every traditional culture about the origins of natural phenomena such as how people obtained fire, why mosquitoes buzz in people's ears, where the moon came from, and why rivers run into the ocean.

She introduced the concept of a pourquoi tale at the beginning of the unit by engaging the class in read aloud response journal activities (Leu & Kinzer, 1995), using *The Fire Bringer* by Margaret Hodges, *Star Boy* by Paul Gobel, and several others. Then she had students work in one of three different literature discussion groups, using text set activities suggested by Short (1993) and response journal activities. Each group had a large set of pourquoi tales to read from. One group read and discussed tales from the Americas, another read tales from Asia and Australia, and a third read tales from Africa, Europe, and the Middle East. Individuals chose different books to read and then members of each group got together twice a week to share their literary experiences in a student-led discussion organized around a "grand conversation" (McGee, 1992). At the end, each group had to make a presentation to the class on at least one culture using only the information in their explanatory myths. They had to infer aspects of that culture from the stories, indicating what they inferred and the evidence that supported their inferences.

"I was doing a search for some stories like we are reading and I found a cool site!" It was Monday morning and Marcus was directing an Internet Workshop session with the rest of the class. "It's this school in Tasmania. I found it on the map. They made a page with all kinds of stories from different cultures and they had other kids e-mail them from where they were in the world. . . . like from Japan, and Indonesia, and from Amsterdam. I found that place, too, on a map. Ms. Meyer, could we do that, too? You know, ask people to send us their pourquoi stories? Then we could do the same thing. . . . write them on our class home page so other kids could read them."

"Yeah. Cool!" A chorus of thoughts emerged from the class.

"Set a bookmark, Marcus, and show me after school. We'll see."

"Yes!" several students said simultaneously. In this class, a "we'll see" from Ms. Meyer was almost as good as gold. Ms. Meyer smiled. Everyone was excited about the possibility of using their new computer to collect stories from other places in the world.

After school, Marcus showed Ms. Meyer the location he had found at the Fahan School's homepage in Tasmania (http://www.tas.gov.au/fahan/stories.html). He also showed her another site at Heinemann Publishers that had a similar collection of stories from around the world contributed by students (http://www.reedbooks.com.au/heinemann/global/mythstor.html). These were nice models. It seemed like a great opportunity to develop a better understanding of different cultures by communicating and sharing stories with children around the world. Ms. Meyer had to do some quick planning.

She visited the NickNacks location (http://www1.minn.net:80/~schubert/NickNacks.html#anchor 100100), a site she had heard about from a friend. (See Figure 5-1.) Here, she read up on Internet Projects on the Internet and quickly linked to a number of useful resources that told her exactly how to set up a project, announce it to others, and where to post her announcement. In just a few minutes, she had posted an announcement at a number of different locations asking teachers and students to contribute pourquoi tales from their culture. By exchanging stories, they would each develop a deeper appreciation for differences and for important aspects of other cultures. She posted her announcement, explaining the project and asking for other classes to join hers, at four different locations:

- **Classroom Connect's Teacher Contact Database** (http://www.classroom.net/contact/)
- **The Global Schoolhouse Projects Registry** (http://www.gsh.org/gsh/class/projsrch.htm)
- **Intercultural E-mail Classroom Connections** (http://www.stolaf.edu/network/iecc/)
- **Kidproject** (http://www.kidlink.org:80/KIDPROJ/)

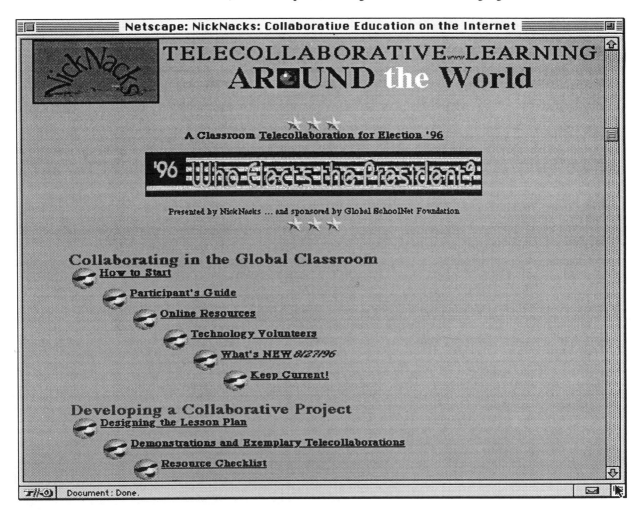

Figure 5.1   The homepage for NickNack's Telecollaborative Learning, a useful location to find out more about collaborative Internet projects (http://www1.minn.net:80/~schubert/NickNacks.html#anchor100100).

She also joined the Kidsphere listserv (kidsphere-request@vms.cis.pitt.edu) and posted a description of the project on this mailing list for teachers.

By the end of the week, Ms. Meyer had received messages from eight different schools around the world: Darwin, Australia; Bristol, England; Haifa, Israel; Kyoto, Japan; Newburgh, New York; Dublin, California; Rapid City, South Dakota; Beaumont, Texas; and Clearwater, Florida. Each had promised to collect traditional myths from cultures in or near their location and share them in two weeks.

As she announced the results of her work to the class, everyone was full of new ideas. Each group, they decided, would work with schools from their part of the world: the Asia and Australia group would coordinate work with the schools in Darwin and Kyoto; the Americas group would work with schools in the United States; and the Europe, Middle East, and Africa group would work with schools in Bristol and Haifa. Also, each group now had a new assignment: to uncover explanatory myths from cultures in their own community so that they could share them with their partner schools on this project. This would involve interviewing parents and relatives to see what they could find from them. Then they would draft versions of these stories and work with their parent informants to revise them. Finally, they would polish off the final version using an editing conference with peers in class before sending it to their partner schools. The class was humming with planning and discussion as each group set to work.

Lessons from the Classroom

There are at least three important lessons we can learn from this experience in Ms. Meyer's class. First, the story of Ms. Meyer's classroom illustrates the important benefits of project-based learning for integrating the language arts. By creating this project and connecting with other classrooms, students were supported in developing all of the language arts: reading, writing, speaking, listening, and viewing. Students learned from one another and from their parents as they gathered pourquoi tales, developed and refined their drafts, debated the correct punctuation, the correct spelling, or the correct way to end their story in drafting, revision, and editing conferences. These were important learning opportunities in the language arts. Speaking skills were also enhanced as students planned and discussed their work. So, too, were listening skills as students had to carefully listen to the stories they collected from their parents and the ideas from their colleagues during conferences. In short, project-based learning experiences on the Internet can provide important support for students in the language arts.

This story also illustrates a second important lesson: The Internet is an exceptional tool for supporting literacy learning by connecting reading and writing. The Internet provides natural opportunities for your students to communicate in writing about their work and to read the responses of others.

Reading and writing are similar processes. They have been compared by various authors as the two wings of the same bird or two sides of the same coin. In busy classrooms with increasing additions to the curriculum, we need to seek ways in which to combine subject areas which have traditionally been viewed as separate and which benefit from being combined. This is possible when we connect reading and writing in learning experiences.

After she announced the project, Ms. Meyer's class read and wrote as they had never done before. Students worked hard in the ensuing weeks to gather explanatory myths from the Vietnamese, Cambodian, African American, Italian, Iroquois, and Chinese cultures in their own community. They wanted very much to have good stories to share with those classes in distant places, some of which they had just heard about. Not only did students read more because of this experience, but they read better because their interest was so high and they were supported by members of their literature discussion group. As students shared stories they had found at home, the library, and the Internet, one could often see students helping other students as they read them together. In addition, important new writing opportunities opened up as students needed to collect stories from their community and carefully draft, revise, and edit them before sending them to other schools. The Internet can be an important tool for supporting literacy learning by connecting reading and writing.

Finally, this story also illustrates a third lesson: while the Internet does contain many original works of literature for students to read, it is especially useful to enrich the literary experiences of students as they read books away from the computer. Immediately after Ms. Meyer announced the project, each group independently decided to search their school library for pourquoi tales for their part of the world. As one student said, "We want to be ready when we start to get our stories from Japan and Australia." As students brought their stories back to each group, many discussions took place as they shared ideas about each culture. These experiences enriched the literary potential of the initial assignment by taking students beyond their set of books and into their local community, their library, and even the rest of the world through the Internet. Many opportunities to enrich children's literary experiences may be developed by integrating the Internet into classroom instruction.

Using Project-Based Learning with the Internet to Integrate the Language Arts

Classrooms have usually organized learning around separate subject areas. Recently, a thematic approach has sometimes been used to organize learning, with a single theme integrating learning experiences in several content areas. Some teachers are now beginning to take a third approach as they seek to capitalize on the learning opportunities available on the Internet. These teachers organize learning experiences around

Internet projects with other classrooms around the world. This can be a very powerful way to develop learning experiences for your students. Project-based learning experiences are especially useful to integrate the language arts as students naturally engage in reading, writing, speaking, listening, and viewing experiences during the course of a project. One sees in these classrooms a rich interplay between content learning and language arts activities, often with common method frameworks such as cooperative group learning, response journals, readers' theater, process writing, inquiry projects, and other highly effective techniques combined with Internet experiences.

What is an Internet project? An Internet project is a classroom learning experience for students that allows them to collaborate with students in other classrooms around the world to complete an activity that integrates the language arts and at least one other curricular area. Examples of projects include:

- Presidential Election.   In this election research and balloting project, students research the presidential candidates in the United States, write and publish editorials at a central location to convince voters, and then conduct a mock election at school sites around the U.S. The results are then displayed by school and state so that students can analyze voting patterns. Math, social studies, and language arts are integrated within this learning unit.
- Paddington Bear Travels the World.   This project sends a stuffed Paddington Bear to primary grade classrooms around the world. When Paddington arrives, he has to keep a journal describing his adventures, the cultures he visits, the sites he sees, and the students he meets. His travel journal is published at the home page of the school that first sent him on his journey and is continuously updated by the classroom he is currently visiting. Other students write to him and ask him questions which are answered by the class where he is at any point in time. Other activities such as calculating mileage and locating Paddington on the map are also used. This project integrates social studies, science, math, and language arts.
- K–1 Students Request Postcards.   This project requests that postcards from classes around the world be sent to a K–1 class in Georgia to help them develop a better understanding of locations around the world. The postcards are read in class and then fastened to a map of the world next to the country they came from. Students answer each postcard with another postcard from their area as well as an e-mail message.

The special advantage of an Internet project is that it contains the potential for very powerful learning opportunities in the language arts in addition to other subject areas. Communicating with students in other locations motivates your students in ways you probably have not seen in your classroom and opens the door to important cross-cultural understandings. Done correctly, Internet projects can be the cornerstone of your language arts program.

How do you get started? You may wish to visit several locations where teachers register Internet Projects for other teachers to find. Reading about other projects will give you ideas for your own. You may find projects by visiting some of these locations:

The Global SchoolNet Projects Registry—(http://www.gsn.org/gsn/proj/index.html)

This is one of the best locations on the web to register a project and to review projects posted by other teachers.

The Global School House: The Connected Classroom—(http://www.gsh.org/class/default.htm)

Search projects posted by teachers by grade level, topic, or time. A useful resource.

KIDPROJ—(http://www.kidlink.org:80/KIDPROJ/)

Another nice location to find current projects, past projects, and possible project topics.

After you have viewed a number of examples, consider a visit to NickNack's Telecollaborative Learning page (http://www1.minn.net:80/~schubert/NickNacks.html#anchor100100). Here you can learn about some great ideas for starting a project.

Additional Instructional Ideas

Initially, you may wish to join someone else's project. After several experiences, though, you could develop your own project, post it, and see if you can get other classrooms to join you. For example, you may wish to adapt literature discussion groups to the Internet. Post the works of literature your students will be reading and see if other classes would be interested in reading the same work(s) and sharing responses. Comparing responses to literature on the Internet will provide many opportunities to integrate the language arts.

If you work with very young children, you may also wish to visit a wonderful site called the Monster Exchange Project (http://www.csnet.net/minds-eye/home.html). Here, students first draw a picture of a monster and then communicate it in writing to another child or class. The recipient tries to draw the monster from the verbal description. Then both sides post their images at the site so they can compare their work. This is great for integrating the language arts in the primary grades. You could also combine the activity with reading literature related to monsters such as *There's a Nightmare in My Closet*. The e-mail message from Brian Maguire describes how this project was developed by a third grade teacher in New York. While this has evolved into a much more complex project than you may wish to develop at the beginning, it does show you what is possible on the Internet. Visit the site and explore the potential of this activity.

Connecting Reading and Writing On the Internet

An important aspect of the Internet is that it provides students with a vehicle for communicating with others around the world through reading and writing experiences. In this electronic environment, students may publish their writing, write to others, and read their responses. Publishing work on the Internet provides students with opportunities to write for an audience other than the teacher. It requires students to be precise and clear in their writing so that their readers understand their meaning. It moves students to naturally seek out opportunities for drafting, revision, and editing conferences as they seek to make meaning clear for their Internet audience. While some might argue that publishing on the Internet means lower standards for writers, we would argue that just the opposite is the case for many writers, especially after they have heard from a reader that their writing wasn't clear or their spelling wasn't accurate. Peers can have a powerful effect on young children as they think about their writing.

Reading the responses of others leads to important critical thinking and analysis experiences as students evaluate others' opinions. Writing back to authors about their responses requires students to express themselves clearly and to think clearly. While some might argue that technology will reduce the importance of literacy for future generations, we would argue just the opposite; the Internet will increase the importance of clear thinking, precise writing, and efficient reading for generations to come.

How can you connect reading and writing through Internet experiences? In addition to the project-based units described earlier, there are at least three important ways in which this may be done: publishing students' work on the Internet, directing students to special locations on the Internet that support young writers, and communicating with keypals.

Publishing Student Work on the Internet

As students engage in writing projects in your classroom you should encourage them to publish their work on the Internet. You may publish student work on a classroom homepage (see Chapter 12). You may also publish student work at a wide variety of locations on the Internet. You should take advantage of these locations to engage students in comprehensive writing process activities which include prewriting, drafting, revision, editing, and publishing. Take advantage of these opportunities to support learning through peer revision and editing conferences, helping your students to see new things in their writing through the eyes of others. When a students' work is prepared, think about submitting it to one of these locations:

E-Mail for You

The Internet has become an invaluable vehicle for teaching my third grade curriculum. I have not been able to find a better tool for removing the walls of the classroom and opening it to an incredible learning environment. It makes a vast amount of information available to the class, provides real-life experiences, and allows kids to publish their work to a world-wide audience.

I began incorporating the Internet into my classroom about two years ago when I created a writing project that I believed would meet many curriculum goals and, at the same time, excite the students. By means of a bulletin board message in CompuServe's education forum, I looked for a classroom that would participate in a Monster Exchange Program. This called for students in two classes to form small groups and design a monster, vividly describe their monster, and then e-mail their descriptions to the other class. Then the student groups in the partner class would attempt to recreate the monster solely from the descriptions. The two classes would finally exchange their pictures to compare the originals with the new ones. John Thompson, the dedicated parent of a Brunner Elementary student in New Jersey loved the idea. He suggested that we publish the monster pictures and descriptions on the WWW and committed to help his home school become involved in the project.

The project was met with enthusiasm by both classes and proved to be a multifaceted learning activity. Students were introduced to and were given the opportunity to practice various computer skills such as word processing, e-mailing, and digital scanning. They were also challenged to refine and integrate their descriptive writing, creative design and drawing skills, and to work together as a team.

What began as a project for two classes increased to a party of over 100 classes from all the world (Siberia, Japan, Australia, etc.). So, not only did we become participants, but we also took on the task of organizing. I suggest teachers first find an already existing Internet project that meets their current classroom goals, is well organized, and offers curriculum integration. It should also require computer skills that you already have. Good features that one should look for are tools such as frequently asked question listings, electronic bulletin boards, chat capabilities, and a support team to answer questions.

When participating with a cooperating class or school always remember to maintain a common timeline, especially with foreign countries. Many countries have opposite seasons, different school years, vacation dates, and time zones. If they are well planned it can actually be to everyone's advantage. Try a collaborative project. I am certain it will excite your students and lead to important learning experiences!

```
Brian Maguire
(Home)  maguireb@norwich.net
********************************************************
Grade 3 Teacher Gilbertsville-Mount Upton CSD
http://www.csnet.net/mindseye/gmu/
********************************************************
Minds Eye Monster Exchange
Project Coordinator
http://www.csnet.net/minds-eye/
```

The Book Nook—(http://i-site.on.ca/booknook.html)

This outstanding location provides a location for students to publish reviews of books they have read. All reviews are published. Students will find examples of reviews organized by grade level clusters and genre. They also are given guidelines for developing their review as well as a list of books in a "Lonely Book Club" in need of reviews. An excellent site that deserves a permanent bookmark on your computer.

Children's Voice—(gopher://vmsgopher.cua.edu.:70/0R37196-39416-gopher_root_eric_ae%3A%5B_edres.feb%5D9502.txt%3B5)

At this location you will find directions for subscribing to a listserv which publishes student writing in grades K–8. Any classroom teacher may publish a child's writing on the listserv at their discretion to be shared with other subscribers.

Cyberkids—(http://www.cyberkids.com/)

This is a magazine for kids. Each year, the magazine invites submissions for writing, art, and musical compositions from students, ages 7–11, for a contest. After a preliminary screening, readers then vote for the winners which are published. A great location for free reading time. Set a bookmark!

KidPub—(http://en-garde.com/kidpub/intro.html)

All work is published at KidPub, a publishing location for kids maintained by a parent in Massachusetts. Directions for submissions are provided. Students can even see how many people have read their work. Set a bookmark!

Locations on the Internet That Support Young Writers

There are also a number of locations on the Internet that support young writers. These locations are often important sources of support for a student who aspires to become a writer. You may wish to set a regular bookmark to some of these locations and consider regular assignments for your students.

Inkspot for Young Writers—(http://www.inkspot.com/~ohi/inkspot/young.html)

Arguably the best location to support aspiring writers with many types of help, including words of advice from authors and editors, interviews with young writers, and a Young Writers Forum. At the Young Writers' Forum, students can network other writers and exchange ideas.

Inkspot for Young Writers: Useful Sites—(http://www.inkspot.com/~ohi/inkspot/young.html)

Another Inkspot location containing a rich array of sites on the WWW to support young writers.

The Quill Society—(http://www.quill.net/)

The Quill Society consists of young writers from around the world who enjoy creative expression and wish to learn from one another. This site includes a message board for discussions between young writers, a place to publish your work, a board of critics who will respond to your work with helpful suggestions, and a fun activities area. A great location for your writers!

Communicating with Keypals

Communicating with keypals is also a wonderful way to connect reading and writing experiences and support students' literacy learning. The more we read and write, the better we read and write; keypals is a great way to increase reading and writing in your classroom. There is something very special about sharing messages every day with another student and it really motivates children. You may wish to use your email account for younger children so that you can screen messages. You may also wish to supervise older students when they are at the computer using their own e-mail accounts. Many locations for keypal lists may be found by using a search engine and typing in the word "keypals." You may also wish to visit these locations:

Global Heinemann Keypals—(http://www.reedbooks.com.au/heinemann/global/global1.html)

A large set of listings by interested keypals. You may also post your own message on their bulletin boards which are organized by age. There is a list here for teachers who wish to have their students communicate with other classes. Be certain students read their excellent netiquette guide or print this out and post it next to your computer.

Pitsco's Launch to Keypals—(http://www.keypals.com/p/keypals.html)

This site contains an extensive set of keypal lists that link teachers to teachers, students to students, and classes to classes. On most lists you can post your own as well as read others' requests.

WeNET Keypals—(http://www2.waikato.ac.nz/education/WeNET/key/keypals.html)

A bulletin board maintained in New Zealand with a list of many classrooms around the world interested in becoming keypals.

Enriching Literary Experiences

There are a variety of ways in which the Internet may be used to enrich your students' literary experiences. We will organize our discussion by the types of locations you are likely to find. We will begin the section by describing the best single location we have found for children's literature on the web and then discuss several other resources: using on-line literature to supplement book experiences and using author information locations to supplement literary experiences. We will conclude with a discussion of instructional ideas you may wish to consider for your classroom as you seek ways to enrich your students' literary experiences.

The Children's Literature Web Guide

The best single location we know of for children's literature is a site maintained by David Brown, a librarian at the University of Calgary. The Children's Literature Web Guide (http://www.ucalgary.ca/~dkbrown/index.html) contains a comprehensive and organized array of links to children's literature resources. (See Figure 5-2.) The types of resources on this page are too exhaustive to list, but they include everything from links to locations about movies developed from children's books, to resources for parents, resources for teachers, on-line works of literature, resources for storytellers, resources for writers and illustrators, discussion groups about children's literature, lists of award winners, and information about authors.

The site is designed to enrich your students' literary experiences without taking them away from books. As the developer of this site indicates, "If my cunning plan works, you will find yourself tempted away from the Internet, and back to the books themselves!" If you are serious about children's literature, you should explore this site, set a bookmark for this location, and incorporate its many resources into classroom learning projects.

Enriching Literary Experiences with On-line Literature

There is an extensive collection of children's literature that is on-line and may be used in your classroom. While we tend to prefer books for central literary experiences in a classroom, it is often useful to read other works related to ones you use in class on the Internet. It is especially nice to know that any work you find on-line may be printed out so that others may read it in the class or so that it may be read at home with the family. There are several types of on-line literature resources: older classics with expired copyrights, traditional tales, excerpts of contemporary best-sellers, works of literature written by children, and master sites containing extensive collections of many literature selections.

E-Mail for You

From: LYNN GATCHELL <lgatchel@moe.coe.uga.edu>
Subject: Keypals

Greetings from Georgia! I have used the Internet with students for at least 2 years now. This has been a self study for the most part, but an exciting new venture and one that has challenged me as an educator of 26 years. Realizing the power of this tool for breaking down classroom walls and entering the global village has provided a new vitality to my approach to teaching. I have thought quite a bit about all the experiences I have either given my students as a resource teacher of the gifted, or assisted with in the regular classroom.

The experience I have chosen to share with you is quite simple, and yet it is one that has been most rewarding to me as a professional. I have been a member of several educational listservs over the last few years. This is an excellent way to set up classroom projects as well as gain information from other colleagues in the field. From one of these listservs, I obtained the name of a teacher who was located in British Columbia, where my husband and I had just visited during the summer break. I wrote to him mostly to reflect on the beauty we had enjoyed in his province. This began a weekly keypal relationship which has continued now for 2 years. We talk "school" and we talk "family"; we commiserate with each other and we discuss technological things that are the latest and those that work for us in the classroom.

Having such a meaningful keypal relationship has caused me to know the power of this tool for students as well. And just think how many years they have left to keep up these relationships and how many problems they might solve over the Internet!

Lynn Gatchell <lgatchel@moe.coe.uga.edu>
http://bob.coe.uga.edu/~bbiddle/bshoals/welcome.html
Barnett Shoals Elementary School
3220 Barnett Shoals Road
Athens, Georgia 30605 USA

You will find many older classics with expired copyrights on the Internet. Because their copyright has expired, these works may now be published by anyone. This allows them to be posted on the web without violating copyright law. Older classics often are used by teachers to provide additional literary experiences for students who have read one work by an author and are interested in reading more, especially when your library's holdings are a bit thin. This is especially nice when you are doing a unit on a classic author and are in need of a few additional works. The problem with these classics is that they usually appear in a text-only form without illustrations. This sometimes takes away from the literary experience. You may, of course, do a search for a particular work or a particular author by using a search engine. Some of the best locations for classic works of literature include:

Lewis Carroll Home Page Illustrated—(http://www.cstone.net/library/alice/carroll.html)

The major works of Lewis Carroll are located here, including *Alice's Adventures in Wonderland*, *Through the Looking Glass*, and *The Hunting of the Snark*. Each contains color illustrations.

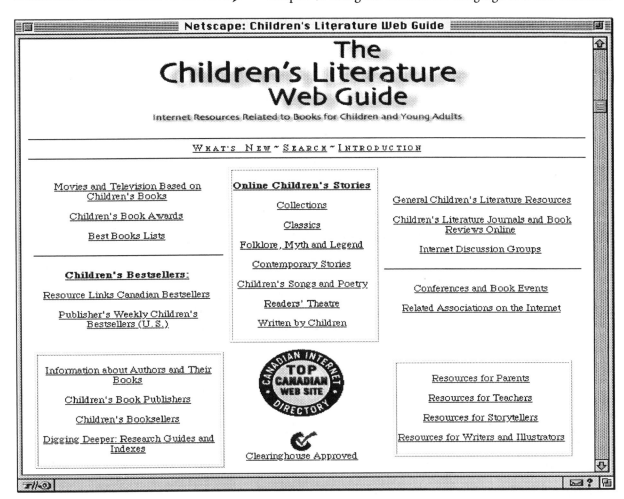

Figure 5.2   The homepage for The Children's Literature Web Guide (http://www.ucalgary.ca/~dkbrown/index.html).

Classics for Young People—(http://www.ucalgary.ca/~dkbrown/storclas.html)

A comprehensive set of links to classic works, some of which are illustrated. These include *Little Women, The Wonderful Wizard of Oz, The Wind in the Willows, Rip Van Winkle, The Gift of the Magi, Anne of Green Gables*, and many, many others.

How The Leopard Got Its Spots—(http://www.sff.net/people/karawynn/justso/leopard.htp)

The classic pourquoi tale by Rudyard Kipling from the *Just So Stories*. Illustrated with photographs.

Another form of on-line literature includes traditional tales. These include folktales, fairytales, myths, and legends. Because so many were published some time ago and their original copyrights are out of date, many are now in the public domain and available on-line. Usually these exist in text-only versions, although, occasionally you will find illustrated versions.

Because traditional tales come from an oral tradition, there are many different versions of most stories. The richness of the web allows us to share multiple versions of the same story and to engage students in critical analysis of each story by evaluating how the versions differ, what types of response each provokes in readers, or what characterizes a "typical" traditional tale. Some of the best locations for traditional tales include:

Mythtext: Mythology from All Over the World—(http://www.io.org/~untangle/mythtext.html)

This is the most comprehensive site for myths we know of. It contains links to a vast array of myth locations on the web including FAQs, Arthurian sites, Celtic sites, Classical sites, Egyptian sites, myth listservs, and myth newsgroups. Great to bookmark for your units on myths and legends.

Stories from the Grimm Brothers—(ftp://ftp.std.com/obi/Fairy.Tales/Grimm/)

Here is an ftp site that has been around for a while. It contains over 50 tales from the Grimm Brothers, including *Beauty and the Beast, Cinderella, Ali Baba and the Forty Thieves, Aladdin*, and many others.

The Little Red Riding Hood Project—(http://www-dept.usm.edu/~engdept/lrrh/lrrhhome.htm)

This site contains 16 different versions of this tale from 17th- to 19th-century Europe. A nice site for comparative projects. Includes illustrations of the original pages.

Folklore, Myth and Legend—(http://www.ucalgary.ca/~dkbrown/storfolk.html)

A comprehensive site with many useful links to sources of information and copies of traditional tales.

At some locations on the web, you will find excerpts of contemporary best sellers. Publishers do not usually put the complete work of a recently published work on the web. They will, however, put a chapter or two in order to interest readers in the complete work. Teachers will sometimes bookmark these locations or print out a copy so that students may see what the book is like before going to the library where the complete work may be found. Other, more creative activities are also possible. Locations with excerpts from contemporary best sellers include:

Concertina—(http://www.iatech.com/books/intro.html)

This publisher has decided to put several complete works at this location for young children to read. They contain sounds as well as illustrations and text. Very nice for younger children.

Selected American Library Association Children's Newbery Award Winners—(http://dab.psi.net/ChapterOne/children/index.html)

At this site you may print out or read the first chapters of many award-winning children's books, including *The Giver, Missing May, Maniac McGee, Number the Stars, The Whipping Boy, Lincoln, a Photobiography*, and many others.

Other locations contain children's voices, literature written by children. These sites are effective in motivating the writers in your class and showing them what is possible. Some of these locations include:

Cyberkids—(http://www.cyberkids.com/)

This is a quarterly on-line magazine written by kids for kids ages 7–11. It includes articles and stories by young writers.

KidPub—(http://en-garde.com/kidpub/intro.html)

A wonderful collection of stories written by children and maintained by a father in Massachusetts who wanted a place for his daughter to publish her work. Many great stories here.

Parents and Children On-line—(http://www.indiana.edu/~eric_rec/fl/pcto/menu.html)

Sponsored by ERIC, this regular magazine contains materials written by children and is intended to support family reading at home.

Enriching Literary Experiences with Information about Authors

Reading a great story is one of the better experiences we can provide students in school. Often, though, our students' experience with a story is limited by knowing little about the author. Often we can provide richer literary experiences by sharing information about the person who wrote their book. This helps to contextualize the literary work and provides important information to children about why an author wrote a story, what experience in their life prompted the story, how they write, other books the author has written, and issues the author often writes about. Knowing this information enriches children's literary experiences. They are many sites on the web that will provide your students with this information. You may, of course, use one of the search engines to locate information about authors. Some of the sites we value include:

Into the Wardrobe: The C.S. Lewis WWW Site—(http://www.cache.net/~john/cslewis/index.html)

This is the best author site around. It contains many rich resources, including a biography, an album of photographs, recordings of the author's voice, many links to other Lewis sites, a listserv address, a usenet address, and even a live chat location.

Kindred Spirits—(http://www.upei.ca/~lmmi/cover.html)

A site with information about Lucy Maud Montgomery, the author of *Anne of Green Gables* and other works. The location includes information about her life, additional links to related sites, information for subscribing to a listserv about her books, and sites on Prince Edward Island, her home.

Ask the Author—(http://www.ipl.org/youth/AskAuthor/)

This location of the Internet Public Library contains information about a number of popular authors, including Lois Lowry, Avi, Matt Christopher, Natalie Babbitt, Daniel Pinkwater, Jane Yolen, Gary Paulson, Charlotte Zolotow, and others. Photos of the authors, a biography, and answers to questions submitted by kids are available.

Laura Ingalls Wilder Home Page—(http://webpages.marshall.edu/~irby1/laura.htmlx)

This site contains much useful information about the author of the "Little House" series. Historical information about the characters and the locations where they lived is provided. The site also has a useful link for teachers which will take you to plans for instructional units about this author and her work.

Additional Instructional Ideas

There are as many good ideas for enriching literary experiences with the Internet as there are creative teachers who have a few moments to plan a new activity. We cannot be exhaustive here. We can, however, provide some examples that might serve to inspire you to think of your own creative uses.

Cinderella Studies—Engage your class in a study of Cinderella tales from around the world. Nearly every culture has its own version of this classic tale. Compare and contrast different versions and see if students can infer what these differences might suggest about the culture associated with each story. Begin with beautifully illustrated versions from your library such as *Mufaro's Beautiful Daughters* by John Steptoe. Then have students explore the web for other versions. They may wish to start at the Cinderella Project (http://www-dept.usm.edu/~engdept/cinderella/cinderella.html) and Cinderella Stories (http://www.ucalgary.ca/~dkbrown/cinderella.html). Then have students begin exploring the web using various search engines for even more versions. A great project for combining web use and literature in very effective ways.

Studying Indigenous Peoples' Literature—If you engage students in a project studying Native Americans or other indigenous peoples, be certain to set a bookmark for Indigenous Peoples' Literature (http://www.indians.org/welker/framenat.html), an outstanding site developed by George Walker. Have students explore this rich site to find out information about the culture behind each of the books they read. Have them share the information they find during Internet Workshop.

This Door Leads to the Internet—Cover the outside of your classroom door with butcher paper, or another type of large paper. Have a group of students design a bookcover on this paper entitled "This Door Leads to the Internet." At the same time, set bookmarks to locations with collections of stories on the Internet such as Contemporary Writing for Children and Young Adults (http://www.ucalgary.ca/

~dkbrown/storcont.html). Have students read a story that is interesting to them during their time on the computer and then print it out. Then have students sit in a "reader's chair" at the front of the room and share their favorite selection with the class. As they finish, post the printed version of their story on the bookcover the students have designed on the door.

E-Mail for You

From: "Karen Auffhammer" <Sangerski@msn.com>
Subject: Maniac Magee

    Hello!
    I have recently read the story Maniac Magee by Jerry Spinelli and it is by far one of my favorites. I was so excited to see a site on the WWW on this story. Here's the URL—(http://www.crocker.com/~rebotis/titles/maniacmagee.html).
    Check it out!! It provides a brief summary of the story, character descriptions, things to discuss with your class, activities and related books. From here you can click to see other popular books that have been reviewed.

A Final Thought

Probably one of the most powerful uses of the Internet for the classroom is the potential that exists to support the language arts. The Internet permits communication between people all over the world and is quickly fulfilling the dream many have had of a global village. Currently, most of this communication takes place through reading and writing. As a result, you have a very special tool to support literacy learning in your classroom. As you work with the Internet in your classroom, you and your students will discover many new ways to exploit this potential.

Language Arts and Literature Resources on the Internet

KIDLINK—(http://www.kidlink.org/)

The goal of KIDLINK is to create a global dialog among the 10- to 15-year-old youth of the world. It is run by KIDLINK Society, a grassroots organization. Here you will find many wonderful forums for your students to communicate with children around the world. Language translation services are available as well as IRC chat sessions. There are locations for student-to-student as well as classroom-to-classroom contact.

Helping Your Child Learn to Read—(http://www.ed.gov/pubs/parents/Reading/index.html)

An on-line book for parents written by recognized experts in the field of reading for the U.S. Department of Education. This book contains useful information on how parents may help their child to read. Print out copies of one of the chapters for "Back-to-School Night." A great resource.

How a Book Is Made—(http://www.harpercollins.com/kids/bkstep1.htm)

Here is a wonderful on-line book written by Aliki, a widely recognized author/illustrator of books for young children. This is a great reading experience for younger children that provides important information about the work of a professional author. Use it in an author study on Aliki or in a unit on writing.

Help Your Child Learn to Write Well—(http://www.ed.gov/pubs/parents/Writing/)

A brochure for parents from the U.S. Department of Education that may be printed out and distributed at "Back-to-School Night." This provides useful information for parents about ways they might assist their child with writing.

Stone Soup—(http://www.stonesoup.com/siteindex.html)

Stone Soup is a hard copy magazine with stories, poetry, and art created by young children. This location takes you to a number of stories and poems written by young children and provides directions for how students may submit work.

Greek Mythology—(http://www.intergate.net/uhtml/.jhunt/greek_myth/greek_myth.html#GreekMythIntro)

Is your class studying Greece? Here is a great site with much useful information on Greek mythology. It provides useful reference information on the gods and goddesses of the Greeks as well as additional Internet resources.

Language Arts and Literature—(http://pen1.pen.k12.va.us:80/~mchildre/langarts.html)

Here is a site with many useful links to sources on the Internet for teachers related to language arts and literature. It even contains links to a site for the Goosebumps series.

Listservs/Mailing Lists for Language Arts

CHILDRENS-VOICE—(llistproc@schoolnet.carleton.ca)

This listserv publishes writing from children ages 5–14.

KIDLIT-L—(listserv@bingvmb.bitnet)

A listserv on children's literature.

MY-VIEW—(listserv@sjuvm.stjohns.edu)

A global creative writing exchange for kids in a listserv format.

TAWL—(listserv@listserv.arizona.edu)

A listserv discussion group on teaching from a whole language perspective.

WAC-L—(listserv@vmd.cso.uiuc.edu)

A listserv on writing across the curriculum.

Usenet Newsgroups for Language Arts

K–12 Teacher Chat Area—(k12.chat.teacher)

Discusses issues of K–12 instruction, including language arts.

Language Arts Curriculum in K–12 Education—(k12.lang.art)

A newsgroup on the language arts curriculum in schools.

Writing Instruction in Computer-based Classrooms—(comp.edu.compostion)

Discusses issues of writing in electronic environments.

Chapter 6

Social Studies: A World of Possibilities

```
To:      Our readers
From:    djleu@sued.syr.edu (Don Leu),
         ddleu@syr.edu (Debbie Leu)
Subject: Social Studies: A world of possibilities

   As you plan integrated, cross-curricular learning expe-
riences with the Internet, a great place to begin is with
the social studies curriculum. There is probably more infor-
mation for social studies than any other subject area on the
Internet. The possibilities for learning experiences in this
area are so rich it becomes easy to integrate learning expe-
riences from other curricular areas. There are several dif-
ferent models for using the Internet in integrated, cross-
curricular units: Internet Activities, Internet Projects,
Internet Inquiry, and Kids Teaching Kids. Each seeks to
present your students with the many learning experiences
possible through the Internet as they explore history, cul-
ture, politics, and important social issues.
   The extensive resources for social studies makes it
possible to design very rich learning experiences for stu-
dents. At the same time, though, this richness presents an
important challenge to teachers and students: how do you
quickly find the information you require on the Internet
when there is so much information that is available? Using
master web sites, developing search engine strategies, using
listservs, and using individual bookmark folders are espe-
cially useful as you explore the Internet for learning op-
portunities in social studies.

   Don and Debbie
```

Spring was in the air as Mr. Guzman entered his room in the morning. He sat for a few moments enjoying his coffee and thinking about his first full year with an Internet connection in his 8th grade social studies classroom. It had been a busy year, filled with new learning as he and his students explored this new resource together to enrich their study of American history.

At the beginning of the year, Mr. Guzman felt a bit intimidated by all of the information on the Internet related to social studies and how he was going to keep track of everything without getting lost. He decided to start simply; he set up a single Internet Activity for students to complete each week. This used the Internet in a manner similar to the other center activities he used in his classroom. He set a bookmark to a location related to the topic they were covering that week and developed a task for the information at that location. Each student was required to complete the task he set up for them. Initially, he developed scavenger hunts to develop navigational skills. Gradually, he moved into other short learning experiences. These required students to think critically about the information at a site related to their current unit. During one week of the colonial period, for example, he set a bookmark to a wonderful site about Benjamin Franklin (http://sln.fi.edu/franklin/rotten.html). (See Figure 6-1.) He then directed students to explore this site and write a short essay about what they thought was the most important accomplishment in Franklin's life, explaining why this accomplishment was so important. At the end of the week, during a short Internet Workshop session, students had a chance to compare their ideas and discuss their conclusions. The discussion really made the totality of Franklin's life come alive as students described his many accomplishments.

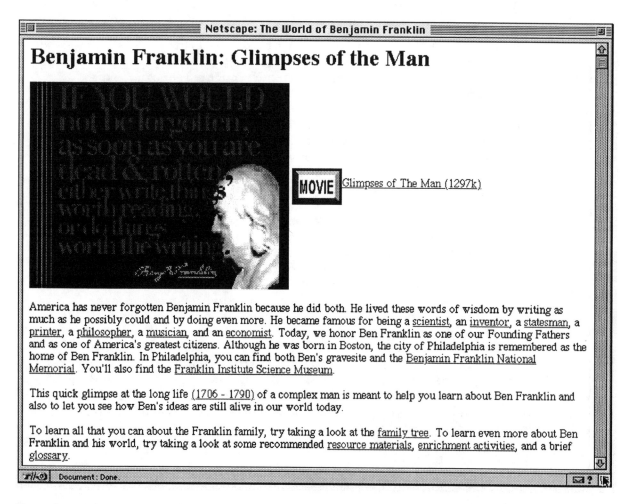

Figure 6-1.   The Home Page of Benjamin Franklin
(http://sln.fi.edu/franklin/rotten.html)

During the middle of the year, as he felt more confident and knowledgeable about Internet resources, Mr. Guzman decided to try developing an Internet Project, connecting with other classrooms around the world. He wanted his students to see how people in other countries interpreted historical events that were important for the United States. He posted a project at The Global SchoolNet Projects Registry (http://www.gsn.org/gsn/proj/index.html) and The Global School House (http://www.gsh.org/class/default.htm) that would compare perceptions of World War II by students from several different countries. Classrooms from Japan, Russia, Germany, England, Italy, and the Canada agreed to participate in the project. After studying this event in their individual classrooms, students in each of the classes wrote an essay describing the meaning of World War II to their country. These essays were exchanged by e-mail between each of the participating classes so that students could read them and understand that history is often interpreted differently by different societies. Each student then had to write a second essay describing what they had learned from reading the essays of students in the different countries. It had been a powerful experience for each of the classrooms. Some classes in the project continued exchanging information throughout the year with his class.

As the end of the year approached, he decided to try something called Internet Inquiry. Each student identified a question in American History they wanted to explore on their own using the Internet and the resources in the school library. Before they started their project, Mr. Guzman set up individual bookmark folders for each student in his class so that students could keep track of good locations and not get them mixed up with those of other students. He also conducted several Internet Workshops, focusing on the use of different search engines to locate information. He had learned there were so many sites related to social studies education that finding useful locations required extra assistance for his students.

Mr. Guzman had students complete the planning form in Figure 6-2. This helped to focus their efforts and provide a road map for their initial work. After one week, he had individual conferences with students to check their progress and to make revisions in their project if any were necessary.

At the end of their Internet Inquiry, Mr. Guzman had each student develop a Kids-Teaching-Kids Activity. This had each student develop a learning activity related to the Internet Inquiry they had just completed and then create a poster advertising this experience. Students had to provide the address of the location on the Internet, explain the learning activity for this site, and advertise the virtues of completing their activity. Mr. Guzman required each student in his class to participate in at least four of these activities during the last two weeks of school. This was a nice way to wrap up their study of American History during the year.

Lessons from the Classroom

Mr. Guzman's first year illustrates a number of important lessons about integrating social studies experiences on the Internet into your classroom. First, it illustrates how it is often helpful to begin with simple Internet experiences as you consider how to use the Internet in your classroom. Using a single Internet Activity each week in your classroom is an easy way to get started with this new resource. As you develop more confidence, it is easy to develop additional experiences for your students.

Second, we again see the power of Internet projects for bringing classroom learning alive through collaborative experiences with students at other locations around the world. Internet projects can be an especially powerful way of organizing classroom learning experiences in social studies; it enables your students to understand how students in different parts of the world view historical, political, and social events as they begin to understand different cultural experiences.

Third, Mr. Guzman's experiences show how Internet Inquiry may be used to support independent learning. This helps students to develop greater responsibility for their own learning as they explore questions that are especially important to them.

Fourth, it shows how an activity such as Kids-Teaching-Kids may be used to support the social learning experiences that are especially important with the Internet. This activity is also a nice way to wrap up a unit in your classroom, allowing students to teach one another about what they have learned.

Planning for Internet Inquiry

Directions: This form will help you to plan for Internet Inquiry, help to keep you on track as you complete your work, and help you to evaluate your work when you finish. Please complete each item as completely as possible and then schedule a conference with me to discuss your planning.

Name(s): _____   Date: _____

Title of my (our) Internet Inquiry: _____

The project will be completed on: _____

The purpose of my (our) project is: _____

_____

_____

As I (we) planned my (our) project, I (we) used the following resources: _____

_____

_____

I (we) will do the following during this project: _____

_____

_____

I (we) will evaluate the project in the following manner: _____

_____

_____

I (we) will begin by using the following Internet sites or by using the following words/phrases with a search engine: _____

_____

_____

I (we) had a conference with Mr. Guzman about this project on the following dates:

_____   _____   _____

Figure 6-2.   The Internet Inquiry Planning Form Used in Mr. Guzman's Class

Finally, Mr. Guzman's experiences demonstrate how extensive the resources on the Internet are for social studies. This abundance of resources is great for developing learning experiences, but it often requires you to help students sort through the many resources to find ones that are useful for them. Often it is helpful to provide special assistance with using the various search engines to locate information. It is also helpful to develop individual bookmark folders so that students may keep track of their own bookmarks.

Central Sites for Social Studies Education

As you begin to consider how you wish to use the Internet as part of your social studies education program, you may wish to visit (and set a bookmark) for several comprehensive sites in this area. The most comprehensive sites we have found include:

- **History/Social Studies Web Site for K-12 Teachers** (http://www.execpc.com/~dboals/boals.html)
- **Lesson Plans and Resources for Social Studies Teachers** (http://www.csun.edu/~hcedu013/index.html)
- **Nebraska Department of Education Social Science Resources HomePage** (http://www.nde.state.ne.us/SS/ss.html)

You may wish to begin your exploration of the Internet for social studies at these locations. Each contains a wealth of links to other sites, as well as ideas about how to best use the Internet for social studies.

Keeping It Simple: Internet Activity Assignments

Sometimes, it is easiest to begin using the Internet in your classroom with weekly Internet Activity Assignments. This may be especially useful as you begin to explore the extensive resources available on the Internet in social studies. There are probably more sites to support learning in social studies than in any other content area.

Internet Activity Assignments use the Internet in a fashion similar to a traditional learning center in your classroom. All you need to do is to locate a site on the Internet with content related to the learning you have planned for that week in your classroom. Then you develop an activity related to that site and assign the activity to your students. They may complete it during their time at the computer. Often, teachers will develop several different activities related to the site they have selected and ask students to pick one, or several, from the list to complete during the week.

The following are several examples that you might consider using in this fashion. First, during a unit on World War II, have students visit the **HomePage of Movietone News** (http://www.iguide.com/movies/movitone/contents.sml). Set a bookmark for the Movietone News Archives and have students view the news footage and text describing the Nuremberg Trials (http://www.iguide.com/movies/movitone/archive/). Then have them write an essay on whether or not the death penalty should be available to prosecutors during a war trial.

For younger students studying the political geography of the United States, set a bookmark for the interactive game, **Do You Know Your State Capitals?** (http://www.cris.com/~Kraft/capitals/). Have them visit each state and try to guess the capital, until they know each of the state capitals.

For students studying the Civil War, set a bookmark for the **Civil War Timeline** (http://rs6.loc.gov/ammem/timeline.html) in the **Civil War Photograph Collection** (http://rs6.loc.gov/cwphome.html). Have your students read the captions and view the pictures, printing out one picture and then writing a description of its significance. Post these photos and descriptions on a bulletin board in your classroom for everyone to see.

Setting up Internet Activity Assignments such as these in your classroom is a good way to ease yourself and your students into simple projects before attempting the richer, but more complex, experiences that are also possible.

Internet Projects

Previous chapters have described the important role that Internet Projects may play in your classroom. They have also identified locations such as **Global SchoolNet's Internet Project Registry** (http://www.gsn.org/gsn/proj/index.html), **Classroom Connect's Teacher Contact Database** (http://www.classroom.net/contact/), or **The Global School House** (http://www.gsh.org/class/default.htm) where you may search for Internet projects others have developed. Internet projects are especially useful in social studies since they allow you to compare your students' experiences with those of students in another culture. Often, communicating with a class in another part of the world will make your study of that culture come alive for your students because they can exchange information.

If you are just beginning to try Internet Projects with your class, it is often easiest to find a project posted by another teacher and seek to join a learning experience defined by someone else that seems appropriate for your class. Then, as you develop more experience with Internet Projects, you will have a better sense of where to advertise for cooperating classes and how to develop a project that others will be interested in joining. We encourage you to visit the sites listed above and explore the many opportunities available for your class through an Internet Project. Examples of projects posted in the past at these sites include:

- **Neighbors to the North and South.** Posted by a middle school teacher in Illinois, this project sought collaborating classrooms in Canada and Mexico to learn more about each other's country and cultures. Each week, classes would exchange information on one topic: What is your school like? Which holidays do you celebrate and what is the significance of each? What is unique about the economy in your state or province? What are current political issues that people in your state/province do not agree on? How do you spend a typical weekend?

- **Passage to Hiroshima.** Developed by a teacher in Nagoya, Japan, this class sought other classrooms interested in studying about the importance of peace and international cooperation. They proposed to begin by exchanging useful sites on the world wide web related to peace. This class also indicated that they would be visiting Hiroshima in November and sought interview and research questions from a collaborative classroom. They volunteered to interview citizens of Hiroshima and then share the results, including photos, upon their return.

- **Culture and Clues.** In this project for 7 to 9 year olds, a teacher proposed exchanging boxes of cultural artifacts from the culture where each participating school is located. Students would use these artifacts to make inferences about what life was like at each location and then write descriptions of this culture. These would be exchanged by e-mail and then students would compare how close their guesses were.

E-Mail for You

```
From: Gary Cressman (cressman@inspire.ospi.wednet.edu)
Organization: Enumclaw Junior High School
Subject: An Internet Project in Social Studies


     Hi! When studying our Civil War, students always come up to
me and say how they are related to such and such or that their
ancestors fought in such and such a battle. I decided to find out
if I could link my students to other students and they could
discuss their ancestors and relate their stories to our unit on
the Civil War. I listed an Internet project with I*EARN which
stands for International Education and Resource Network (http://
www.iearn.org/iearn/). They have many different project areas,
```

and I chose to put it in the Social Studies area (http://
www.iearn.org/iearn/projects.html). I did this project with my
six 8th grade U.S. History classes, with about 175 students total.

There is a monthly fee to join I*EARN. I was in contact with
them from home and school using text-only e-mail. Usually I had
my students compose their work during class and I would send them
off at night when the I*EARN connection charges were lower. I
also would collect messages during the evening at home and post
them the next day on the wall. But often my students wanted to
know if there was any mail that day, so I said OK and we checked
our mail. It was wonderfulllllllll when a message would come in
and the student it was addressed to was there to receive it. All
mail came to me; my students did not have their own accounts or
addresses.

One of the I*EARN moderators in Spain picked up my message
and passed it on to a Belgium UN relief worker. The next day I
received a message from a 16 year old Bosnian boy with a cry for
help from his refugee camp in northern Bosnia. The message was
actually sent in Serbo-Croatian, and an English translation came
a day later; I do not know who did the translating. I had no
thoughts of including our study of the US Civil War with civil
wars in our society today. But things changed quickly. So I shared
this message with my students and they started writing letters of
support to this boy. This got my students following current
events in a way that would not have been possible otherwise.

A few days later, a message came from some high school students in New York who were writing a newspaper about human rights
abuses, which a civil war is. They asked if my students could
join in their discussion. Of course we did. And 27 of my students
were included in the paper, Liberty Bound, published by the Cold
Spring Harbor High School. The age difference between the students did not make a difference as it turned out. In fact, it
made my students become more concerned that they did not sound
too young.

We were also contacted by a High School in northern Israel
and asked if my students could help teach their students about
our civil war. This connection was again made for us by one of
the I*EARN moderators. In return, their students sent us stories
about their experiences during the Gulf War.

Internet projects have had a powerful impact on my students'
learning. I have found that the best projects are those where you
have a tight bond/connection/commitment from the people on the
other end to stick to the project. Often these happen in unex-
pected ways.

    Gary Cressman
    Chair, History Department and Computer Resource Teacher
    Enumclaw Junior High
    Enumclaw, Washington
    cressman@inspire.ospi.wednet.edu

Internet Inquiry

Once your students have become familiar with locating Internet resources, Internet Inquiry may be a useful means to develop independent research skills and allow students to pursue a question which holds a special interest for them. Internet Inquiry projects may be developed by small groups or by individuals. They usually begin with students identifying a topic and a question they wish to explore related to the current unit. The question may be as specific as "What happened to Benedict Arnold after he betrayed his country in the Revolutionary War?" or as general as "What is it like to live in Japan?" The important aspect of Internet Inquiry is that the students should do research on a question which they find to be important. Usually, the teacher works with individuals or groups to support their selection of an interesting issue and the resources that may be useful starting points for their research. Often, teachers will also help students to identify how their work will be shared and evaluated when they complete it. Involving students in self-evaluation experiences is thought to be helpful in getting students to become more aware of what defines successful research and learning experiences.

Some teachers will introduce Internet Inquiry by reading aloud the book *What Did George Washington Have for Breakfast?* by Jean Fritz, the story of how a young boy went about finding the answer to this question and the many things he learned along the way. It nicely illustrates the wonderful learning opportunities that happen when someone pursues the answer to a seemingly simple question.

Figure 6-2 shows an example of a worksheet that may provide students with important assistance as they begin the planning phase of Internet Inquiry. Using a form such as this supports students in their work, especially when they are new to Internet Inquiry.

Internet Inquiry is often effectively combined with Internet Workshop sessions. During this time, students and groups may share what they have learned in their research and what they haven't yet discovered. These conversations enrich the study of your unit and at the same time they provide students with useful new ideas to explore as they seek answers to their questions.

Kids-Teaching-Kids

One of the best ways to learn something is to teach it to someone else. This is the idea behind Kids-Teaching-Kids activities. As your students use the Internet during a unit, consider using this type of experience at the end of the unit as you summarize and review the learning that has taken place. During a Kids-Teaching-Kids activity, students first identify a useful web location related to the unit you have been studying and then develop a learning experience around it for other students to complete. Examples of these learning experiences might include:

- a student completing a unit on twentieth century U.S. history sets a bookmark to the **Langston Hughes Page** (http://ie.uwindsor.ca/jazz/hughes.html) and asks other students to read each of the poems there, selecting one and writing a response in their poetry journal about it;
- another student, completing a unit on diversity, invites others to visit the **Indigenous Peoples Literature page** (http://www.indians.org/natlit.htm) and asks them to list the two stories they liked the best on a list of favorite stories identified by everyone who visits this site;
- another student, completing a unit on ancient civilizations, invites classmates to play one of two simulations of Greek warfare, **Empire** or **The Peloponnesian War** (http://www.duke.edu/~kuhlmann/warhorse/index.html) and describe their experience in a letter to their citizens.

After students develop a learning activity, they design a poster, advertising the site and describing what students will be required to do there. These poster advertisements are then displayed around the room so that everyone can read them to select the site they wish to visit and the activity they will complete. Often, teachers will distribute a list of the sites and ask students to obtain the signature of the person who developed the activity they complete. This indicates that they have successfully completed their activity.

Kids-Teaching-Kids can be useful for organizing Internet activities during the final weeks of a unit in your classroom. It may be used, of course, in all subject areas but, because there are so many resources on the Internet for social studies, it is especially useful for social studies units.

Search Strategies in Social Studies

There are so many wonderful resources on the Internet for teachers and students it is sometimes hard to find what you want. It is easy to get lost as you explore first one site and then another and then still another. There are several strategies you may wish to try as you explore the many resources in social studies.

The easiest strategy is to visit one of the comprehensive social studies sites listed earlier in the chapter and begin to explore the many resources located there. Usually these are organized by topics. The best of these is the **History/Social Studies Web Site for K-12 Teachers** (http://www.execpc.com/~dboals/boals.html), an extensive listing of hundreds of locations on the WWW useful for supporting social studies education. It is likely that you will find many useful resources by visiting this single location.

If you are seeking something very specific on the WWW, you may wish to use one of the search engines by clicking on the "Net Search" button in Netscape Navigator. On a rotating basis, this will connect you to one of several search engines such as Excite, Yahoo, Infoseek, Lycos, or Magellan. Then you can type in the words that best describe what you are looking for and click on the button that says "Search" or "Find." This will search the Internet for related web sites.

These search engines usually try to match the words you provide to words that appear on various pages in the WWW. Thus, it is usually best if you only use key descriptive words likely to be on the pages you are seeking. For example, the best way to search for something about the pyramids of Giza in Egypt is to simply type in "pyramids Giza Egypt." Avoid the use of words like *the, of,* or *a* since the search engine will look for these in addition to the other words you enter, listing every page it finds containing the word *the, of,* or *a.* Some search engines will allow you to do a more advanced search by clicking on a button. At this location you can usually ask the search engine to search by an entire phrase or sentence. This will permit an even more precise search for the type of information you are looking for.

Finally, you may wish to subscribe to a listserv or mailing list for teachers who may have found sites for units you are about to begin. This often leads to many useful locations since these teachers will have already used them in their classrooms. You may wish to subscribe to SOCSTUD-L, a listserv for teachers of social studies (mailserv@hcca.ohio.gov). Other listservs or mailing lists are described at the end of this chapter. If necessary, see Chapter 3 to review the procedures for subscribing to listservs/mailinglists.

Using Individual Bookmark Folders

When you have an entire class doing Internet Inquiry and many individuals setting bookmarks for sites they find useful, your list of bookmarks will become lengthy and confusing for any single student. Versions 3.0 and later of Netscape Navigator allow you to solve this problem. It is possible to make an individual bookmark folder for each student in your class.

To make individual bookmark folders, you must first open the bookmark window by clicking on the Window menu item at the top of your Netscape Navigator screen. Select the item called "Bookmarks." This will open a separate window for editing and adding new bookmark folders, one for each student. To add a folder for each student, click on the menu item called "Item" at the top of your screen and select "Insert Folder." A window will then open asking you to name this new folder. Simply type in the name of a student and then select OK to close the window. Repeat this for each student in your class and you will have a bookmark window that looks similar to Figure 6-3.

Now that you have a location for each student to place their bookmarks, you will need to show students how to make certain they designate their folder to receive new bookmarks. That way, when they add a new bookmark, it will be placed within their folder and not within a folder belonging to someone else.

Designating a student's folder to receive new bookmarks is not difficult. Show students how to open the bookmark window in Netscape Navigator by clicking on the Window menu item at the top of your screen and selecting "Bookmarks." As you did before, this will open the window for editing bookmark folders. Now, highlight the folder of the student who is working at the computer by clicking on it once. Then, click on the menu item at the top of your screen called "Item" and select "Set to New Bookmarks

E-Mail for You

From: Jeanette Kenyon (jkenyon@ahoynet.com)
      (jkenyon@pen.k12.va.us)
Organization: Anne E. Moncure Elementary School
Subject: Social Studies through the Internet

Dear Colleague,
     Every March, my 3rd grade class follows the Iditarod Sled Dog
Race using the Internet as our main source of information. We
work in cooperative learning teams in my class and each team
selects a musher to follow and we post a large Alaskan map on the
board. There are wonderful sites on the World Wide Web which post
daily race updates as well as a wealth of background information
about the race, the mushers, and life in Alaska. This last year,
the sites that I used included:
     http://www.alaska.net/~Iditarod/
(lots of good background info, photos, and links to many
Alaska sites)
     http://www.starfishsoftware.com/idog/
(our main site this year for up to date results, current news
and info, and even sound files)
     http://info.alaska.edu:70/ls/Alaska/iditarod
(although this site didn't have current information for this
year's race there is good background information. It is from
Willoughby Middle School in Ohio who used to compile the results
daily for previous races)
     These change nearly every year and you may wish to do your
own search with one of the search engines that are available.
     It is very easy to incorporate map skills, math practice
including reading charts and graphs, weather information, cultural lessons, geographical land forms, and even animal rights
issues into the unit. There is always a high level of excitement
as the students scan the latest race standings and move their
musher's pin along the trail marked out on the map. I also rely
on works of literature by Gary Paulsen and Shelley Gill to "round
out" the unit. Shelley Gill has compiled a very comprehensive
curriculum guide for the Iditarod which is available.

     Jeanette Kenyon
     Third grade teacher
     Anne E. Moncure Elementary School
     Stafford, Virginia

Folder." Whenever this student adds a new bookmark, it will be placed in his or her folder, since this is now the active bookmarks folder.

Next, go back up to the menu item at the top of your screen called "Item" and select "Set to Bookmark Menu Folder." This will make only the bookmarks in this student's folder appear when the Bookmark menu item is selected at the top of the Netscape Navigator screen. Close the bookmark window (the one showing in Figure 6-3) and this student is ready to begin.

Before students begin their session, have them open the bookmark window, designate their folder by clicking on it, and then select the "Set to New Bookmarks Folder" and "Set to Bookmark Menu Folder." This will make their folder the active bookmarks folder. You may wish to cover this strategy during an Internet Workshop session.

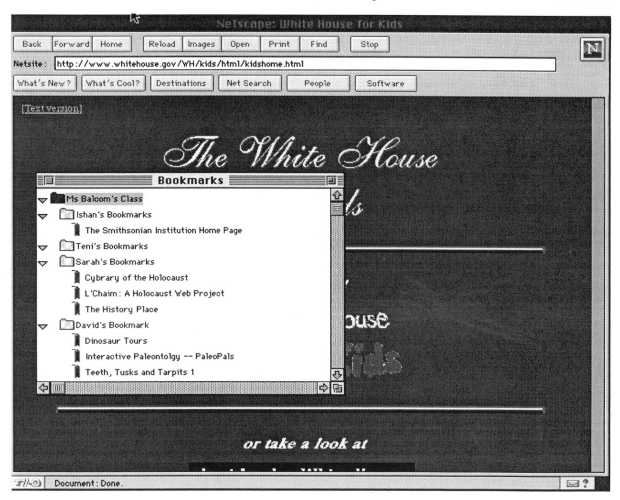

Figure 6-3. Setting Individual Bookmark Folders

Instructional Resources on the Internet

Civil War Photograph Collection—(http://rs6.loc.gov/cwphome.html)

This site contains over 1,000 photographs from the Civil War, many by Mathew Brady. Viewing these images makes you feel the national conflict and struggle during this period. The time line at this site is especially valuable since it provides an ongoing story of the struggle along with photographs of key events.

Cybrary of the Holocaust—(http://remember.org/)

This is an cyber library or resources for individuals wishing to study the Holocaust. Audio interviews from survivors, written recollections by survivors, works of literature, images, and a wide array of resources depict this dark period in our history to ensure that we do not forget.

History/Social Studies Web Site for K-12 Teachers—(http://www.execpc.com/~dboals/boals.html)

If you are going to stop at one site for social studies this should be it. A massive set of links to sites on the WWW useful for social studies education organized in a set of categories. One of the richest sites we have found on the Internet and it is continuously updated. Set your bookmark.

Lesson Plans and Resources for Social Studies Teachers—(http://www.csun.edu/~hcedu013/index.html)

Developed by a professor at California State University at Northridge, this location contains useful lesson plans and Internet resources for busy social studies teachers. Links to many useful sites.

Africa Homepage—(http://www.seas.upenn.edu/~cardell/africa.html)

A rich site devoted to the peoples and cultures of Africa, including people in the Americas from Africa. This site contains links to many sites with information about the history, culture, and arts of many rich heritages, all of which trace back to the African continent.

Gateway to World History—(http://library.ccsu.ctstateu.edu/~history/world_history/)

This is just what the title says it is. It is a great starting point for beginning any study of history from native American history to the history of current crises in the world. This site contains many links to useful historical resources.

Movietone News Online—(http://www.iguide.com/movies/movitone/contents.sml)

Remember watching the Movietone News just before the Saturday matinee came on at the Bijou? Here it is online. Download a short black and white news clip each week and see who can do the research to describe its significance. A great way to get kids back to the history books. They can also send a historical image in a postcard, take a history quiz, and rewrite a caption for a historical photograph.

PBS Teacher Connex—(http://www.pbs.org/tconnex/index.html)

PBS Teacher Connex seeks to reach U.S. teachers with valuable program information, as well as cross-curricular applications, lesson plans, and links to Internet sites related to television programs appearing on the Public Broadcasting Service stations in your area. Many teachers use videos of these programs in the class. Here is a great Internet connection for these experiences.

The White House for Kids—(http://www.whitehouse.gov/WH/kids/html/kidshome.html)

Have your students take a tour of the White House and visit the president and his family. Students may also leave a message for the president, read a newsletter for students, and experience several important historical moments that have recently taken place.

National Geographic Society Home Page—(http://www.nationalgeographic.com/main.wd)

The home page of the National Geographic Society provides a wealth of information for students related to the programming and books of this organization. Within the site is a great location (http://www.nationalgeographic.com/ngs/geo_ed/geoed7.wd) for lesson ideas on geography, an area of the curriculum that is often neglected. Also located at this site are maps which may be printed out by students for reports.

Virtual Tourist II—(http://www.vtourist.com/vt/)

Have your students start here to take tours of various countries and cities around the world. They travel by clicking on the location of the map they wish to visit and, once they arrive, find pictures, information about that location, and links to other sites with more information about their travel destination. A great initial activity to orient your students to the WWW.

Listservs/Mailing Lists for Social Studies

CIVNET—(listserv@listserv.syr.edu)

Conversations about the teaching of civics.

MEMORIES—(listserv@sjuvm.stjohns.edu)

This listserv allows students to talk with survivors of World War II.

SOCSTUD-L—(mailserv@hcca.ohio.gov)

Conversations about teaching social studies.

SS435-L—(listserv@ualtavm.bitnet)
Conversations about teaching social studies in the elementary grades.
TAMHA—(listserv@cms.cc.wayne.edu)
Conversations about teaching American history.

Usenet Newsgroup for Social Studies Education

The Social Studies and History Curriculum in K-12 Education—(k12.ed.soc-studies)
Discusses instruction in social studies at all grade levels.

Chapter 7

Science: Using the Internet to Support Scientific Thinking

```
To:    Our readers
From:  djleu@sued.syr.edu (Don Leu),
       ddleu@syr.edu (Debbie Leu)
Re:    Using the Internet for Science Education


    Some teachers lack confidence in their ability to teach sci-
ence. Approached with the proper perspective, however, science
education can become the center of your classroom as you use it
to integrate language arts, math, social studies, and other sub-
ject areas. Science is all about helping students to think scien-
tifically, asking questions and seeking logical answers through
observation, thinking, reading, writing, and critical analysis.
As noted in the National Science Education Standards, science
education needs to provide both a "hands on" and a "minds on"
experience.
    The Internet can be a valuable tool in this process. Learning
to use the Internet, itself, is a scientific process as you and
you students make hypotheses about how the Internet works and
then test these with your browser. Internet Workshop may be very
useful here. In addition, the Internet provides extensive re-
sources to help your students as you cultivate their ability to
look at the world scientifically. These include an extensive set
of science museums where your students can interact with exciting
demonstrations of scientific principles, experts available to
answer students' questions about any aspect of science, on-going
scientific studies where your students may contribute their ob-
servations and help to interpret the results, listservs on teach-
ing science where you may obtain valuable ideas to bring to your
classroom, and lesson plans to help you with your science teach-
ing.


    Don and Debbie
```

As Ms. Thomas walked into Room 301, a full week before school started in the fall, she saw the quotation behind her desk and smiled. It was a simple sentence, a sentence she had found during her first attempts at navigating the Internet several years ago. She had copied the quotation onto an index card and posted it behind her desk so she would see it every time she entered the room. The worn card, quoting an early rocket scientist, said:

> It is difficult to say what is impossible, for the dream of yesterday is the hope of today and the reality of tomorrow.
>
> —Robert Goddard

This card held many meanings as it greeted her each morning. It reminded her of the passionate belief she had in the potential of every child in her room. It also reminded her of all that she had accomplished in learning to use the Internet, especially in the area of science.

When she first started teaching, three years ago, she did not feel comfortable teaching science. She quickly formed a team teaching relationship with her friend next door. The team taught social studies and science that first year and the following year, each focusing on the subject area they knew best. She learned a lot about science teaching from this relationship as she increased her understanding of the Internet.

Her mind drifted to last year, the third year her school had been connected to the Internet and the first year she had actually taught science by herself. She smiled again as she recalled some of her experiences. She had started the year cautiously, doing a unit on the solar system and integrating language arts experiences by reading *This Planet Has No Atmosphere* by Paula Danzinger and *A Wrinkle in Time* by Madeleine L'Engle. She set bookmarks on Netscape Navigator for **The Nine Planets Tour** (http://seds.lpl.arizona.edu/billa/tnp/), **The Hubble Space Telescope** (http://www.stsci.edu/), and the home page for the current **Space Shuttle** mission at NASA (http://www.ksc.nasa.gov/shuttle/countdown/). She developed several short Internet Activity Assignments for students to complete at these locations. She also subscribed to several listservs for science educators, following the conversations to see if she could get some good ideas for her class. One of the conversational threads discussed the **National Standards for Science Education** and gave the URL for this document (http://www.nap.edu/readingroom/books/nses/html/). She explored this site and its links, learning about the new science standards and getting several useful ideas, especially the concept of science as inquiry.

Over a holiday break, she discovered the **Shuttle/Mir Online Research Experience** (http://quest.arc.nasa.gov/smore/), an Internet Project site related to science in space. (See Figure 7-1.) This contained an outstanding set of science experiences related to the Space Shuttle and MIR collaboration, including information about science projects taking place, biographies of the scientists on the project, experiments students can complete, a discussion group for teachers and students, and many outstanding lesson plans. This allowed her students to collect data and contribute to an on-going science study. They enjoyed comparing their observations with observations made by other students around the world.

Toward the end of the year she decided to try Internet Inquiry with cooperative group science projects. Students worked in groups of twos and threes to identify an important question in science they wanted to answer. Then they used the Internet and their school library to try to discover the answer. Internet Workshop sessions twice a week seemed to help students a lot on their projects. At the end of the unit, the class held a science fair with each group setting up a "poster session," describing their question, their work, and what they had discovered on a large poster board.

She remembered the project Tyronne and Alex had shared at their science fair. Tyronne and Alex had both been interested in the ant farm Ms. Thomas brought into the classroom after the winter holidays. They were fascinated by the continuous activity of the insects. The question they wanted to answer in their Internet Inquiry was "Do ants ever sleep?" When they shared this question during Internet Workshop, other students had all kinds of suggestions. They could check in the library for books about animals. They could check on the Internet by doing a search with one of the search engines for "ants" and "sleep." Someone also gave them the URL for **The Mad Scientist Network**, a place on the Internet where they could ask a scientist this question (http://128.252.223.239/~ysp/MSN/). And someone else suggested they mark one ant and watch it for 24 hours to see if it ever stopped to sleep. The idea of staying up all

Figure 7-1.   The home page for S/MORE: Shuttle-Mir Online Research Experience

night caught their attention and they pleaded with Ms. Thomas to take the class ant farm home over the weekend. She finally relented and, after they selected one ant ("Hooty") and marked him with a non-toxic marker, Ms. Thomas dropped the ant farm off at Alex's house Friday after school. They made observations every fifteen minutes in their science journal for an entire day and learned that Hooty never stopped to take a rest or stopped working. They even took some pictures for their poster session at the science fair. They created a wonderful poster that presented their work. It included their photos, a written report describing their reseach, and the conclusions they reached. They also included the e-mail message in Figure 7-2 from a scientist in Australia. They were pleased they had figured out a way to answer their question using a method that even the adult scientist had not considered.

Lessons from the Classroom

This story from Ms. Thomas's classroom has several important lessons for all of us to consider. First, the Internet provides many helpful resources that can assist you in developing an exciting and dynamic science program in your classroom, a program consistent with the National Science Education Standard's emphasis on thinking scientifically through inquiry.

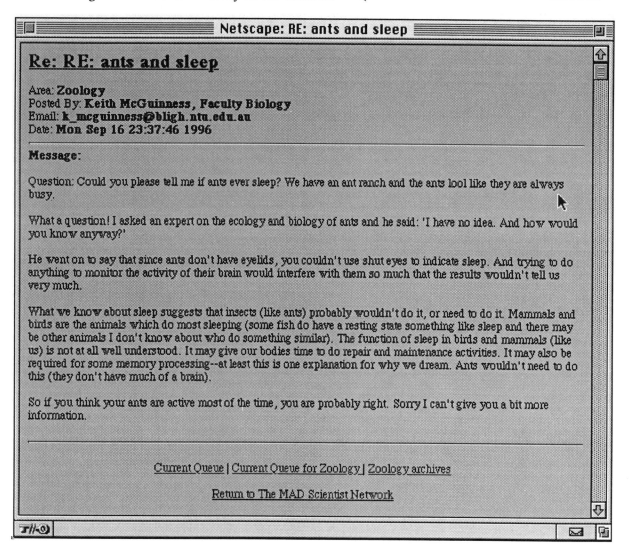

Figure 7-2.   Alex's response from an Australian scientist on the Mad Scientist Network
(http://medinfo.wustl.edu/~ysp/MSN/posts/841965056.Zo.r.html)

Second, Internet Activity Assignments may be used in your classroom to enrich your science program, especially when you are just beginning to use the Internet in your classroom. These take little time but provide important experiences for your students.

Third, Internet projects are a powerful way of helping your students to think scientifically as they work collaboratively with others to gather data and interpret the results. Several locations on the WWW provide opportunities for your class to engage in Internet projects, or to develop your own projects and invite others to join.

Fourth, Internet Inquiry is an excellent vehicle to help your students think scientifically as you develop a science-as-inquiry program in your classroom. Science is as much a verb as it is a noun. Having students identify questions they wish to answer and then helping them to develop techniques for answering their questions is important in preparing students who not only know science but also do science.

E-Mail for You

From: Jan Barth (wex018@mail.connect.more.net)
Organization: Brookfield Middle School
Subject: Using the Internet for Science in the Middle
               School Classroom

One of the first ways I used my Internet connection was during a 7th grade unit on Earth processes where we were studying about earthquakes. I had my students do a word search on the Netscape search engine called Yahoo. They typed in the word earthquake and found several sites listed. The one I wanted them to use allowed them to plot the daily earthquake activity around the world (http://www.civeng.carleton.ca/cgi-bin/quakes).

We then decided to take a large world map and pinpoint the sites by the latitude and longitude that was reported on the Internet site. (This is a good tie in to Social Studies!) We did this for several days and immediately saw a pattern developing—earthquakes occurred along regular lines in the Earth's crust. My students wanted to know why. This led us to read about plate boundaries and the motion of the plates. Because we had used the Internet and seen this pattern, our discussion about plate tectonics was so much more exciting than if we had only read about this. The Internet made the concept come alive for my students.

The students were also excited by getting daily information that listed the magnitude of each earthquake. They wondered why they didn't read about some of the larger earthquakes in the newspaper which led to a discussion of journalism. (This is a good tie in to Language Arts!)

I found the Internet very useful in making this unit a valuable learning experience. One of the things I would suggest is for you, the teacher, to do the search beforehand and find the site that you would like your students to reach. You can provide better assistance with their search if you have done it before they do. You can also bookmark the site you want them to use and then call it up every day whenever you want to use it.

My students and I learned as we went and enjoyed our first experience on the Net. I would be glad to answer any messages about how I use the Internet in my class. Just e-mail me and I'll do my best to answer. Good luck!

Jan Barth
Brookfield Middle School
Brookfield, MO 64628
wex018@mail.connect.more.net

Central Sites for Science Education

There are a number of locations on the Internet that will provide you with important assistance as you determine how best to use this resource in your classroom for science education. One type of site provides you with a wide array of links to useful curricular and other resources for science education. Another will provide you with information about the national science standards. Others will provide you with science units, ideas for science demonstrations, and/or lesson plans. Finally, some locations will be useful if you wish to subscribe to listservs related to science education. Each will be useful to you as you consider the broader issues of your science education program.

If you only have time to visit one central site, pay a visit to the **Eisenhower National Center for Mathematics and Science Education** (http://www.enc.org:80/index.htm). This federally-funded project provides K–12 teachers with a central source of information on mathematics and science education. One section contains links to a monthly "Digital Dozen," 13 great sites on the Internet for math and science education that change each month. Another section contains an excellent collection of lessons and activities for your students. In addition, there is a location where you may ask experts in the field of science education any question that will improve your classroom program. These experts will provide you with answers and resources to help you meet your students' needs. It also has a resource finder which will allow you to search an extensive set of instructional resources by topic or key word. Finally, this site contains a section where you may read various publications related to science education. Clearly, this WWW location is of tremendous utility as you seek to use the Internet to improve your classroom science program. It is especially useful as a jumping-off point.

Another excellent site to use as a jumping-off point is **Frank Potter's Science Gems** (http://www-sci.lib.uci.edu/SEP/SEP.html). This site contains over 2,000 links to outstanding science resources on the WWW. What is especially nice about this location is that it is organized by science area (e.g., physical science, Earth science, life science, etc.) and by topic within each area (e.g., within Earth science there are locations for measurement, earth, solar system, astronomy, atmosphere, land/oceans, and natural resources). Each topic is also organized, this time by grade level. The organizational scheme used at this site allows you to quickly find resources for units you are planning to teach in your class.

If you wish to keep up with the most recent developments in earth science, take a look at **Web Earth Science for Teachers** (http://www.usatoday.com/weather/wteach.htm), a location within *USA Today*. This has a list of links that are often related to items in the news or weather. At the bottom, there are links to other sections with information on other topic areas, as well as lesson plans and activities for your classroom.

You may also be interested in taking a look at the **National Science Education Standards** (http://www.nap.edu/readingroom/books/nses/html/overview.html), which outline what students need to know and be able to do in order to be scientifically literate at different grade levels. Many teachers have found that this provides important support.

Another type of central site provides teaching plans for busy teachers. Many of these are good beginning points as you consider ways in which to help your students become scientifically literate and think scientifically. One of the most comprehensive sites is **Lessons and Activities for Science** (http://www.enc.org:80/lessci.htm), a location at the Eisenhower National Center for Mathematics and Science Education site mentioned earlier. This site contains links to outstanding locations containing more lesson plans and activities than you would be able to complete in a lifetime of teaching. Exploring these locations will give you many good ideas for your science program. Another outstanding location with teaching plans and wonderful resources is located at **Inquiry Resources** (http://www.sln.org/resources.html), a location in the Science Learning Network. Here you may search by grade and topic for a wide variety of teaching resources. It is especially useful when you have a unit and are looking for related web resources. **The Science Learning Network** (http://www.sln.org/) also has wonderful resources for collaborating with other science teachers around the world, including an on-line chat area, a projects area, and a bulletin board. Finally, you may wish to visit the home page for the **Elementary Science Center of the Minnetonka Public Schools** (http://WWW.minnetonka.k12.mn.us/support/science/), an excellent example of a district providing important support to its teachers.

Teachers often use demonstrations to catch students' interest and get them to think scientifically. There are a number of useful locations on the WWW that describe demonstrations you can share with your class to illustrate scientific principles or to initiate conversations about causes and effects. One of the best collection of demonstrations is **The Exploratorium Science Snackbook** (http://www.exploratorium.edu/publications/Snackbook/Snackbook.html). This allows you to quickly replicate many of the exciting exhibits at one of the world's premier science museums. Another location, **Forty Demos to Make Science Come Alive** (http://nesen.unl.edu/methods/nerds.html), was developed by N.E.R.D.S. (Nebraska Educators Really Doing Science). A third location with exciting demonstrations is **Whelmers** (http://www.mcrel.org/whelmers/). Developed by Steven Jacobs, these demonstrations catch students by surprise and get them to really think about physical principles.

Finally, you may find it useful to follow the discussions in several listservs/mailing lists. One you may wish to consider is **T321-L**, a discussion group for teaching science in elementary schools (istserv@mizzou1.missouri.edu). Another is **CYBERMARCH-NET**, a discussion group for teachers interested in environmental education (majordomo@igc.apc.org). Additional listservs/mailing lists as well as several science education newsgroups are listed at the end of this chapter.

Keeping It Simple: Internet Activity Assignments

Internet Activity Assignments are a good way to begin using the Internet in your classroom for science education. Internet Activity Assignments are easy to set up and require the possession of minimum navigation knowledge by either you or your students. Locate a site on the Internet with content related to your science unit and set a bookmark for this location. Then develop an activity that requires students to use that site and assign the activity to your students to complete during the week. Alternatively, you may develop different activities related to the site and encourage students to complete as many as possible during their computer time.

Excellent Internet Activity Assignments may be developed from the many resources located at science museums around the world. These often provide exciting simulations, demonstrations, or science puzzles for students. By developing appropriate Internet Activity Assignments, you can engage your students in scientific thinking as you encourage them to consider the information at the WWW location. A good place to begin is the **Science Learning Network** (http://www.sln.org/), a central location for museums and science educators around the world. Their **Inquiry Resources Page** (http://www.sln.org/) contains links to many great science activities at different museums and a searchable data base that allows you to quickly find science activities by topic and grade level. You may also wish to visit an excellent collection of links to interactive science museums around the world at **Hands-on Science Centers Worldwide** (http://www.cs.cmu.edu/~mwm/sci.html). The best science museum we know of for students is San Francisco's Exploratorium. It used to be that only Bay Area students were fortunate enough to access the many exciting and informative science exhibits there. Now, anyone with an Internet connection can participate. Be certain to pay a visit to the **Exploratorium Home Page** (http://www.exploratorium.edu/). You won't regret it. Another museum with great interactive exhibits is **London's National Museum of Science and Industry** (http://www.nmsi.ac.uk/).

Here are several examples of Internet Activity Assignments that might be developed for science units.

- **A Virtual Dissection of a Cow's Eye.**   If you are doing a unit on physiology or on vision you may wish to set a bookmark for The Cow's Eye Dissection (http://www.exploratorium.edu/learning_studio/cow_eye/index.html). Here students are taken step-by-step through the dissection with supporting glossary terms for the parts of the eye; RealAudio sound clips from the Exploratorium staff explain what is taking place. This location also contains a program students can download to your computer that will help them to learn the physiology of a cow's eye. Have students explore the entire WWW location in order to draw an accurate illustration of a cow's eye with each of the important parts labeled. On a separate page, have them explain how this important body part works. Post these next to your computer as they are completed.

Afterwards, have them ask an expert from the Exploratorium via e-mail a well-thought-out question about how a cow's eye works. Post questions and answers.

- **Storm Science.**   During a unit on weather for third or fourth graders, set a bookmark to Hurricane: Storm Science (http://www.miamisci.org/hurricane/), a location at the Miami Science Museum. Have students track several hurricanes on an interactive map, make a storm hunter plane, read narratives from the members of a family that survived a hurricane, make several weather instruments, and contribute a story of a personal disaster or a work of art to the healing quilt. After the experience, have students send a challenging question about the weather to a scientist on the Mad Scientist Network (http:128.252.223.239/~ysp/MSN/). Post questions and answers as they arrive.

- **Optical Illusions.**   If your students are studying optical illusions have them visit a wonderful science museum in Australia, **Questacon** (http://sunsite.anu.edu.au/Questacon/Act.html), and complete the "Challenge of the Curves" experience. Have them write an explanation for the optical illusion at this site and e-mail it to the museum staff. Don't forget to explore the other wonderfully interactive experiences for students at this location.

Internet Activity Assignments such as these will enable you to support science units with Internet experiences that require little preparation time yet provide important experiences for your students.

Internet Projects

Internet projects are especially useful in science for several reasons. First, they create situations in which students help one another to discover important concepts. Internet projects take natural advantage of opportunities for socially mediated learning, opportunities that are so powerful within the Internet. For example, as a class in Florida communicates with students around the world about the ecological needs of manatees, they teach others about an endangered species at the same time they learn about endangered species in other parts of the world. Internet projects are a powerful tool for a teacher who takes the time to explore their potential for classroom learning.

Second, Internet projects in science provide natural opportunities for curricular integration with other subject areas within thematic units. Internet projects in science require students to engage in language arts experiences as they communicate with others via e-mail. These experiences also lend themselves to social studies as students learn about different parts of the world and the social and cultural characteristics that define those locations. In addition, Internet projects in science often require students to engage in math experiences. A project comparing weather patterns in different parts of the world, for example, will require students to record rain amounts, wind speed, and temperature and calculate the means for these over an extended period of time. Students may also have to compare and perhaps graph meteorological data reported from other locations. Thus, Internet projects in science contain inherent possibilities for curricular integration, an important concern for busy teachers who have to continually squeeze new additions to the curriculum within school days that do not expand.

Finally, when Internet projects in science are designed appropriately, they can foster scientific thinking. Thinking scientifically involves developing and evaluating best guesses about why things are the way there are. This can be an important part of any Internet project in science. Classes in different parts of the world often see the same issue in different ways because of different cultural traditions. Science allows these students to question one another, decide upon appropriate ways of evaluating competing hypotheses, gather information, and evaluate that information to reach conclusions that are agreed to by all parties.

As you begin to consider Internet projects around science topics, be certain to visit **Telecollaborative Learning Around the World** (http://www1.minn.net:80/~schubert/NickNacks.html). This location provides the best tutorial on designing Internet projects we have found, as well as wonderfully complete examples of successful Internet projects (http://www1.minn.net:80/~schubert/NickProjects.html). Pay a visit, too, to NASA's **Online Interactive Projects** (http://quest.arc.nasa.gov/interactive/index.html#archives).

E-Mail for You

From: Beverley Powell (bpowell@globalx.net)
Subject: My Romance with SchoolNet

Based on my experience in elementary teaching and information consulting, I think that all the teachers reading this book should be aware of the educational potential of **Canada's SchoolNet** (http://www.schoolnet.ca).

SchoolNet is a collaboration between federal and provincial governments, the education profession and industry. Already far advanced, SchoolNet is scheduled for implementation in all of Canada's elementary and secondary schools, libraries and museums by 1998. It is a world-class educational resource offering a vast range of informational opportunities.

What's there already, and growing, is a rich list of information entrées in a global menu of databases, for example:

* SchoolNet RINGS Projects (http://www.stemnet.nf.ca/Projects/RINGS/)—involves students working in groups or RINGS to contribute and discover new information using the Internet as a medium.
* SchoolNet Grassroots Projects (http://www.schoolnet.ca/grassroots/)—seeks to motivate Canadian teachers and students to create and implement pedagogically sound, Internet-based classroom projects.
* CANADISK (http://www2.schoolnet.ca/cdisk/)—features a database of images and documents on Canadian studies.
* SchoolNet's MOO (http://www.schoolnet.ca/moo/)—offers a text-based virtual environment where students from around the world can communicate via computer.
* Special Needs Education Network (http://www.schoolnet.ca/sne/)—provides Internet services specific to parents, teachers, schools, and others involved in the education of students with special needs.
* Other services teachers and students have access to: resources by subject, gopher, CHAT, mailing lists, newsgroups, and FTP.

SchoolNet is designed to support educational adventures by students in diverse regions and countries. It includes a pioneering program to support native schools. It has already been instrumental in several outstanding educational accomplishments, including new lesson databases and dissemination of CDs on leading-edge student projects. In short, SchoolNet is the Crown jewel of the Canadian educational establishment. Teachers all over the world are invited to use SchoolNet's avenues of communication and first-class technology. They can inspire and inform student experiments in international learning, so direly needed in today's fractioning world.

Beverley Powell
Elementary School Supply Teacher
Ottawa, Canada

You may also wish to visit **Global SchoolNet's Internet Project Registry** (http://www.gsn.org/gsn/proj/index.html), **Classroom Connect's Teacher Contact Database** (http://www.classroom.net/contact/), and **The Global School House** (http://www.gsh.org/class/default.htm) to find additional examples of Internet projects. Examples of projects posted previously at some of these sites include:

- **Night of the Comet**—(http://ccf.arc.nasa.gov/comet/index.html). Sponsored by NASA at their page for **Online Interactive Projects** (http://quest.arc.nasa.gov/interactive/index.html#archives), this project provided a forum for observing and discussing the passing of Comet Hyakutake. Students at over 100 locations around the world contributed their observations, questions, and answers to this "First Virtual Star Party." Students could ask experts at NASA questions, send in their photos of the comet for viewing by others, read about comet facts, and participate in a series of experiments. Be certain to visit this location and see what new projects are being planned. Set a bookmark!

- **Worldwide Weather Watch**—A first grade teacher from Macedon, New York and second grade teachers from Mound, Minnesota posted this science project and attracted classrooms from the United States; Canberra, Australia; and Tasmania. Primary school students around the world compared global weather conditions by sharing monthly e-mail reports about their weather, what they wore, and what they were did outside. Students learned about different temperature scales, seasonal change in different hemispheres, measurement, math, cultural variation, and language arts.

- **Earth Day Groceries Project**—(http://www.halcyon.com/arborhts/earthday.html). Each year participating classes obtain grocery bags from local supermarkets, decorate them with environmental messages, and then return them to be used at the grocery store by customers. Students share photos and reports of their accomplishments at a central site. A teacher at the Arbor Heights Elementary School in Seattle, Washington has developed this wonderful environmental awareness project. Over 180 schools around the world participated last year, distributing over 75,000 grocery bags decorated with messages about the environment.

FAQ (Frequently Asked Question)

I am using Netscape Navigator 3.0 in my fourth grade class. Why do I always get an "Out of Memory" message after several students use the Internet in the morning?

There are a number of reasons for an "Out of Memory" message. This message is telling you that your RAM (Random Access Memory) or the memory allocated to Netscape Navigator has reached its limit. There are three possible solutions. First, see if you can obtain additional RAM. This requires inserting one or several new chips. You will need to talk to the technical support person at your school about this. Second, try having each student quit Netscape Navigator when they finish their session. Netscape keeps track of each site you visit and this list often gets lengthy, taking up much of Netscape's memory allocation. Quitting Netscape deletes this list and frees up memory. Third, you may choose to use an earlier version of Netscape. These require less RAM and will give you more memory to use as you navigate the WWW.

Internet Inquiry

Internet Inquiry is a perfect vehicle for helping your students to think scientifically, critically, and carefully about the natural world. Children have so many questions about the world around them and there are so many resources on the Internet to engage them in careful study of natural phenomena that Internet Inquiry should be an important part of your science program.

Internet Inquiry usually contains five phases: question, search, analyze, compose, and share. In the first phase, students identify an important question they wish to answer; usually this is related to the unit you are studying. You can support this phase by participating in group brainstorming sessions or by conducting an Internet Workshop around the topic of important questions that might be explored. In addition, you may wish to brainstorm individually with students who are having difficulty identifying an intriguing question. Another very nice strategy during this phase is to set a bookmark for science museums or other science sites and encourage students to explore these locations for an interesting question to address.

During the second phase—search—students look for information and/or perform experiments to address the question they have posed. They may search on the Internet for useful resources, experiments, and demonstrations. Students should also be encouraged to use more traditional resources that may be found in their classroom or school library. They may also wish to ask an expert via e-mail about the question they are trying to answer. Communicating with experts via e-mail can be very helpful to students. A list of e-mail addresses and WWW locations where students may contact experts in science is provided in Figure 7-3.

During the third phase—analyze—students need to analyze all of the information they have in order to respond to the question they initially posed. Sometimes this phase leads to a straightforward answer derived from several supporting lines of evidence: the results of an experiment, a graph of data, an e-mail response from a scientist, documentation from several books or Internet locations, or an e-mail message from another student studying the same question. Often, the analysis phase may be supported by peer conferences in which students share their results and think about their meanings. Or, you may wish to use Internet Workshop to support students' analytic skills.

The fourth phase—compose—requires students to compose a presentation of their work. This may be a written report, a poster board display, or an oral report with displays of evidence. You may wish to follow process writing procedures to support this phase by engaging students in drafting, revision, and editing conferences.

The final phase—share—is an opportunity for students to share their work with others and respond to questions about their investigation. Some teachers set aside a regular time one day a week for sharing Inquiry Projects as they are completed. You may wish to use a variation of an Author's Chair in your classroom by designating a Scientist's Chair for use during presentations of Inquiry Projects. Alternatively, you may wish to have a science fair in your classroom at the end of each unit during which students may display their work and answer questions as students circulate around, visiting each of the presentations.

Internet Inquiry can be an exciting aspect of your classroom and your science program. It provides independent explorations of the scientific world, opportunities to contact real scientists about important issues, and opportunities to support the development of scientific thinking.

General Locations for Contacting Experts in Science

Ask an Expert—(http://www.askanexpert.com/p/ask.html)
This is a general site with links to a wide range of experts.

Ask a Mad Scientist—(http://128.252.223.239/~ysp/MSN/)
This wonderful resource will put you in touch with a wide range of scientists around the world.

Locations for Contacting Specific Types of Experts in Science

Ask an Agriculture Expert—(http://spiderweb.com/ag/)
e-mail: agrihlp@wco.com
Obtain answers to questions about cultivated plants, gardens, farming, etc.

Ask an Architect—(http://www.4j.lane.edu/aiab/aquestion.html)
Obtain answers to questions about designing spaces.

Ask an Antarctic Expert—(http://icair.iac.org.nz/education/resource/askaques/askagues.htm)
e-mail: psommerv@icair.iac.org.nz
Obtain answers to questions about Antarctica.

Ask an Astronaut—(http://www.nss.org/askastro/home.html)
e-mail: rpearllman@nss.org
Obtain answers to questions about space science and being an astronaut.

Ask an Astronomer—(http://www2.ari.net/home/odenwald/qadir/qanda.html)
e-mail: starman@unc.edu
Obtain answers to questions about stars, planets, comets, and other aspects of astronomy.

Ask an Atmospheric Expert—(http://hyperion.gsfc.nasa.gov/Reading_room/ask.html)
Obtain answers from NASA about air quality, air pollution, and other issues related to the atmosphere.

Ask a Bug Expert—(http://wworkin.com/bugdoctor.html)
e-mail: bugdoc@orkin.com
Obtain answers to questions about bugs and insects.

Ask a Dinosaur Expert—(http://denr1.igis.uiuc.edu/isgsroot/dinos/rjjinput_form.html)
e-mail: jacobson@geoserv.isgs.uiuc.edu
Obtain answers to questions about dinosaurs and paleontology.

Ask Dr. Science—(http://www.ducksbreath.com/index.html)
Obtain answers to all kinds of questions about science.

Ask an Earth Scientist—(http://www.soest.hawaii.edu/GG/ASK/askanerd.html)
Obtain answers to questions about the natural workings and natural history of the Hawaiian Islands and the world.

Ask a Geologist—(http://walrus.wr.usgs.gov/docs/ask-a-ge.html)
e-mail: Ask a Geologist@usgs.gov
Obtain answers to questions about rocks, geology, and earth forms.

Ask a Gravity Expert—(http://www.physics.umd.edu/rgroups/gen_rel_the/question.html)
Obtain answers to questions about gravity.

Ask a Health Expert—(http://linear.chsra.wisc.edu/chsra/chen-fu/qmail.htm)
Obtain answers to questions about health.

Ask a Hydrologist—(http://wwwdwatcm.wr.usgs.gov/askhyd.html)
e-mail: pubinfo@maildwatcm.wr.usgs.gov
Obtain answers to questions about water and water quality.

Figure 7-3 continued on the following page

Figure 7-3. WWW locations and e-mail addresses for contacting experts in various fields

Figure 7-3 continued

Ask a Nutritionist—(http://www.cornell.edu/cgi-bin/dialogs_all?nutriquest)
Obtain answers to questions about food and nutrition.

Ask an Ocean Animal Expert—(http://www.whaletimes.org/whaques.htm)
e-mail: whaletimes@whaletimes.org
Obtain answers to questions about all types of marine animals.

Ask a Paleontology Expert—(http://ucmp.berkeley.edu/museum/pals.html)
Obtain answers to questions about dinosaurs and paleontology.

Ask a Science Expert—(http://www.npr.org/sfkids/resources.html)
e-mail: mentors@npr.org
Obtain answers to questions about science from the Science Friday Kids Connection by National Public Radio.

Ask an Animal Keeper—(http://www.libertynet.org/iha/valleyforge/writeus.html)
Obtain answers to questions about pets and animals.

Instructional Resources on the Internet

Bill Nye the Science Guy—(http://nyelabs.kcts.org/)

A great resource related to the popular series on your local Public Broadcasting System television station. There is, of course, information on programming, including home science demonstrations and lessons for upcoming topics. There is also a location to send the science guy e-mail. More importantly, there is a search engine that will connect you to outstanding science sites on the WWW. Science rules, indeed!

Jumbo—(http://www.jumbo.com/)

Looking for shareware and freeware to download and use in your classroom for science units? Here is the location with the largest set of programs to download on the WWW. Check out the science and the education sections for many useful resources.

Live from Antarctica—(http://quest.arc.nasa.gov/antarctica/index.html)

Here are enough resources for an entire year's project on science taking place in Antarctica. Dates and times for a series of related television programs are listed, as well as a teacher's guide and classroom lessons, questions and answers between students and scientists, a bibliography of related resources, links to other sites with information on the Antarctic, weekly newspapers published in the Antarctic, and contact with scientists studying the plant life and the ozone hole.

Monarch Watch—(http://monarch.bio.ukans.edu/)

Here is a wonderful opportunity to participate in science studies of the Monarch butterfly, sponsored by the Department of Entomology at the University of Kansas. The site contains an extremely comprehensive set of resources for studying Monarchs and sharing your observations, especially of their migration through your area. Find out about migration patterns, join one of several science projects, learn how to raise and release Monarchs in your classroom, learn how to start a butterfly garden near your classroom, and communicate with scientists who study these beautiful creatures. Set a bookmark!

NASA's Online Interactive Projects—(http://quest.arc.nasa.gov/interactive/index.html#archives)

This is one of the best locations for science study available. Students can participate in a number of scientific studies, ask questions of experts, see demonstrations, and really come to understand what scientific investigation is all about. Many useful resources for the teacher, too. Make a bookmark!

The Hubble Space Telescope's Public Page—(http://www.stsci.edu/public.html)

Here is the location for the Hubble Space Telescope and all of the wonderful science taking place with this instrument. There are many incredible photos of deep space that illustrate a number of new insights discovered with this technology. Many links for teachers and students interested in space study are also found here.

The Nine Planets: A Multimedia Tour of the Solar System—(http://seds.lpl.arizona.edu/billa/tnp/)

Want to get your upper elementary grade and middle school students interested in space science? Have them take this tour of the solar system, visiting each of the planets and their major moons. This site contains many stunning photographs and the latest science resulting from recent probes to these unusual worlds. Set a bookmark!

The Why Files—(http://whyfiles.news.wisc.edu/index.html)

Funded by the National Science Foundation and located at the University of Wisconsin, this location provides you and your students with science information behind recent news stories. What evidence is there of life on Mars? Does a climatologist study changes in the Earth's climate? What causes Mad Cow disease and how do humans catch it? How does amber preserve DNA? These and many more questions are answered here along with related links to other sites on the WWW.

Virtual Frog Dissection Kit—(http://www-itg.lbl.gov/vfrog/)

An outstanding demonstration of the potential of the Internet for science education. Think of all the poor frogs that will be saved! This site, developed by the Lawrence Berkeley National Laboratory, contains a great dissection experience where students learn about a frog's internal organs and systems. Videos are also available. At the end, students may also play the Virtual Frog Builder Game, in which they try to put a frog back together. Set a bookmark!

VirtualEarthquake—(http://vflylab.calstatela.edu/edesktop/VirtApps/VirtualEarthQuake/VQuakeIntro.html)

VirtualEarthquake is an interactive computer program designed to introduce you to the concepts of how an earthquake epicenter is located and how the Richter Magnitude of an earthquake is determined. Concepts such as seismometer, seismograph, and epicenter are explained and students see how scientists study earthquakes.

You Can with Beakman and Jax—(http://pomo.nbn.com/youcan/)

Based on the television program, Beakman's World, this location is great for curious young scientists who want to figure out how the world works. It has a location where students can ask questions about the natural world and also an interactive set of demonstrations illustrating answers to questions such as: What does smoking do to your lungs? How does a thermometer work? Why does the moon look bigger on the horizon? How does a sundial work? How does the moon power the tides? A good question is a powerful thing!

Listservs/Mailing Lists for Science Education

CYBERMARCH-NET—(majordomo@igc.apc.org)

A discussion group for teachers interested in environmental education.

IMSE-L—(listserv@uwf.cc.uwf.edu)

A discussion group sponsored by the Institute for Math and Science Education .

T321-L—(listserv@mizzou1.missouri.edu)

A discussion group on the teaching of science in elementary schools.

TIMS-L—(listserv@uicvm.uic.edu)

A discussion group sponsored by the Teaching Integrated Mathematics and Science (TIMS) Project.

Usenet Newsgroups for Science Education

k12.ed.science—Discussion about the science curriculum in K–12 education.

misc.education.science—Discussion of issues related to science education.

k12.chat.elementary—Informal discussion among elemtary students, grades K–5.

k12.chat.junior—Informal discussion among students in grades 6–8.

k12.chat.teacher—Informal discussion among teachers in grades K–12.

Chapter 8

$\mathcal{M}$ath:
Thinking Mathematically on the Internet

```
To:    Our readers
From:  djleu@sued.syr.edu (Don Leu),
       ddleu@syr.edu (Debbie Leu)
Re:    Using the Internet for Math Education
```

Since 1989, when the National Council of Teachers of Mathematics published *Curriculum and Evaluation Standards for School Mathematics*, a change in the way we view mathematics education has taken place. We see it in school classrooms where teachers increasingly engage students in critical thinking and communication through math experiences. These require basic skill knowledge but also emphasize mathematical insight, reasoning, and problem solving. Increasingly, children realize math is a sense-making experience as they become active participants in creating knowledge and communicating that knowledge to others.

The Internet can help you to realize the potential all children have for thinking mathematically. There are many useful sites to engage your students in important math experiences and to help them communicate with others about what they are learning. We were certainly surprised to find such an active and exciting math community on the Internet. There are sites with intriguing puzzles, software to download, weekly math challenges, biographies of famous women in math, mathematicians who answer your students' questions, lesson plans, and even a counting sheep who will solve any four-function math problem for you (in Sheepese, of course). We hope you enjoy all of these locations.

Don and Debbie

"I want to show you our Web Math." Clarissa pulled her mom over to the Internet computer in their classroom and they sat down to see what Clarissa had been talking about every night at dinner. It was Open House evening at Eastwood Elementary school and Clarissa had her mom come early so they would have the Internet all to themselves. "See, here is what we do each day at the beginning. We read about the numbers for today and Ms. Johnson has a quiz to see if somebody knows this when we go home. I print it out for my group so we all know it." Since today was the first of the month, they read a portion of the page for the number one at **About Today's Date** (http://acorn.educ.nottingham.ac.uk/cgi-bin/daynum), a site located at Nottingham University in England:

> "An ace is number one in playing cards. French playing cards are marked '1' instead of
> 'A'. A cyclops is a creature with one eye and a dromedary is a camel with only one hump.
> There is only one of lots of things. There is only one President of the United States,
> there is only one Atlantic Ocean and there is only one you. All of these are unique."

"Today she asked us what a dromedary was and we knew the answer in my group," Clarissa said proudly.

"See, now here we got the Brain Teasers . . . . These are to tease our brains and make us smarter and we got to work together 'cause that's the best way to learn, Ms. Johnson says. Julie and me, we always figure it out, but sometimes we ask Alisa to help."

Clarissa had selected the bookmark for **Brain Teasers** (http://www.eduplace.com/math/brain/), a site with a new math problem each week that really challenged students to think. (See Figure 8-1.) This was a regular, weekly assignment in Ms. Johnson's room. Often there would be a group of students at the computer talking about the problem and trying to figure out the best strategy to arrive at the answer. Usually she didn't mind, because she wanted her students to learn how to learn together. Sometimes, however, she had to tell them to be a bit quieter when they got too excited and noisy. This was a good noise, though. She could usually hear them arguing about how to solve the problem as they learned from one another.

"See, and here's what I'm doin'. It's a report on famous women in Math and it's about Hypatia. She discovered parabolas but she was killed in Egypt 'cause they thought she was a witch. She was just smart. I'm gonna send them my report with e-mail when I'm done. Ms. Johnson's helping me." As she spoke, Clarissa showed her mom the site called **Past Notable Women of Mathematics** (http://www.cs.yale.edu/homes/tap/past-women-math.html). They saw how you could read biographies of famous women and how students could submit reports to be posted at this site.

"And here is where we did our fractals project," Clarissa said as she showed her mom the site called **A Fractals Lesson** (http://cml.rice.edu:80/~lanius/frac/). (See Figure 8-2.) "Fractals are cool! Here is the Sierpinski Triangle we made when we did this. We had to measure and find all the midpoints in our triangles." Clarissa pointed to the bulletin board and the large fractal made from students' separate fractals.

Then, Clarissa took her mother over to another location in the room where there was a display called food prices around the world. Their class had posted an Internet project designed to compare the price of a Big Mac, regular fries, and soda, along with other food items, around the world. Each class reported on the price for each item and then calculated the cost as a percentage of the average hourly salary for their country. The participating classes shared the results with one another so they could compare the price of common food items in each of their countries. Each class was completing a unit on statistics. They studied common statistical concepts by working through the lessons at a site called **Statistics Every Writer Should Know** (http://nilesonline.com/stats/) and then linked to an excellent resource containing economic statistics for each participating country, **Finding Data on the Internet: A Journalist's Guide** (http://nilesonline.com/data/links.shtml). "See, we can eat 8.5 Big Macs for each hour we work," said Clarissa. "And in Russia they get only .2 Big Macs for each hour of work."

Clarissa's mom was thinking that math had certainly changed since she went to school. She had a conversation about this with Ms. Johnson because she wasn't certain how she could help at home. Ms. Johnson gave her a copy of an article she had obtained and printed from the Internet, **Helping Your Child Learn Math** (http://www.ed.gov/pubs/parents/Math/index.html). It contained all kinds of useful ideas

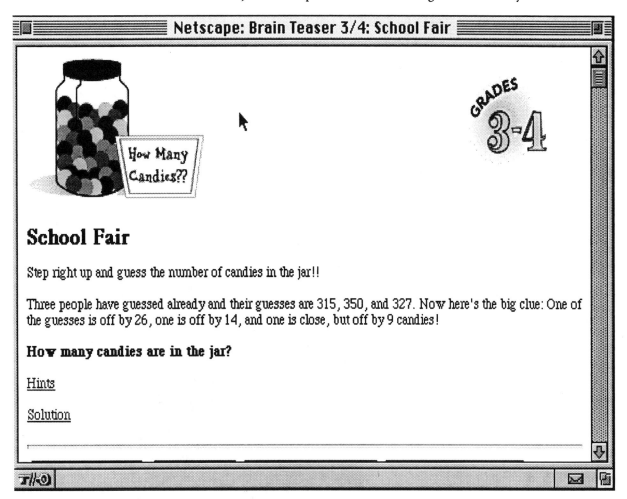

Figure 8-1. An example problem for students in grades 3–4 from the Brain Teaser site
(http://www.eduplace.com/math/brain/)

that parents could use at home to assist their children. "Yes," Clarissa's mom thought to herself on the way home, "Math certainly has changed."

Lessons from the Classroom

Clarissa's experience in Ms. Johnson's classroom illustrates several useful lessons for us to consider as we look at the Internet for Math education. First, the Internet profoundly changes the possibilities for Math education in fundamental ways. The availability of extensive resources on the Internet enriches the nature of mathematics education and changes it as much as when school textbooks first appeared for elementary students during the eighteenth and nineteenth centuries. The Internet allows teachers and students to study mathematics in important new ways that are consistent with the recent standards adopted by the National Council of Teachers of Mathematics and the emphasis on mathematical insight, reasoning, and problem solving. As with other areas of study, we will see that Internet Activity Assignments, Internet Projects, and Internet Inquiry are all possible in Mathematics education. Each may be used to integrate learning with other subject areas.

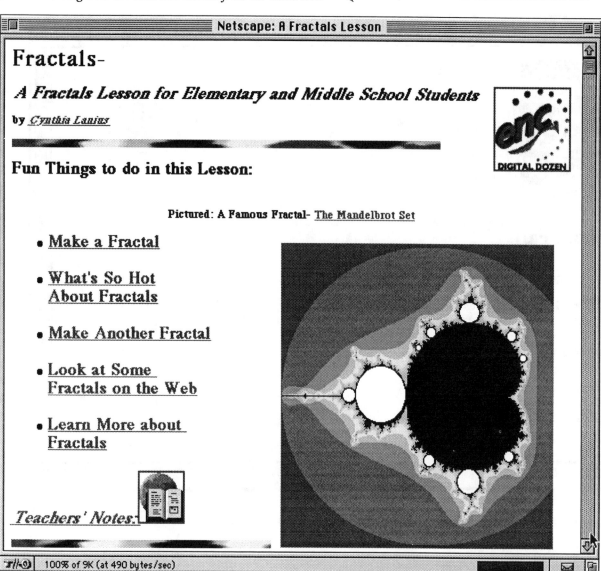

Figure 8-2. The home page for A Fractals Lesson
(http://cml.rice.edu:80/~lanius/frac/)

In addition, the Internet provides a wealth of mathematical data that may be used to help students learn more about themselves and the rest of the world. Just as Clarissa's class developed new insights about living standards around the world, your class may use the Internet to reach new conclusions based on data available through the Internet.

Finally, the Internet provides opportunities for students to communicate their developing insights and to compare them with those of other students, both in their class and around the world. A recent emphasis in Mathematics education is to support students as they communicate their insights about patterns they see in the world around them. The Internet provides important opportunities to accomplish this.

E-Mail for You

From: Jodi Moore (jbmoore@pen.k12.va.us)
Subject: Using the Internet for Math

Hi! The Internet is a tool that will motivate and excite all your students, especially in math. There are countless web sites available to entice even the most reluctant learners. I print a problem for my class each week from **Brain Teasers** (http://www.eduplace.com/math/brain) or **The Elementary Problem of the Week** (http://forum.swarthmore.edu/sum95/ruth/elem.pow.problems.html). The problems provide an avenue for healthy competition as well as practice and discussion within the classroom.

My students also frequent various web sites which provide useful information for research and reference on mathematicians and related mathematical topics such as the MacTutor History of Mathematics archive (http://www-groups.dcs.st-and.ac.uk/~history/). This information enhances classroom instruction and math takes on a new face. Enlivening the classroom environment with the real world is motivating. Students display confidence in locating information readily and they are able to apply the knowledge they have collected.

Lastly, students in my class have been able to integrate history and math, joining seven other schools from the U.S., Newfoundland (Canada), Germany, Saudi Arabia, and Australia in an Internet project. During a three-month period we all agreed to write four different articles with information about our school and the history and geography of our area. After composing each short research project, students at each school wrote five math problems based on the research. This was then sent using e-mail to the other six schools. Students in the participating schools solved the problems and sent back their answers. We were able to check the solutions as well as analyze any errors. It was especially interesting to listen as students decided if it was a computational error, an error in writing the problem, or a misinterpretation of the data. My students also benefited from the submissions of the other six schools. Each of the teachers in the project often collaborated to "lead" the problems in a particular area to provide appropriate practice and subsequent mastery.

I thoroughly enjoy the opportunities the Internet allows me to provide my students. Just like any other new toy, limits must be set and specific rules must be devised. Still, this powerful tool will literally make all the difference in the world with students. I can honestly say I am glad technology has arrived!

—

Jodi Moore, 6th grade teacher   Battlefield Middle School
jbmoore@pen.k12.va.us   11120 Leavells Rd.
                                Fredericksburg, VA 22407

Central Sites for Math Education

You can use a number of sites for a jumping-off point as you begin to explore the Internet for math education. Most of these have links that will take you to a wide range of locations designed to support your math program. These will include sites that may be used for Internet activities, Internet projects, or Internet Inquiry. Central sites may also contain links to lesson plans and locations where you can share ideas with other teachers about math education. A few will contain links to publications that allow you to keep up with developments in this area. Usually these central sites are more permanent and stable locations; they will be less likely to move to another location, disappear, or turn into a subscription service that will require a fee. They are often supported by a state or federal unit or by a non-profit organization or university. We encourage you to begin your explorations at one of these central sites.

As with science, the best single site may be the **Eisenhower National Center for Mathematics and Science Education** (http://www.enc.org:80/index.htm). We especially like the location here called the "Digital Dozen," 13 great sites on the Internet for math and science education that change each month. There is also an archive for sites that have received this award in the past. Another helpful feature is the "ENC Services" location, where you may ask experts any question you might have about math education. In addition, there is a great selection of lesson and activity locations and a "Resource Finder" that will help you locate curriculum resources for classroom projects. Be certain to begin your exploration in math at the Eisenhower National Center for Mathematics and Science Education.

A second very useful jumping-off point is the **Math Forum** (http://forum.swarthmore.edu/) at Swarthmore College, funded by the National Science Foundation. The goal of this location is to " . . . to build a community that can be a center for teachers, students, researchers, parents, educators, citizens at all levels who have an interest in mathematics education." They have done an exceptional job by providing many useful resources for teachers, students, and others. In addition to links to useful math sites on the web, the Math Forum maintains chat areas and listservs/mailing lists that students and teachers can use to share ideas and questions about math. **Dr. Math** (http://forum.swarthmore.edu/dr.math/) is also on call to answer questions from you or your students. This is an exceptional site on the web. Be certain to explore the many resources here.

Another central location you may wish to visit is the **Math Archives** (http://archives.math.utk.edu/newindex.html). Located at the University of Tennessee, this site has an especially good collection of software you may wish to download and use in your classroom. The Math Archives provide resources for mathematicians at all levels, not just K–12 educators, but if you look in the "Teaching Materials" section you will find a category for "K–12 Materials." There is also a nice collection of links to WWW resources for math in a section called "Topics in Mathematics." You will find a visit to this location well worth your time.

The **Math Department at Canada's SchoolNet** (http://www.schoolnet.ca/math_sci/math/) may also be useful as you begin to explore links to math resources. This location contains a number of links to math sites you will find useful. At the present time, this list is not organized by topic or grade level, but SchoolNet is quickly evolving and it looks like this will be an important resource.

The **Math** (http://www.csun.edu/~vceed009/math.html#Math) section of **Web Sites and Resources for Teachers** (http://www.csun.edu/~vceed009/) is also very useful as a jumping-off point into the web for math education. These locations are located at California State Northridge and are maintained by two professors in the School of Education. At the Math location, there are many links to locations with lesson plans for busy teachers. There are also links to a number of good board games. Another section contains links to ideas and activities to support your math program. All of the sites at this location contain resources that are useful to classroom teachers. It appears to have been developed by people who really understand teachers' classroom needs.

Finally, you may wish to subscribe to one of several listservs/mailing lists and participate in the conversations that are taking place each day about math education. One of the more important conversations taking place is on **NCTM-L** (listproc@sci-ed.fit.edu), the listserv sponsored by the National Council of Teachers of Mathematics. Join in and share your questions, concerns, and insights. Other useful listservs/mailing lists and math education newsgroups are listed at the end of this chapter.

Keeping It Simple: Internet Activity Assignments

If you explore some of the central sites described above you will quickly find many exciting locations related to the units in your math program. These are great places to use as you develop Internet Activity Assignments, the fastest way to bring the resources of the WWW into your classroom for math and other areas of your curriculum. Developing an Internet Activity Assignment is easy. Locate a site on the Internet with content related to your math unit and set a bookmark for this location. Then develop an activity that requires students to use that site. Assign this activity to your students to complete during the week. Some teachers will develop a number of different activities related to the site and then ask students to complete as many as possible during their computer time. Work completed during Internet Activity Assignments may be shared at the end of the week during Internet Workshop.

Many teachers will develop Internet Activity Assignments from one of several locations on the web that provide a weekly math challenge for students, a math problem that requires careful thinking to solve. Alternatively, some teachers will just print out this math problem each week and duplicate copies for their students. One location with weekly problems for students is **Brain Teasers** (http://www.eduplace.com/ math/brain/), a location sponsored by Houghton Mifflin. Each week, a new problem is presented by grade level. If students require it, they may click on a "Hint" or a "Solution" button. There is also an archive of problems used in the past.

The Little Math Puzzle Contest (http://www.odyssee.net/~academy/mathpuzzle/ mathpuzzlecontest.html) is another site with a weekly math problem for students. This site presents a single, ungraded problem for students. There is also an archive and a winner's list. You must have a password to access the answer at this site. Teachers may obtain the password via e-mail.

A third site with a weekly math problem is the **Elementary Problem of the Week** (http:// forum.swarthmore.edu/sum95/ruth/elem.pow.html). Each week a new problem is listed. There is an archive, as well, of past problems. A unique aspect of this site is that individual students, groups, or classes may register for the yearly set of problems. If they do so, their answers will be responded to by a "Visiting Math Mentor." Students, groups, and classes may also apply to be a Visiting Math Mentor for other students who submit answers to these problems. So, after participating for a while, you may wish to have your class volunteer to respond to answers submitted by other students during the year. This can be very exciting for your students as they take on the role of the teacher and help others solve challenging math problems.

Word Problems for Kids (http://juliet.stfx.ca/people/fac/pwang/mathpage/math1.html) is another location with graded math problems. For each, there is a linked "hint" button. Answers are provided to teachers with a registered e-mail address.

Other sites, too, may be used for Internet Activity Assignments. These may be located by exploring some of the central sites for math education described earlier. Here are just a few:

Dr. FreeMath—(http://www.omahafreenet.org/ofn/drfreemath/drfreemath.html)

Dr. Freemath is an electronic mail project where one mathematics question per month will be researched and answered from each elementary class. Past examples of questions include: How much water evaporates in the ocean each year? Why is any number to the zero power equal to one? What is pi not really equal to 22/7?

Biographies of Women Mathematicians—(http://www.scottlan.edu/lriddle/women/women.html)

This site contains a developing set of biographies. The group creating this site is looking for others to research famous women mathematicians and submit additional biographies.

MacTutor History of Mathematics archive—(http://www-groups.dcs.st-and.ac.uk/~history/)

Extensive links to sites with information about the history of math. A nice location to set up a weekly question related to math history that will help students develop a richer understanding of math concepts.

The Fruit Game—(http://www.2020tech.com/fruit/f752.html)

A simple interactive game with a hidden trick. See if your students can explain the trick in writing.

Interactive Mathematics Miscellany and Puzzles—(http://mars.superlink.net/abogom/)

Forget the title. Check this site out! It has an incredible list of links to games, activities, and puzzles that will keep your class busy all year! Set a bookmark!

?

FAQ (Frequently Asked Question)

Sometimes when I go to a site on the WWW it tells me that I need a "Java-capable browser." How do I know if I have this? What does this mean?

You have a Java-capable browser if you are using Netscape Navigator 3.0 or later or if you use Internet Explorer 3.0 or later. A Java-capable browser is one that will run special programs put on the web to assist with animation, sound, or video. These enhance the multimedia capabilities of web locations. You are using a Java-capable browser if you see animated objects at some web sites. These might be a message that moves along the bottom of your window or objects that spin around in place. Java-capable browsers also permit multiple windows to be open at any single web site.

Internet Projects

While they take more time and planning, Internet projects with other classrooms are an important instructional tool for several reasons. First, Internet projects are important because they support cross-curricular learning experiences. Language arts is almost always a part of any Internet project since it requires students to communicate with others about their thinking in mathematics. In addition, social studies and science are also frequently a part of these projects. An insightful teacher will plan to take advantage of these natural opportunities for cross-curricular integration.

Internet projects in math are also important because they encourage students to work together to develop the ability to think mathematically. Part of thinking mathematically is being able to communicate problem-solving strategies to others and to listen as others describe different approaches to proofs. This is supported when classrooms are communicating with one another, modeling their approaches to solutions, and explaining their answers.

There are several Internet projects in math that run continuously and have a separate site on the WWW. **Good News Bears** (http://www.ncsa.uiuc.edu:80/edu/RSE/RSEyellow/gnb.html), a year-long stock market game for middle school students is one such location. Here, students participate in a contest using on-line stock market data as they do research and then buy and sell stocks in an attempt to maximize their portfolio. It is an excellent experience that brings mathematical thinking to real-world problems and solutions. Another site you may wish to visit is the **Elementary Problem of the Week** (http://forum.swarthmore.edu/sum95/ruth/elem.pow.html). After solving a number of problems at this location, have your class volunteer to serve as a visiting mentor, responding to others' answers and assisting them with the solutions. This can be an exciting experience for your class.

Other projects may be joined by reviewing projects posted at the traditional locations on the Internet, such as **Global SchoolNet's Internet Project Registry** (http://www.gsn.org/gsn/proj/index.html), **Classroom Connect's Teacher Contact Database** (http://www.classroom.net/contact/), or **The Global School House** (http://www.gsh.org/class/default.htm). If you see a project that will fit in with an upcoming unit, be certain to join.

Alternatively, you may wish to work with your class during Internet Workshop to develop an Internet project in math that you post and invite others to join. Be certain to plan this far enough in advance that you can attract enough participants and develop communication links. Examples of projects that you may wish to post for others to join include:

- **Problems for Problem Solvers.** Invite other classrooms to join you in exchanging interesting math problems to solve together. Appoint one class each week to be the lead class on a rotating basis. The lead class is responsible for developing five problems or puzzles that are sent to participating classes which then have a week to return the answers. The lead class is also responsible for responding to each class and the solutions they suggested. Each week, another class becomes the lead class and circulates five new problems or puzzles for everyone to solve.

- **Heads or Tails?**   Here is a simple project for younger students. Invite other classes to flip a coin from their country ten times and record the number of times that heads turn up. Repeat this ten times. Then have them send the results to your class, which will record all of the data, write up the results, and send back a report with the percentage of times heads turn up during a coin toss. You may wish to invite participating schools to exchange the coins they flipped so that young children become familiar with different currency systems.

- **Statisticians Unite!**   Here is a project for middle school students who are exploring statistics. Invite a group of participating classes to join you in working through the experiences at **Statistics Every Writer Should Know** (http://nilesonline.com/stats/). After completing these experiences, have each class develop group projects to analyze and report comparative statistics from their country, state, or nation on some category where numerical data is kept. Use the site **Finding Data on the Internet: A Journalist's Guide** (http://nilesonline.com/data/links.shtml) to obtain these data. Then share the reports that were developed and provide responses to each report.

- **Graph your Favorite**   (http://www1.minn.net:80/~schubert/Graph.html). This activity was completed by students in grade 2, 4, and 6 classrooms in Michigan, Minnesota, Canada, Australia, and California. Students in eight participating classes voted each week on their favorite item in one category: pets, holidays, sports, school subjects, food. The data was calculated separately for boys and for girls. Participating classes sent their data to the project coordinator who compiled the results each week and e-mailed it to everyone for further analysis. Students used the data in raw form to make their own spreadsheets, both manually and by computer. They also made computer bar graphs and pie graphs as well as manually drawn bar graphs. Then they analyzed the graphs and drew conclusions.

Internet Inquiry

Part of thinking mathematically involves identifying questions that are important to you and then seeking answers to those questions. Internet Inquiry allows you to support these more independent experiences among your students.

You will recall from the previous chapters that Internet Inquiry usually contains five phases: question, search, analyze, compose, and share. Students identify an important question they wish to explore, search for resources to help them understand the information related to this question, analyze the data they have obtained, compose a presentation of their work, and then share their work with others. These steps may also be used to structure Internet Inquiry in mathematics.

Sometimes, it is possible to organize Internet Inquiry around interesting sites that already exist on the Internet. Examples include the very rich sites that exist for the following:

Pi Mathematics—(http://www.ncsa.uiuc.edu:80/edu/RSE/RSEorange/buttons.html)

Have students read about the history of pi, view a video, complete several different activities, calculate the best deal on several pizzas, and share their favorite pizza topping with students around the world. Have them write up a report on their experiences and share them with others. Soon, you will have to have a sign-up list for this site during Internet Inquiry.

A Fractals Lesson—(http://cml.rice.edu:80/~lanius/frac/)

Have students explore this site during Internet Inquiry, making a fractal, learning how fractals are related to chopping broccoli, and viewing many fractals on the WWW. Then have them prepare a poster session on fractals for the class including examples they printed out from sites on the WWW.

Mega Mathematics—(http://www.c3.lanl.gov/mega-math/) (See Figure 8-3.)

There are so many wonderful Internet Inquiry possibilities at this site that it is hard to know where to begin. From a seemingly simple coloring problem that has perplexed cartographers for centuries, to the mathematics of knots, to issues of infinity, to graphs and games, this site has enough intriguing issues to keep any student thinking mathematically for a year. Point students to this site and stand back. Set a bookmark!

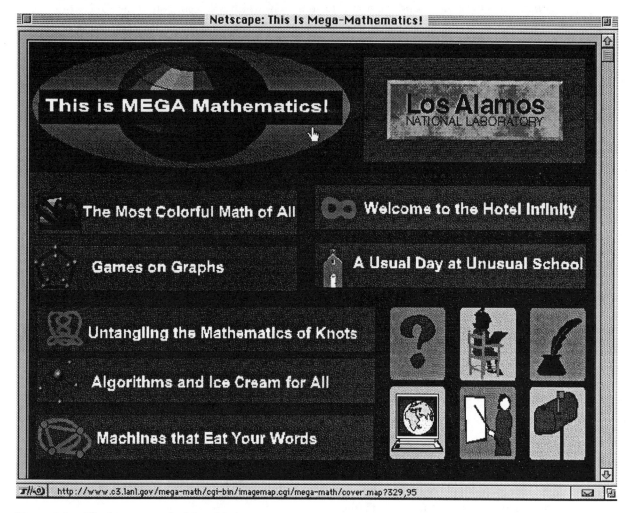

Figure 8-3.   The home page for Mega Mathematics
              (http://www.c3.lanl.gov/mega-math/)

Another approach to Internet Inquiry is to encourage students to explore sites containing links to many different topics in mathematics. As students explore these sites, encourage them to explore and define a project they wish to complete. You could direct them to any of the central sites described earlier in the chapter or you could direct them to some of these locations:

Knot a Braid—(http://www.mta.ca/~rrosebru/kbl/knotlinks.html

Here is a great math location for students exploring for an Inquiry project. Each week a new site is selected in math. Previous links are available so that you can go down the list until you find something really interesting. It won't be hard at this location.

Interactive Mathematics Miscellany and Puzzles—(http://mars.superlink.net/abogom/)

Have students do an Internet Inquiry on one of the puzzles or problems at this site. Be certain to encourage them to report on the history behind the problem as well as the problem itself. They may wish to visit some of the history sites mentioned earlier to gather information.

As you do more and more Internet Inquiry with your students, consider having a Math Fair in which students present their projects in a "poster session." If you can, schedule this at a time when parents can attend so that they can witness all the wonderful things you are doing with your students.

Instructional Resources on the Internet

About Today's Date—(http://acorn.educ.nottingham.ac.uk/cgi-bin/daynum)

Have students visit this page each day to find out interesting information about each of the numbers from 1 to 31. Your kids will learn a lot by just reading the information at these pages. Post the information in class, too, in your math center. Make a bookmark!

Big Sky Telegraph Math Lesson Plans—(gopher://bvsd.k12.co.us/11/Educational_Resources/Lesson_Plans/Big%20Sky/math)

Any site with a name like this has to be good! A good location for lesson plans in math. This is a gopher site but it contains many useful math activities.

Educational Sites for Math—(http://www.enc.org/resmath.htm)

Here is a set of great links to wonderful sites for mathematics education selected by the Eisenhower National Center for Science and Math. From a fractal microscope, to a location for Googolplex, to Virtual Polyhedra, this resource has great sites for students and teachers. Set a bookmark!

Explorer—(http://unite.ukans.edu/)

The Explorer is a collection of educational resources including instructional software, lab activities, and lesson plans for K–12 mathematics and science education.

A nice collection for busy teachers. Even though the interface is not always easy to understand, it is still worth the time you may spend to explore and figure it out.

Finding Data on the Internet—(http://nilesonline.com/data/)

Here is the place to get nearly every piece of statistical data on states, countries, cities, and other geographical and political units. A treasure trove for data snoopers and a great place for older students to explore during Internet Inquiry.

Jumpin' Jehosaphat the Counting Sheep—(http://www.tiac.net/users/sdodds/Java/Jj.html)

Here is a sheep that will solve addition, subtraction, multiplication, and division problems for your younger students. It jumps and counts out the answer, in Sheepese. Much fun, but it requires Netscape 3.0 or later to run.

MacTutor History of Mathematics archive—(http://www-groups.dcs.st-and.ac.uk:80/~history/)

Interested in the history of mathematics? Here is the URL 4 U. Find out who the mathematician of the day is or read the biographies of famous mathematicians and learn about their accomplishments. It contains many unique links to sites about the history of mathematics.

NCTM Standards—(http://www.enc.org:80/online/NCTM/280dtoc1.html)

This is the document that has had a powerful effect on the way many people think about mathematics instruction. Reading it can provide you with useful insights about this area of the curriculum.

On-line Mathematics Dictionary—(http://www.mathpro.com/math/glossary/glossary.html)

Need to know what amicable numbers are? How about a deficient number? Or a rusty compass? Boy, could your students have fun with this page. This is a great resource when you encounter an unusual word in math.

Past Notable Women of Computing & Mathematics—(http://www.cs.yale.edu/homes/tap/past-women.html)

Here is a great location to help students become aware of the many contributions made by women to the development of mathematics. Many interesting biographies and also a location for students to submit their own reports on notable women in mathematics.

Statistics Every Writer Should Know—(http://nilesonline.com/stats/)

This is an excellent tutorial for students learning about simple statistics, including means, medians, per cent, per capita, and more. A great interactive tutorial to help middle school students understand these concepts.

The World of Escher—(http://www.texas.net/escher/)

M.C. Escher was a wonderfully talented and self-taught artist who employed many principles of mathematics in his tessellations (repeated geometric patterns). Visit this site and marvel at the images he created. How about an Inquiry study of this person and his work?

Listservs/Mailing Lists for Math Education

IMSE-L (listserv@uwf.cc.uwf.edu)

A discussion group on math and science education sponsored by the Institute for Math and Science Education.

MATHSED-L (listserv@deakin.edu.au)

A discussion group on mathematics in education.

NCTM-L (listproc@sci-ed.fit.edu)

A discussion group on math education sponsored by the National Council of Teachers of Mathematics.

TIMS-L (listserv@uicvm.uic.edu)

A discussion group sponsored by the Teaching Integrated Mathematics and Science (TIMS) Project.

MATHEDCC (listserv@vm1.mcgill.ca)

A discussion group focusing on technology in math education.

SUSIG (listserv@miamiu.bitnet)

A discussion group on math education.

Usenet Newsgroups for Math Education

k12.chat.teacher—Informal discussion among teachers in grades K–12.

k12.ed.math—Mathematics curriculum in K–12 education.

pnet.school.k-12—Discussion about K–12 education.

pnet.school.k-5—Discussion about K–5 education.

Chapter 9
Special Ideas for Younger Children: Using the Internet in the Primary Grades

```
To:     Our readers
From:   djleu@sued.syr.edu (Don Leu),
        ddleu@syr.edu (Debbie Leu)
Re:     Using the Internet in the Primary Grades

    The primary grades are aptly named. In these grades (K-3),
children receive their primary learning experiences, experiences
that will last them a lifetime. If you are a primary grade
teacher, you are already aware of this fact. You are very con-
cerned about the start you provide for your students and you have
shouldered this additional responsibility because you believe you
have something special to contribute to their young lives.
Thoughtful Internet use becomes especially important at these
grade levels.
    You will find in this chapter a number of ideas to assist you
with these responsibilities and a number of web sites that are
especially useful when working with young children. Electronic
coloring books, dogs that bark out the answers to math problems,
stories that are read aloud by young children in other class-
rooms, a guided tour of the White House by Socks the cat, and a
number of other resources are all available to assist you. We
expect you and your students will enjoy these experiences as you
discover new things about the world around us.

    Don and Debbie
```

Justin, Leo, and Marisa were working together at the Internet computer in their kindergarten classroom.

"Make it yellow. Make the worm yellow."

"No. Worm's aren't yellow. They brown. Where's brown."

"There's brown. Click brown. Now click the paintbrush. Now click the worm."

"Cool!"

They were at **Carlos' Coloring Book** (http://www.ravenna.com/coloring/), a site their teacher had bookmarked for her students. (See Figure 9-1.) Ms. Dye's class was exploring color names and she thought this site would be good for her students, getting them to talk about color names as they learned simple computer skills such as clicking the mouse and using bookmarks. It had worked out well; she found students using the names of the colors as they worked together to electronically color pictures in this coloring book.

"Look, the message says we gotta read the ABC book today," Marisa said. "Go to the ABC book. Click on the bookmarks and go to the ABC book."

Each morning, Ms. Dye read a morning message to the children. Each morning message mentioned an Internet Activity for her students to complete. She knew their interest in this new classroom resource would mean that many would try to read this part of the message on their own. Today the message was:

Wednesday, October 10

It is a rainy day.

Today we will have music.

Please read the ABC book on the computer.

I made a bookmark.

　　Ms. Dye

Justin printed a copy of the apple he had just finished on the class's new color printer. Then the three of them selected the bookmark Ms. Dye mentioned in the morning message and explored the alphabet book at **ABC Educational Games** (http://www.klsc.com/children/Alpha.html). They talked about the pictures and letters as they worked their way through the alphabet.

"My turn," announced Kevin as he walked over to the computer corner. He pointed to the clock. "The big hand is on 12 and Ms. Dye said it's my turn when the big hand's on 12. You got to stop now. My turn."

Justin, Leo, and Marissa moved over for Kevin and watched as he selected the bookmark for the **What is it?** location (http://www.uq.oz.au/nanoworld/whatisit.html) of **Nanoworld** (http://www.uq.oz.au/nanoworld/nanohome.html), a site in Australia with many strange-looking pictures of objects taken with an electron microscope. Each week, she selected a picture from the files at this location or from **Scanning Electron Microscope** (http://www.mos.org/sln/sem/index.html) and had students draw a picture of the object and then write a description of what they thought it was. It was always great fun to have students share their pictures and read their invented spelling for this activity during a brief Internet Workshop.

"Cool. It's a snake."

"No, it's a fish bone."

"It looks like a tunnel."

Ignoring all of these suggestions, Kevin carefully drew his picture of the strange shape and wrote below his picture:

KEVIN

I THK S A FRS

"What you say?" asked Justin.

Proudly, Kevin read his work, "I think it's a forest."

Figure 9-1.   One of several interactive coloring books available on the Internet:
Carlos' Coloring Book (http://www.ravenna.com/coloring/)

Lessons from the Classroom

This episode from Ms. Dye's classroom demonstrates how the Internet contains many locations that may support classroom learning among even the very youngest learners at school. In a short period of time, these students had many important experiences with letters, words, pictures, and colors. There are many locations on the Internet that can support children as they learn lessons important to their emerging understanding of the world around them.

The episode also illustrates how thoughtful teachers can integrate Internet Activities into instructional practices that already take place in their primary grade classrooms. In this class, Ms. Dye always listed an Internet Activity in her message of the day experience with the class. She used the message of the day at the beginning of school to expose students to print and to encourage them to use print to obtain information. She found that students paid particular attention to the Internet Activity she wrote in the message and would refer to it often throughout the school day. Children would come up to the message and point to each word as they tried to read it. Others would point to it from the computer as they reminded others of what they were supposed to do.

The episode in Ms. Dye's class also illustrates a third lesson: it is important for lower grade classrooms to obtain the best technology possible, since this provides important support for students, especially in its ability to provide multimedia resources to students who are not yet fluent readers. Ms. Dye had one of the few color printers in her school and a powerful multimedia computer, capable of playing speech, animation, and sound very quickly.

Last year she had written a memo to her principal. She pointed out that the kindergarten always had the oldest computer in the school and that this was not fair. She suggested that her young students really deserved the very best technologies so that they could benefit from having stories read aloud to them on the Internet, so that they could learn color names faster, and so that they could view the memory-rich, multimedia resources available on the Internet. She pointed out that older students could read text but that her students needed the new speech technologies to be able to learn to read and write. She also noted that a color printer would help her children learn color names. Apparently, her arguments were compelling; at the beginning of the year she found a multimedia computer and color printer in her classroom. Ms. Dye was taking full advantage of their potential to support her young children.

E-Mail for You

From: Isabelle Hoag <hoag@eruronet.nl>
Subject: Permission Slips

Dear Teacher,

   I was both nervous and excited when my class got hooked up to the internet! I asked several people for their ideas about having the kids surf around and about making our own page. I hope this helps you, too.

   First, I was worried that my third graders might find a site that I would not want them to see for some reason. To guard against this I made up the "Bookmark plus four" rule. They must ask to use Netscape. Then they must start with a site that I have saved on our list of favorites or "bookmarks." They can follow four links from that starting point and then they must return or start with another bookmark. They can show me sites they would like to add to our bookmarks.

   Next, I was worried that the kids would buy something or download a virus or sign up for something. There are many attractive blinking icons tht scream "click here!" and children are being taught to follow instructions! So my class has strict instructions to never, ever write their name or give out any information when they are surfing. They must come and get me if they are asked for information.

   When setting up my own pages, I wrote a permission slip similar to the ones I use for field trips. Only photos, work and first names of children for whom I have permission slips are used. I only use first names and never identify children in photos.

   This is a new technology and if treated with respect and caution it is a valuable resource in the class! Have fun!

   Isabelle Hoag
   Primary School Teacher
   The Internatioal School of Amsterdam

General Issues for the Primary Grades

There are several issues that require special attention if you are fortunate enough to work with children in the primary grades: child safety, supporting emergent navigation skills, and seeking supportive technologies. Each is essential to keep in mind as you work with young children on the Internet.

Child safety is a critical concern for young children unfamiliar with the Internet. As a teacher you are responsible for your students' physical safety in the classroom. You are also responsible for new safety issues that now arise because of the Internet. Chapter 2 described the nature of acceptable use policies often used to establish rules for the appropriate use of the Internet and prevent young children from viewing objectionable locations.

Primary grade teachers, because their children are especially naive about the world, will need to pay particular attention to child safety on the Internet. We have always discussed fire safety and traffic safety in primary classrooms. Now we must begin to discuss Internet safety. You may wish to discuss issues of Internet safety as they arise in your class within an Internet Workshop as described in Chapter 4.

Often teachers in the very youngest grades (K–1) will limit children's use of the Internet to sites with a bookmark. While children may travel out from the locations you have bookmarked through hyperlinks to other sites, this does limit the viewing of inappropriate locations.

Internet safety is not limited to the viewing of inappropriate sites; it also applies to e-mail. Most school districts will require that all incoming and outgoing e-mail messages for primary grade students go through the classroom teacher's account so that you may monitor the e-mail communication of your students and ensure their safety. Should you find any inappropriate messages from strangers, you should immediately report the incident to your principal or another designated person in your district. You should also respond to the message, indicating that you have reported it to a supervisor.

Another important aspect of Internet use in the primary grades is to help children learn basic navigation strategies. Learning about hyperlinks, bookmarks, mouse skills, and other emergent navigation strategies are important for the very youngest learners. You should not assume that your students have these skills but, rather, plan systematically to support their development. Having students work with partners during computer time, using Internet Workshop, and developing very simple scavenger hunts for your young students are all ways to support this aspect of Internet use. Simply worded scavenger hunts that students complete in pairs or small groups are especially useful. These develop navigation strategies as students also practice functional reading and writing tasks. When you ask students to write down an answer during a scavenger hunt, look for words that are displayed on the screen so that they may copy them onto their worksheet. This will make it easier for your youngest students to successfully complete this literacy experience.

Finally, we want to speak up in support of primary grade teachers seeking and receiving supportive technologies to assist the youngest learners. Often, schools follow a hand-me-down policy with computers; primary grade classrooms receive the oldest computers that are passed down from the high school, to the middle school, and finally to the elementary school. This is unfortunate since the youngest learners benefit the most from the latest technologies and the most powerful computers. These enable stories to be read aloud, provide animations to explain challenging meanings, and play audio clips to enhance meaning. In order to take full advantage of these types of resources on the Internet, you will require a computer with at least 16 MB of RAM (a type of memory). This much memory is required to run Netscape 3.0 or later versions with multimedia plug-ins. If you find yourself teaching in the primary grades without a computer capable of using the multimedia technologies at web sites, consider Ms. Dye's approach—take your concerns to your principal, explaining the greater need young children have for the latest technologies.

Central Sites for the Primary Grades

We have been unable to locate a site on the Internet that contains an extensive set of links exclusively for students in grades K–3. Perhaps someone out there is now working on such a site to support our younger learners. In the meantime, you will have to visit central sites designed for all of the elementary grades and sort through those that may be most appropriate for your students. As you visit these locations, consider setting a bookmark for each place that looks like it has possibilities for your students, even if it will be used later in the year. You may wish to make separate folders to organize bookmarks for units you will be teaching later in the year.

Most central sites for young children tend to be located at commercial locations on the Internet that are open to everyone. These commercial sites can be identified by the ".com" at the end of their URL. Some tend to disappear after a while, perhaps because they were economically unsuccessful. Some will contain commercial advertising.

One place to begin your search is at **Yahooligans** (http://www.yahooligans.com/). This is one of the largest collections of useful sites for children with links that are screened before being accepted. As with all lists, though, one can never guarantee the contents of links that move away from these sites. Thus, you must still monitor student use. You may wish to set a bookmark for Yahooligans and allow students in the older primary grades access to this information. For younger students, you may wish to preview locations, set bookmarks, and only allow children to use the bookmarks you have set.

There is also an excellent set of sites for young children located at **Berit's Best Sites for Children** (http://www.cochran.com/theosite/KSites.html). These have been screened and rated. Each of them also contains a short review describing the contents. Many will indicate the approximate grade level for the activities at the location.

You may also wish to visit Magellan's **KidZone** (http://www.mckinley.com/browse_bd.cgi?KidZone). This location contains many sites of interest to children. The list of links at this location contains short descriptions of each site, along with a star rating used to identify the better sites.

If you are looking for a master list of central sites for children, pay a visit to **Berit's Other Sites for Children** (http://www.cochran.com/theosite/Ksites_part5.html#more). This lists many locations where you may find useful links.

Keeping It Simple: Internet Activity Assignments

If you visit central sites for the primary grades, you will quickly find many locations that will fit into an Internet Activity. These may include coloring books, alphabet books, and stories (some of which are read aloud) for the youngest children. They will also include activities in literature, math, science, and social studies for older students. As you have already discovered, Internet Activities are easy to develop. Simply find a location related to your classroom curriculum, set a bookmark for it, develop a brief activity, and then have your students complete the activity during the week. You may want to develop several activities for your students to explore during the week instead of just one. Often, it is also useful to include a writing activity with the assignment to support young children's developing literacy ability. These writing activities may then be shared during Internet Workshop at the end of each week.

Here are some examples of Internet Activities that might be used with students in the primary grades:

Alex's Scribbles—Koala Trouble—(http://www.peg.apc.org/~balson/story/) (See Figure 9-2.)

This site from Australia features an extensive collection of wonderful stories about Max, the koala bear, by Alex Balsom (5 years old) and his dad. It is quickly becoming a cult classic on the Internet for young children. The stories contain hyperlinks within the illustrations; these require children to click on the correct location in the illustration in order to move forward in the story. Have children draw a picture of Max and write their own story after reading one of these delightful adventures. Then have them read their stories during Internet Workshop.

Internet Coloring Books—There are a number of coloring books on the Internet for very young children to enjoy. Have children print out their work and then write something about what they have completed. Some sites provide interactive opportunities to color illustrations right on the screen. Others only have black-and-white illustrations to be printed out and then colored. Interactive sites include: **Kendra's Coloring Book** (http://www.gcg.com/misc/colorbook/) and **Carlos' Coloring Book** (http://www.ravenna.com/coloring/). Non-interactive sites include: **TV Ontario Colouring Book** (http://www.tvo.org/cb_eng/) and

E-Mail for You

From: Jeff Scanlan < jscanlan@powerup.com.au >
     Queensland, Australia
Subject: My experience with the Internet

I have not yet been able to achieve an Internet connection at
my school so I have had to do it all from home. It is a little
inconvenient but rewarding just the same. To begin with I "surfed
the net" looking for schools that would like to correspond via e-
mail with us. After several blind alleys I found someone in Massachusetts who was interested and we have had an extensive exchange between students in our classes. The very fact that there
is someone on the other side of the world who will listen to you
has a powerful effect on children's writing if there is a chance
that what is done will be shared in another country.

I began by getting the children to write introductory letters
but I found that children need guidance to do this. They tend to
just want to outline details of family and pets which can be a
little boring. What I then did was to ask children to write about
something that had happened recently to them and how they felt
about that experience. This seemed to work much better. I explained that it is always much more interesting to read how someone feels about an experience rather than just learning that
something has happened. When I had it all together I asked a
parent to come to the school and type the letters which were then
put on a floppy disk for me to take home to my computer and send.

There were activities other than letter writing that I used.
One successful idea was to gather data about the children in my
class. I then asked my students to draw graphs to represent the
information we gathered: how many children were born interstate,
how many parents worked locally or in the city nearby, etc. We
also drew a plan of the school which helped the children in understanding measurement. (I posted this information by regular
mail because I did not have a scanner).

It is said that computing is an adventure. Well, I'm still
learning . . .

    Jeff Scanlan, Teacher
    Year 4 (8 year olds)
    Alexandra Hills State School
    12 Princeton Avenue
    Alexandra Hills 4161
    Queensland, Australia

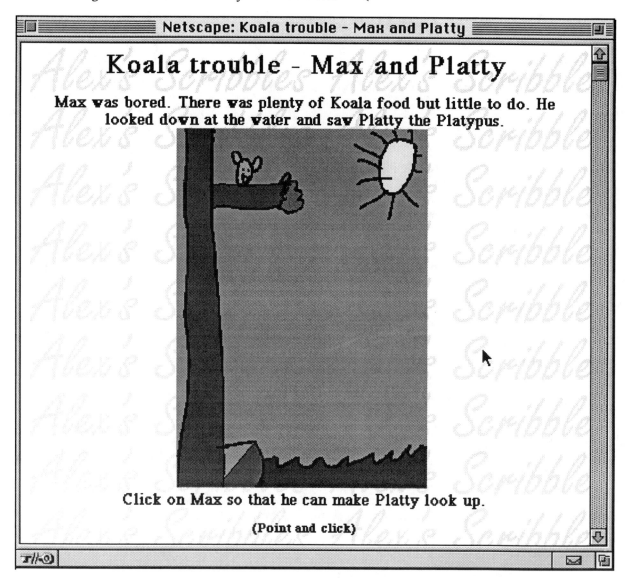

Figure 9-2.   A page from a story at Alex's Scribbles—Koala Trouble (http://www.peg.apc.org/~balson/story/)

NASA's Space Coloring Book (http://tommy.jsc.nasa.gov/~woodfill/SPACEED/SEHHTML/color.html).

Hangman at Kids Corner—(http://www.ot.com:80/cgi/kids/hangman)

Here is a fun site for this traditional game. It is a great place for kids to develop their decoding and spelling talents as they complete an Internet Activity.

Blue Dog Can Count—(http://kao.ini.cmu.edu:5550/bdf.html)

At this location, children can write an addition, subtraction, division, or multiplication problem and listen as Blue Dog barks out the answer. This is a great place to check one's work. Better yet, have one student write the problem while the other predicts the answer. Then see if they agree with old Blue Dog. Great fun. Set a bookmark!

Jumpin' Jehosaphat the Counting Sheep—(http://www.tiac.net/users/sdodds/Java/Jj.html)

This is a site that is similar to Blue Dog, only here Jumpin' Jehosaphat jumps and bleets out the answer.

How a Book Is Made—(http://www.harpercollins.com/kids/book.htm)

If your children enjoy works by the author Aliki, here is a great site for them, because it describes how she writes and publishes a book. Also at this site is a location to download directions to make a pop-up book. Have students read Aliki's article, then have them make a pop-up book.

In addition to these traditional uses of sites for Internet Activities, it is also possible to use your computer as a fixed resource to support very young children's literacy development, as Ms. Dye did. For example, find an unusual image each day to display on the screen and encourage your students to draw a picture of this image and then write down what they think it is. A great source of these images is the **Nanoworld Image Gallery** (http://www.uq.oz.au:80/nanoworld/images_1.html), where you will find images taken by an electron microscope. (See Figure 9-3.) Sometimes images will contain the label for the item. This is also useful for students who may wish to copy the word down as they write a sentence describing the picture they see. This can easily be set up as an Internet Activity for kindergarten classrooms, with children's pictures and writing shared during Internet Workshop.

Figure 9-3.   An image from the Nanoworld Image Gallery used in a writing activity for young children (http://www.uq.oz.au:80/nanoworld/images_1.html)

Internet Projects

Permanent sites with Internet Projects for the primary grades are beginning to appear on the Internet. Given the power of this type of experience, we suspect that more will soon follow. One of the more comprehensive locations has been developed by a third grade teacher and a parent, **The Mind's Eye Monster Exchange Project** (http://www.csnet.net/minds-eye/). (See Figure 9-4.) This site puts together classes that wish to participate. Then, students draw a picture of a monster and write a description of what it looks like. Paired classes exchange their descriptions and attempt to draw a picture of what they think the other students' monsters look like. Finally, the images of all monsters are posted at the Monster Exchange Project so that classes may see the originals and compare them with the descriptions that were written. Many lesson plans and extension ideas are also listed at this location for teachers. Because the site is run without charge, there is a limit on the number of participating classes. Also, it is possible the site may charge a small fee in the future in order to support all of the interchanges between classes.

In addition to permanent sites such as this one, you should also visit locations on the Internet where less permanent Internet Projects are described, inviting you and other teachers to join in classroom inter-

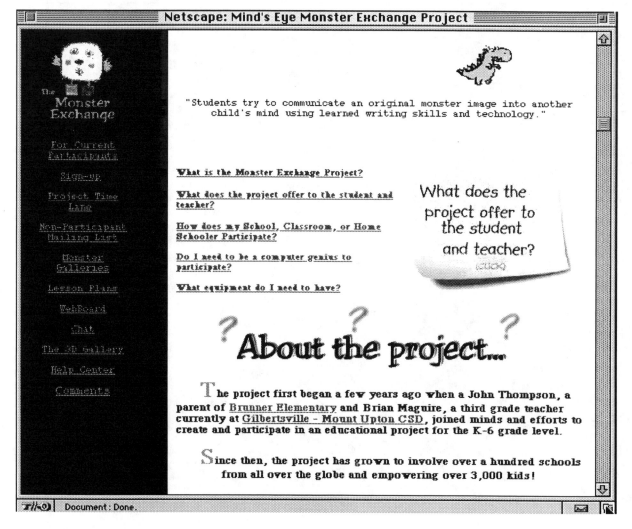

Figure 9-4.   The home page for The Mind's Eye Monster Exchange Project
(http://www.csnet.net/minds-eye/).

changes. Or, you may come up with your own idea for a great project and invite other teachers to join you. Locations where teachers post projects and invite others to join them have been described in other chapters. They include:

- **The Global SchoolNet Projects Registry**—(http://www.gsn.org/gsn/proj/index.html)
- **The Global School House: The Connected Classroom**—(http://www.gsh.org/class/default.htm)
- **KIDPROJ**—(http://www.kidlink.org:80/KIDPROJ/)
- **NickNack's Telecollaborative Learning Page**—(http://www1.minn.net:80/~schubert/NickNacks.html#anchor100100).
- **Classroom Connect's Teacher Contact Database**—(http://www.classroom.net/contact/)

Examples of projects you may wish to consider joining or developing for primary grade students include:

- **The Eric Carle Book Club.**   Invite other classes to read works by Eric Carle (or another popular author). Then, using writing process activities, share children's written responses to these works with each classroom. Also, consider polling each class about their favorite books by this author and sharing the results with other classes. When all of the results are in, have each class develop a graph to display the results. Send the results of your work to the author and see if he/she responds.

- **Amazing Insects.**   Join a third grade class in Minnesota as they study insects during the year and share the results of their studies with classes around the world. Writing, math, literature, and science are woven into this project. This project even has a home web site (http://www.minnetonka.k12.mn.us/groveland/insect.proj/insects.html).

- **Playground Chants Around the World.**   Playground chants are part of every child's culture no matter where they go to school. Have your students write these down carefully and exchange them with classes at other locations around the world. Communicate with classes to find out the meanings of chants that are unfamiliar to your students. This is a wonderful way to support reading and writing in your primary grade classroom and to discover important aspects of other cultures.

- **Teddy Bears Travel the World.**   Have each participating class purchase a small teddy bear and send it to one of the other classrooms. In each class, the teddy must go home with a different child each night. Each child must then write a description of the what they did, where they went, and what it was like at their location. These should be developed with the parent/guardian and returned to school. Each day, these messages go out to each participating class to be read by the students. A map can be marked to show where each Teddy is in the world. At the end, Teddy bears can be mailed back to the home classrooms with souvenirs from its host classroom.

Internet Inquiry

Independent Internet Inquiry projects occur less frequently in the primary grades than they do at other grade levels. Part of the reason for this is child safety. Parents are often reluctant to have their young children independently exploring resources on the Internet. As a result, school boards often will place limits on children's independent Internet use at these younger levels. A more common reason, however, is that children at this age are still developing navigation skills. Because these skills have yet to be completely developed, it simply takes too long for many students to acquire useful information about a topic or project that interests them. Finally, the speed of obtaining information on the Internet is also impeded by young children's emerging literacy ability. Even when children do find resources that are related to their Inquiry project, they are not always able to understand the information. Thus, independent inquiry projects are less common in the primary grades than at older grade levels.

It is useful, though, to spend time supporting children as they develop navigation skills. Indeed, some teachers will focus on navigation as a subject for Internet Inquiry. Usually this is developed during Internet

Workshop time when teachers encourage children to share some new strategy they have discovered and to seek advice about something they do not understand. Teachers, too, will develop navigation skills through the use of regular scavenger hunts on the Internet, usually in groups or pairs. These results will be shared during Internet Workshop as a way of discussing navigation strategies.

Instructional Resources on the Internet

Animal Tracks—(http://www.nwf.org/nwf/kids/)

The National Wildlife Federation has developed this site for kids interested in animals and the environment. It contains interactive games for the youngest users, riddles and jokes for older students, and even articles from past issues of *Ranger Rick*. A nice location during units on animals and the environment.

Carnival World—(http://www.lifelong.com/CarnivalWorld/CarnivalHP.html)

A commercial site, to be sure, but several nice examples of talking storybooks are located here. If you have downloaded the plug-in and text-to-speech software from Monster Math (see below), come to this location and visit the talking storybooks that can be used for Internet Activities. These are very nice for the youngest readers.

Concertina—(http://www.iatech.com/books/intro.html)

Concertina is a new Canadian publisher of children's books. They have placed several nice selections here for young children. Some sounds are available within the books.

Internet Resources—(http://www.sln.org/resources.html)

This location on the Science Learning Network contains many resources for science education. Click on the search button to search for existing science activities for students at your grade level. This is a great location to quickly locate an Internet Activity for your science units. Set a bookmark!

Kid Safety on the Internet—(http://www.uoknor.edu/oupd/kidsafe/start.htm)

This site contains questions and answers to help kids protect themselves and handle emergencies. It covers Internet safety as well as other types of situations. It may be helpful for students in the 2nd and 3rd grades.

Learn the Alphabet—(http://www.klsc.com/children/Alpha.html)

This location has several nice activities for your youngest learners: an alphabet book, a game where you match a letter with a picture, a game where you match a word with the picture, and a counting book.

Monster Math—(http://www.lifelong.com/CarnivalWorld/MonsterMath/MonMathHP.html)

One of the first sites on the Internet to use text-to-speech technology, a real boon for children in the primary grades. At this site you will find a series of easy math problems woven into a story format for young children. Directions and links are provided to obtain the plug-in that will read all of the pages aloud to children. It will even read it in Spanish. Set a bookmark!

Space ABC's—(http://buckman.pps.k12.or.us/room100/abcspace/spaceabc.html)

Here is a great alphabet book on outer space developed during a science unit by the students in a K–2 class at Buckman School in Portland, Oregon. Many of the pages have RealAudio files so your students can have them read aloud by the children who wrote them. If K–2 children can do this, think what your students could do. And think what it would be like if we all developed such wonderful materials for other classes to use. Set a bookmark!

Stage Hands Puppets Activity Page—(http://fox.nstn.ca/~puppets/activity.html)

If you are interested in using puppets in your classroom here is the site for you! Puppet activities are a wonderful way to support language development in the primary grades. This location is rich in resources, including an interactive experience to allow students to design their own puppet on the screen, an on-line puppet theater where you can read plays developed by other children and submit your own play, performance tips from "The Professor" (students can also ask the professor questions and see the answers), paper puppets and patterns to download, ideas for using scraps to make puppets, and links to other puppet sites. Set a bookmark!

The Ant Who Thought He Was a Penguin—(http://www.webmonkey.com/demo/96/34/talkerdemo/index.html

If you have downloaded the plug-in and text-to-speech software from Monster Math (see page 154), pay a visit to this humorous talking storybook. It may be a little challenging for your youngest students to understand, but it is great fun and an example of similar sites that are on the way.

The Dog House—(http://www.unitedmedia.com/comics/peanuts/)

Here is the home of Snoopy, Charley Brown, and the whole gang. Young children really enjoy comics and here they can read many of the strips from Charley Brown. They can also play games and read up on their favorite character from the comic strip.

The Dr. King Timeline Page—(http://buckman.pps.k12.or.us/room100/timeline/kingframe.html)

Who is this teacher and who are these kids at the Buckman School in Portland? Here is another wonderful work of literature for young kids. A great follow-up activity after reading together *My Dream of Martin Luther King* by Faith Ringgold or a unit on this important American.

The White House for Kids—(http://www.whitehouse.gov/WH/kids/html/kidshome.html)

Have your kids take a tour of the White House conducted by Socks, the cat. A fun activity for your students to complete as an Internet Activity. Your students can even write a letter to the president. Set a bookmark!

Listservs/Mailing Lists for the Primary Grades

ECENET-L (listserv@postoffice.cso.uiuc.edu)

A discussion group on early childhood education (0–8 years)

PROJECTS-L (listserv@postoffice.cso.uiuc.edu)

A group interested in using a project approach in early childhood education

RTEACHER (listserv@listserv.syr.edu)

A discussion group on using technology to support literacy learning sponsored by *The Reading Teacher*, a journal of the International Reading Association.

Usenet Newsgroups Lists for the Primary Grades

k12.chat.elementary—Informal discussion among elementary students, grades K–5.

k12.chat.teacher—Informal discussion among teachers in grades K–12.

pnet.school.k-5—Discussion about K–5 education.

Section III

The Internet Classroom: Putting It All Together

Chapter 10
Using the Internet to Increase Multicultural Understanding

```
To:    Our readers
From:  djleu@sued.syr.edu (Don Leu),
       ddleu@syr.edu (Debbie Leu)
Re:    The Internet Brings Each of Us Closer Together

    A really exciting aspect of the Internet's potential in edu-
cation is the opportunity it provides to increase multicultural
understanding and celebrate the diversity that defines our lives.
As we observe conflicts around the world, based largely on the
inability of different cultural and religious groups to respect
and understand one another, it helps us to better appreciate
stable societies with diverse cultural traditions. The United
States, for example, is home to over one hundred different lin-
guistic groups, over 700 religions, and countless ethnic and
cultural groups. The U.S. has the greatest variety of multi-
ethnic households in the history of the world. In the Los Angeles
School District, more than 80 different languages are taught.
Societies like the U.S. only survive if each member develops a
common commitment to respecting the rights of others and the
cultural context from which they come. This is not something that
should be left to chance. Instead, we need to actively support
multicultural understanding at every opportunity. The Internet is
a new and very special tool in these efforts.
    This chapter will demonstrate the potential of this technol-
ogy to draw each of us closer to others who come from different
cultural contexts. Understanding others and the cultural context
from which they come is an increasingly important goal as we
build a global village with this new technology.

    Don and Debbie
```

"But I don't understand why we can't write to Native American students," said Desmon. "I don't understand why it hurts their feelings when we say we are studying their culture."

Desmon was reporting during an Internet Workshop session in Ms. Meadows' class. The students in her class were doing Internet Inquiry in a unit designed to increase multicultural understanding and build a classroom community. Celebrating different cultural traditions helped to accomplish these goals. Students had been working in groups on Internet Inquiry projects. Some had picked a Hispanic theme and were reading literature and studying about the many different Hispanic cultures. They had found many useful locations on the WWW such as the **Chicano! Homepage** (http://www.pbs.org/chicano/). Others had picked an African-American theme and had decided to focus on the connections they saw between the poetry of Langston Hughes, the actions of Rosa Parks and Martin Luther King, Jr., and the civil rights struggle. Another group had picked a Japanese theme and were studying the literature and cultural traditions of this culture. Through **Web66** (http://web66.coled.umn.edu/schools.html) this group had linked up with another class in Kyoto and were exchanging e-mail messages, discovering many important insights about each other's cultural traditions.

Desmon's group was studying Native American literature and cultures, especially the common respect they all expressed for Mother Earth. Desmon's group had read many of the prayers, poetry, and stories located at **Indigenous Peoples' Literature** (http://www.indians.org/welker/framenat.htm) as they developed a growing respect for the traditions, struggles, and views of Native Americans. **A Line in the Sand** (http://hanksville.phast.umass.edu:8000/cultprop/) had been especially useful. In addition, they read a number of books from the library including: *Thirteen Moons on Turtles Back,* by Bruchac and London, *Giving Thanks: A Native American Good Morning Message* by Chief Jake Swamp, *Ceremony—In the Circle of Life* by White Deer of Autumn, *Buffalo Woman* by Gobel, and *Chief Sarah: Sarah Winnemucca's Fight for Indian Rights* by Morrison. They had also been exploring some of the many Native American sites on the web. They were excited when they found a great location, **Native American Indian** (http://indy4.fdl.cc.mn.us/~isk/mainmenu.html, and discovered a place to post a message (http://indy4.fdl.cc.mn.us/~isk/schools/schlbook.html) in hopes of linking up with Native American students who might be interested in becoming KeyPals. But then they came across a message from the author of this site, saying:

> Non-Indians: teachers, kids, please do not say "studying Native Americans and want to correspond with some." This is offensive, racist. This service is primarily a way for Indian kids to get in contact with each other, not a method of providing specimens for study by your class or students.

Desmon was sharing his question with the rest of the class. "I didn't know that I was being racist," he said. "And I don't want to hurt anyone's feelings. I just want to understand more about their culture."

This event prompted a lively discussion in Ms. Meadows' class. Some couldn't understand the reason behind the message until Michelle asked how they would feel if someone wrote: "We are studying girls, or Hispanics, or African-Americans, or boys, and we want to correspond with some."

"It makes you feel like a thing, not a person," she noted. "And, there are many different Native American cultures, not just one." This made many students think again about how the person who developed this web site must have felt when reading this kind of message.

The discussion in Ms. Meadows' class was useful in developing greater respect and sensitivity for others, issues at the heart of effective cross-cultural communication and understanding. It increased children's awareness of the power of words and how the words one uses in a message may unintentionally hurt people. It also helped students develop greater sensitivity to different cultural traditions and how one must be respectful of cultural differences on the WWW.

Toward the end of their conversation, Ms. Meadows pointed out that it was important for Native American students to have a space on the WWW to communicate with other students from Native American cultures and that one needed to respect this right. She also noted that some Native American students were interested in communicating with students from non-Native cultural traditions. She said that she had found a location on the web, **Kids from Kanata** (http://www.web.apc.org/webhome/KFK/ kfkhome.html), where Native American and non-Native American classes who wanted to exchange e-mail could do so on Canada's SchoolNet. She wasn't certain if this was open to students in the U.S., but she said she would send a message and see if this would be possible.

Lessons from the Classroom

Ms. Meadows' classroom has several important lessons for us to consider as we think about using the Internet to increase multicultural understanding. First, it is clear that the Internet provides special opportunities to help everyone better understand the importance of appreciating the unique qualities in each of our cultural traditions. No other instructional resource available in your classroom is as rich in its potential for developing an understanding of the diverse nature of our global society and for helping each of your students walk in someone else's footprints.

Ms. Meadows sought to take advantage of this potential. Each group in Ms. Meadows' class had to define and complete an Inquiry project celebrating a special cultural group. Ms. Meadows said that several guidelines had to be followed: their project had to treat the culture with respect, it had to include literature and Internet experiences as part of the project, and each group had to develop a learning experience for the rest of the class based on what they had learned from that culture. One group was planning on building a display and learning center in the classroom along with a parent who was coming in to share cultural artifacts; another was planning on a poetry reading, a readers theater presentation, and an Internet Activity; another was developing a reading corner and a bulletin board; the fourth group was going to do a read aloud activity and develop an Internet scavenger hunt for everyone to complete.

Using the Internet to celebrate the diversity that exists in our world is important for a variety of reasons. Bringing this information into your classroom sends an important message to your students about the respect and dignity each of us needs to accord every human experience. Integrating Internet resources from different cultures into your curriculum is central to accomplishing this important goal. Children feel pride in themselves and their culture when all cultural experiences are valued for the contributions they make to a rich and vibrant society. In addition, students develop a richer appreciation of the historical forces that have shaped our societies and the contributions made by different cultural groups. Finally, the Internet allows all students to explore issues of social justice. Exploring issues of social justice is essential to preparing children for citizenship in a diverse society where these issues are fundamental to our collective well-being.

The episode from Ms. Meadows' class also teaches us a second lesson: e-mail experiences with others may be very useful as you consider using the Internet to increase multicultural understanding. E-mail allows your students to immediately communicate with others around the world who come from different cultural traditions and learn more about their unique heritage. This opportunity has never before existed in school classrooms; it provides your students with powerful cross-cultural experiences that may be used to develop understanding and respect for others.

E-mail, however, is a two-edged sword in developing multicultural understanding. On one side, e-mail removes many of the visual trappings that normally impede conversations between members of different cultural groups; we tend to ignore physical differences and focus, instead, on considering the ideas and experiences of the person with whom we communicate. This is what the students who studied Japanese cultural traditions experienced in Ms. Meadows' class. On the other hand, when we bring stereotypes about a cultural group to e-mail conversations, these stereotypes often appear unintentionally between the lines of our messages and may be hurtful to the recipient. This is what happened when students left messages at the location called Native American Indian. E-mail communication between different cultural groups requires sensitivity to the recipient and an ability to anticipate how a particular message might be interpreted as you compose it. Often, it forces us to confront stereotypes we may have but may not realize. These are good lessons for all of us to learn.

E-Mail for You

From: Angeles Maitland Heriot < maitl_sh@sminter.com.ar >
      Junior 7 Teacher
      St. Hilda's School
      Buenos Aires, Argentina

Subject: Developing Cross-cultural Relationships

Hello!
    St. Hilda's School, Argentina, is a prestigious bi-lingual
institution located in the Province of Buenos Aires. I teach
Language, Literature, and Religious Knowledge in English as a
second language to 17 boys and girls of 11-12 years old.
    The Internet project for this age group, called "To Be or not
to Be," is one of the few interdepartamental projects linking the
Spanish and English sections (and the work of their teachers).
The departments are separate in that they have their own authori-
ties and time tables, as well as staff and curricula. Therefore,
the project stands as an experimental joint venture.
    The computer teacher renders his lessons in Spanish, and he
has a basic comprehension of English. He is responsible for our
Internet project, and I, the teacher of English to the same group
of students, provide him with translations whenever necessary.
The purpose of the project is to give children a meaningful task
in their computing lessons to connect our children with the outer
world, since our school is located in a small suburb in the Province of Buenos Aires, and the exchange with other schools or
children is scarce.
    From a broader perspective, the Internet allows our young
users to become aware of the geography, history, and culture of
the world. It is hoped that our pupils will enlarge their knowledge, and increase their curiosity about other places and races,
while learning to respect different values and ways of living and
to use English to communicate effectively. The incentive to
"talk" with other children all around the world is extremely
powerful. The Internet is an ideal medium, since it requires an
informal writing style, thus allowing the writers certain "literary licenses" (spelling, misprints, punctuation misuse). Pupils
may feel more at ease when they are not required to rewrite their
messages. The Internet encourages children to write and to practice their typing to enjoy the thrill of receiving a message!!!
    On the other hand, teachers need to guide their pupils' work,
so that the context and content of the letters are not misleading
and/or inaccurate. A little time is required before children
realize that no matter how instantaneous the whole process may
be, there is still the need to think to be able to express their
aims clearly.
    I'll be very glad to answer any question you would like to
ask with reference to the Internet at school. We are only experi-
menting with this service in our Argentine context. More connections and more servers are just beginning to appear in the market, offering lower costs and better services.

Angeles Maitland Heriot
Home address: J. de Garay 1051-(1686) Hurlingham-Buenos Aires-
Argentina
tel: 00 54 1 6622392 - fax: 00 54 1 662 6378
e-mail: maitl_sh@sminter.com.ar

Central Sites to Increase Multicultural Understanding

There are many locations on the Internet that provide you with a comprehensive set of resources for helping your students to develop greater understanding of different cultural traditions. You may wish to review the resources at these sites as you develop Internet Activities and Internet Projects with your students. Some locations are also useful for Internet Inquiry.

It is possible that some of the central sites we identify in this section may contain links that eventually link to locations where issues of sexual orientation are considered. While we believe these issues are appropriate for older students to consider, we recognize that a number of communities may feel uncomfortable about allowing younger students to access these sites. We mention this so that you may make informed judgments about which central locations you make available to your students.

The best central sites to support instruction in multicultural understanding include:

Walk a Mile in My Shoes: Multicultural Curriculum Resources—(http://www.wmht.org/trail/explor02.htm)

If you only have time to visit one central site on multicultural issues, be certain you stop here. It is designed specifically for teachers new to the Internet and includes many links in areas such as multicultural literature resources for teachers, multicultural sites for kids, sites for e-mail exchanges, sites with links on specific cultural groups, and sites with links to schools all over the world. Set a bookmark!

Multicultural Pavilion—(http://curry.edschool.Virginia.EDU/go/multicultural/)

Located at the School of Education at the University of Virginia, this location is very well organized. The most useful area is a "Teachers' Corner" where you will find a set of links to important locations on the WWW for multicultural education, links to on-line resources for teachers and students, several historic archives, and links to on-line literature for students.

Diversity—(http://www.execpc.com/~dboals/diversit.html)

This is an enormous collection of links to sites on the WWW related to diversity and multicultural education. It is part of the larger History/Social Studies Web Site for K-12 Teachers. Sections include: general sources, disabilities, migration and immigrant resources, Jewish resources, Asian American resources, African-American resources, Women Studies resources, Native American resources, and Hispanic resources.

CLNET—(http://clnet.ucr.edu/) (See Figure 10-1)

This location at UCLA has an extensive collection of links to sites about Chicana/o Latina/o cultures and resources. Set a bookmark!

Keeping It Simple: Internet Activity Assignments

Exploring the links at these central sites will immediately give you ideas for Internet Activities designed to increase multicultural understanding. Some teachers develop Internet Activities related to multicultural issues as students study a unit on this theme in class. Other teachers like to have a weekly Internet Activity devoted to increasing multicultural understanding as a regular part of their curriculum, each week exploring a different cultural experience on the Internet and then discussing this experience during Internet Workshop.

When you find a location you wish to include in your instructional program, simply set a bookmark for it, develop a brief activity based on the information at that location, and then have your students complete this activity during the week. You may want to develop several activities for your students to explore during the week instead of just one.

When you are trying to increase multicultural understanding with Internet Activities, it is also important to keep two additional ideas in mind. First, try to provide opportunities for students to work together on these assignments. When two students work on an Internet Activity together, opportunities develop for important exchanges to take place about these issues. This almost always leads to conversations that

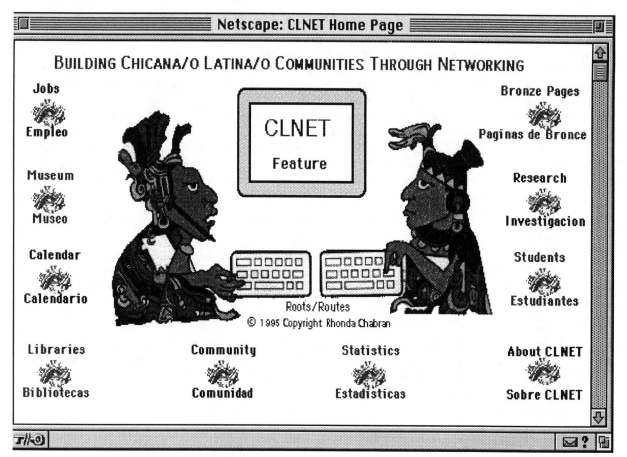

Figure 10-1.   The home page for CLNET (http://clnet.ucr.edu/)

are important to developing greater respect and sensitivity about other cultures, especially if you establish this value in your classroom. Second, provide an opportunity to share students' thoughts and responses after they complete their activity, perhaps during Internet Workshop. This allows you to support the respect and sensitivity about other cultures that you are trying to develop.

Here are some examples of Internet Activities that might be used to support greater multicultural understanding:

Mancala—(http://imagiware.com/mancala.cgi)

This strategy game from Africa is often found in classrooms. Here it is in a virtual form. A great site for your students to play this game against the computer as you study African or African-American cultural traditions. It contains clear directions and the program will even give you hints if your game is not going very well. Set this site up as an Internet Activity during Kwanzaa. Make a bookmark!

Kid's Window—(http://kiku.stanford.edu:80/KIDS/kids_home.html)

There are enough activities on Japan at this site to design Internet Activities for an entire unit. Audio is included throughout this site. It is probably most appropriate for students in grades 1–4. Invite students to read one of several classic Japanese folk tales such as Momotaro or listen to it read aloud in Japanese or English. Have students order lunch and then write what they ordered in both English and Japanese. Have students attend language class in Hiragana, Kanji, or Katakana and then teach one other student in class a few words in Japanese. Have students finish up by following the directions to make an origami crane. Set a bookmark!

E-Mail for You

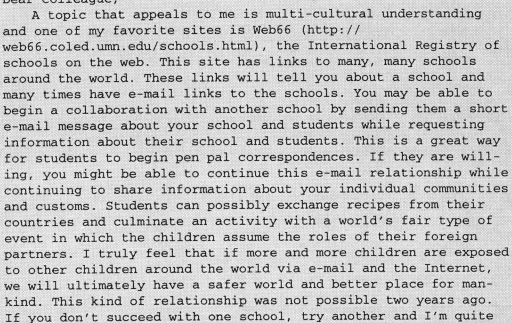

```
From: Bill Farrell < farrellb@ride.ri.net >
      <xyz101@uriacc.uri.edu
Subject: Multicultural Understanding


Dear Colleague,
     A topic that appeals to me is multi-cultural understanding
and one of my favorite sites is Web66 (http://
web66.coled.umn.edu/schools.html), the International Registry of
schools on the web. This site has links to many, many schools
around the world. These links will tell you about a school and
many times have e-mail links to the schools. You may be able to
begin a collaboration with another school by sending them a short
e-mail message about your school and students while requesting
information about their school and students. This is a great way
for students to begin pen pal correspondences. If they are will-
ing, you might be able to continue this e-mail relationship while
continuing to share information about your individual communities
and customs. Students can possibly exchange recipes from their
countries and culminate an activity with a world's fair type of
event in which the children assume the roles of their foreign
partners. I truly feel that if more and more children are exposed
to other children around the world via e-mail and the Internet,
we will ultimately have a safer world and better place for man-
kind. This kind of relationship was not possible two years ago.
If you don't succeed with one school, try another and I'm quite
sure you'll find a school that is more than willing to collabo-
rate on a project with you. I wish you good luck on your Internet
odyssey and hope to run across your school someday on the infor-
mation superhighway.


Bill Farrell
Computer Literacy Teacher
Chariho Middle School


*****************************************
William L. Farrell
Computer Specialist, Grades 5-8
Chariho Regional Middle School
455B Switch Road
Wood River Jct, RI USA 02894
401 364-0651
e-mail: xyz101@uriacc.uri.edu
http://www.chariho.k12.ri.us/cms.html
*****************************************
```

Martin Luther King Jr.—(http://www.seattletimes.com/mlk/index.html)

An outstanding site designed for teachers and students to reflect on the legacy of this famous American. (See Figure 10-2) It includes an interactive timeline of his life and contributions, audio clips of important speeches, reflections on his life from many individuals, a photo tour of the civil rights movement, information about the national holiday in the U.S., classroom ideas, and opportunities to communicate with others about the significance of King's accomplishments. A must for celebrating his life with many resources for Internet Activities. Set a bookmark!

Miracle: The White Buffalo—(http://www.bossnt.com/page16.html)

In 1994, a white buffalo calf was born in Wisconsin, a sign to many Native Americans of great significance. This location chronicles the story of this significant event and the meaning it holds for many Native American cultures. Have your students read the newspaper articles at this location to observe the way in which these are written. Then, have students use the information to write their own newspaper article of this event and its meaning.

Kwanzaa Information Center—(http://www.melanet.com/melanet/kwanzaa/kwanzaa.html)

Kwanzaa is the African-American spiritual holiday initiated by Dr. Maulana Ron Karenga in 1966. Today it is celebrated in an increasing number of homes. This location provides a rich set of information resources about this holiday, how it is celebrated, and what the various symbols mean. Have your students read the information at this site and prepare a short report on this holiday to be shared during Internet Workshop.

Maya/Aztec/Inca Center—(http://www.realtime.net/maya/)

A rich site with many resources designed to help students recognize the many accomplishments in history, geography, geology, astronomy, archaeology, anthropology, and art that existed in the Americas before Christopher Columbus's arrival. Have your students explore these pages and bring one important cultural achievement to share and explain during Internet Workshop. Use this time to discuss the rich heritage that existed in the Americas before its discovery by Europe.

Internet Projects

Internet Projects are, perhaps, the best method to develop multicultural understanding among your students. When your students communicate with students from another cultural context, many important insights are shared about how we are all alike and how we are different. Children have a special way of cutting right through social trappings to share essential information with one another. Their queries, which sometimes might be perceived as offensive to an adult, are often appreciated for what they are by other children—an honest attempt to understand the world around them. Guiding children into these new types of cultural interchanges on the Internet can do much to increase your students' appreciation for cultural differences. It is a wonderful way to celebrate diversity in your classroom.

Visit some of the traditional sites for Internet Projects and seek out projects with classes from different cultural contexts. These locations include:

- **The Global SchoolNet Projects Registry**—(http://www.gsn.org/gsn/proj/index.html)
- **The Global School House: The Connected Classroom**—(http://www.gsh.org/class/default.htm)
- **KIDPROJ**—(http://www.kidlink.org:80/KIDPROJ/)
- **NickNack's Telecollaborative Learning Page**—(http://www1.minn.net:80/~schubert/NickNacks.html#anchor100100).
- **Classroom Connect's Teacher Contact Database**—(http://www.classroom.net/contact/)

Sometimes it takes a special effort to contact classrooms from other cultural contexts. You may have to initiate contact directly with teachers and schools. We encourage you to do so. Not every teacher or

Figure 10-2.   The home page for Martin Luther King Jr. at the Seattle Times
(http://www.seattletimes.com/mlk/index.html)

school will respond to your requests but enough will respond to make this a valuable strategy. Locations that enable you to do this include:

Intercultural E-mail Classroom Connections—(http://www.stolaf.edu/network/iecc/)

This exceptional service is provided by St. Olaf College in Minnesota to bring together schools from all over the world. Your school can take part in a variety of e-mail exchanges and classroom collaborations.

Kid News: Kid Talk—(http://www.vsa.cape.com/~powens/kidtools.html)

A wonderful bulletin board with postings from students around the world. There is also a keypals program with screened messages. You may wish to develop a project around individual keypals in different countries using the resources at this site.

International WWW Schools Registry—(http://web66.coled.umn.edu/schools.html)

Visit this site and travel around the world to visit the home pages of schools in Australia, Japan, Canada, the U.S., Europe, and many other locations. Contact some of the schools to see if they are interested in an Internet Project with your class.

Examples of projects you may wish to consider joining or developing to increase multicultural understanding include:

- **Who Are Our Heroes?** Invite other classes to participate in a heroes project. Each student in classes from different cultural contexts writes a description of their hero, explaining what it is about this person that makes them admirable. Classes then exchange these essays in order to understand who children in different cultural contexts admire. Then, provide an opportunity for students to ask questions of one another about their essays, especially information that may relate to their culture. These essays and conversations provide an ideal opportunity to discover important aspects of different cultures. This project could be extended to include heroes in different categories: parent/guardian heroes, teacher heroes, sports, heroes, etc.

- **Weekly News from Around the World.** Invite classes from around the world to contribute two or three news articles each week from their classroom about local events. Have one class collect these articles via e-mail and distribute a weekly world newspaper to each of the participating classes. Writing about local events for students in another cultural context forces students to develop greater sensitivity to the needs of their readers from different cultural contexts. Reading about these events develops a better understanding of the cultural context in different parts of the world.

- **Explanatory Myths from Around the World.** Every culture contains a set of explanatory myths that explain the creation of natural elements—why the sun comes up each day, where fire came from, how a mountain or lake was created, or where the face in the moon comes from. Invite schools from different cultural contexts to research, write, and share these stories with students from different cultural contexts. Read these stories in your classroom and discuss what each may say about the culture from which it came.

- **KeyPals.** During the course of the year, help your students to develop keypals with several classes around the world. Share these individual messages during Internet Workshop and discuss what each suggests about its cultural context. You may wish to visit **Intercultural E-mail Classroom Connections** (http://www.stolaf.edu/network/iecc/) or **International WWW Schools Registry** (http://web66.coled.umn.edu/schools.html) to make contact with classes who wish to participate.

Internet Inquiry

Using Internet Inquiry strategies to develop multicultural understanding can be especially powerful. Individual students often have an interest in a particular cultural context, either their own or one with which they have a special connection. Supporting students' interests through Internet Inquiry can be an effective approach since it usually combines learning across several different subject areas about questions that are personally significant.

There are several ideas to keep in mind as you pursue Internet Inquiry in this area. First, where appropriate, encourage your students to work in groups. When students work in groups, they often share new insights, interpretations, and resources. This leads to important new directions as students pursue related questions. With support, these groups may also be able to conduct their own regular Internet Workshop sessions focusing on the topic of their Internet Inquiry. If you can accomplish this, you and your students will have established an important vehicle for learning about multicultural understanding.

Second, encourage your students to develop KeyPals with other students from the cultural context they are exploring. This will be an important source of information for your students. Discussing common issues that matter with someone from another cultural context is the best way to understand that context. Encourage your students to share these exchanges with their group and the rest of the class.

Finally, be certain to have students share their multicultural learning within the structure of Internet Workshop on a regular basis. When many students share their new insights and their questions about a variety of cultural contexts, everyone gains new insights about the diversity that exists in this world. Moreover, discussing these matters in the open helps to remove stereotypes and sends your students a powerful message about the respect we should accord each culture.

Instructional Resources on the Internet

China the Beautiful—(http://www.chinapage.com/china.html)

Here is a location with all things beautiful from China. Visit the China Room and learn about calligraphy, view many beautiful paintings, read a timeline of emperors, read classic poetry, and travel to museums around the world with Chinese exhibits. This location also has special software for viewing the Internet in Chinese.

Native Web—(http://www.maxwell.syr.edu/nativeweb/)

This is a nice location for resources on Native cultures. It contains many useful links to a variety of Native American resources, including information about tribal units, literature, newsletters, and journals.

The Amish, the Mennonites, and the Plain People—(http://padutch.welcome.com/amish.html)

This location contains information about the Amish and related cultures, including photographs, an extended explanation of the origins and nature of these traditional communities, and an excellent site where you may ask a question about the Amish as well as read answers to previous questions.

Native American Indian Resources—(http://indy4.fdl.cc.mn.us/~isk/mainmenu.html)

One of the richest locations on the Internet for the Native American community. Information about Native history, literature, biographies, herbal knowledge, environmental concerns, schools, politics—you name it. Set a bookmark!

Africa Online: Kids Only—(http://www.africaonline.com/AfricaOnline/kidsonly.html)

A nice location for your students to learn about Africa. They can read Rainbow Magazine—a Kenyan magazine for kids, play African games and decode messages, learn about the over 1,000 languages in Africa, meet African students on-line, find a keypal, or visit the home pages of schools in Africa. Set a bookmark!

Jewish Culture and History—(http://www.igc.apc.org/ddickerson/judaica.html)

One of the more extensive sites on the Internet on Jewish culture with many links to other locations, including links to Virtual Jerusalem and the Tour of Israel.

Japan Links: Japanese Language and Culture—(http://www.aiai.ed.ac.uk/~timd/japanlinks.html)

This location holds an extensive set of links to all things Japanese. Included are links to Japanese newspapers in English, tours of cities in Japan, links to Japanese language pages, Hiroshima and Nagasaki links, and many more. Enjoy your stay!

Tales of Wonder: Folk and Fairy Tales from Around the World—(http://www.ece.ucdavis.edu/~darsie/tales.html)

This location contains a great collection of stories organized around different cultural traditions: Russia, Siberia, Central Asia, China, Japan, The Middle East, and other locations. As you explore different cultures in social studies, or other areas of your curriculum, have students read and respond to selections from that culture. You may wish to have your students make comparisons between several different selections or look for clues to a culture from the information in a story.

Multicultural Book Review Homepage—(http://www.isomedia.com/homes/jmele/homepage.html)

Are you looking for great literature selections to use in your classroom for multicultural issues? Here it is. This location contains reviews of multicultural literature for kids. One book is featured each month. Set a bookmark!

Listservs/Mailing Lists for Increasing Multicultural Understanding

CULTUR-L (listserv@vm.temple.edu)

A discussion group on cultural differences in the curriculum.

MULTC-ED (listserv@umdd.umd.edu)

A discussion group on multicultural education, K–12.

NAT-EDU (listserv@indycms.iupui.edu)

A discussion group on K–12 education and Indigenous Peoples.

Multicultural Pavilion E-mail Discussion (Grouphttp://curry.edschool.Virginia.EDU/go/multicultural/issues.html)

This is the WWW location for an active discussion group for the multicultural Pavilion web site.

Chapter 11

Including All Students on the Internet

```
To:   Our readers
From: djleu@sued.syr.edu (Don Leu),
      ddleu@syr.edu (Debbie Leu)
Re:   Insuring Internet Equity Within Classroom Communities
```

Internet equity has become an important issue within the educational community. It is important to provide more equitable access and ensure that we do not leave any members of our society behind. Most of this discussion, though, has focused on how to ensure equal Internet access between schools and school districts. It is also important that we do everything we can to ensure equal Internet access *within* individual classroom communities. This aspect of equity has gone largely unnoticed.

Sometimes, for example, a few students in a classroom become so exited about electronic learning they tend to dominate the use of limited electronic resources, inadvertently excluding others in the process. At other times, students who fall behind in navigational skills at the beginning sometimes fail to take full advantage of their computer time because they are uncertain about how to accomplish tasks and are too embarrassed to ask for assistance. At other times, challenged students do not always fully participate in Internet experiences for any of a number of reasons. This chapter recognizes each of these issues as it seeks ways to ensure equitable Internet access for each child in your class.

Don and Debbie

Ms. Hammermill noticed that a group of her students was excited about what they had just discovered on the Internet. "Cool!" someone said again. Each time someone said "Cool!" a few more students were attracted to the computer to see what was taking place. She was pleased with the enthusiasm her students experienced about learning as they used the Internet. She was also concerned.

"Maya, isn't it your turn at the computer?" Ms. Hammermill asked one of the quieter members of her class. She had noticed that Maya was reluctant to claim her computer time when others, because of their excitement, did not leave the computer according to the classroom schedule. Maya was so shy she missed her computer time several times last week. Ms. Hammermill was determined not to let that happen again. She encouraged the group at the computer to quickly finish their work and allow Maya her full turn on the Internet.

"Can I help Tora when I am done?" asked Maya. Tora was visually impaired and she and Maya usually worked together after Maya had worked alone.

"That would be great," said Ms. Hammermill. "And could you change the font size to 72 like I showed you?" Changing the font to this larger size in Netscape Navigator enabled Tora to read the information on the screen. "And then maybe ask Orlando to translate the Spanish message you two received from the class in Argentina. Have him translate your answer, and type it up, too. I would like to send that out today after school."

A little later, she noticed Maya and Tora working on the Internet Activity she had developed for her class this week using the location for **Monster Math**—(http://www.lifelong.com/CarnivalWorld/MonsterMath/MonMathHP.html). (See Figure 11-1.) She could tell that they were using the speech-to-text plug-in because she could hear each of the story problems being read aloud for them. This helped them to understand the problem better. Tora found it especially useful as she followed along with both the text and the speech.

A little later, she saw Orlando concluding the translation of Maya and Tora's e-mail message to students in Argentina. The three of them were talking back and forth as Orlando was trying to complete the translation. This activity was especially nice since it accomplished several things at once. Of course, Maya and Tora were assisted in getting their message out. In addition, however, it gave Orlando a sense of pride in his ability to speak and write in Spanish. Last year, this was seen as a handicap. After the Internet entered his classroom with opportunities to correspond in Spanish, Orlando's linguistic ability was seen in a very different light. Being fluent in Spanish was now an asset that was much in demand, especially after Ms. Hammermill established connections with several Spanish-speaking classrooms around the world. Finally, working on a translation with Maya and Tora helped Orlando develop a better understanding of English at the same time it helped Maya and Tora develop a better understanding of Spanish. Listening to their conversation as they worked on the translation showed that each student was learning much about each language. It was a wonderful experience to observe.

A little later, Ms. Hammermill noticed Orlando working on the Internet Activity with Monster Math. She noticed how he would listen to the problems in English first and then shift to the Spanish plug-in and listen to the same problem in Spanish before he sat down to solve it. Having a site with text-to-speech plug-ins in both languages was especially helpful to bilingual students like Orlando. She was hoping more sites like this would appear shortly on the Internet.

Lessons from the Classroom

This episode from Ms. Hammermill's classroom illustrates an important lesson for all of us to consider: the sensitive orchestration of classroom environments by an insightful classroom teacher can ensure successful Internet access for all students. Just having a computer connected to the Internet does not guarantee equity of access for each of your students. You must work actively to ensure equity in your classroom.

One element of this active orchestration is being sensitive to times when some students' enthusiasm for their work on the Internet impedes others' access to this important resource. Having a regular schedule for Internet use, as suggested in Chapter 4, provides a certain level of equity in your classroom. In addition, however, you will have to carefully monitor student use, as Ms. Hammermill did, watching for those moments when students become so enthusiastic they lose track of time and prevent access by others.

Figure 11-1. The home page of Monster Math, a location using text-to-speech technology in both Spanish and English
(http://www.lifelong.com/CarnivalWorld/MonsterMath/MonMathHP.html)

Another important element in the active orchestration of equity is to be certain you are aware of ways to accommodate the unique learning needs of each child in your classroom. Adjusting the font size for Tora enabled her to access the world of information available on the Intertet. Previously, she had been limited to large-print books and the use of a special magnifier. The Internet permitted Tora to access an enormous amount of information, simply by enlarging the size of the font on Netscape. Text-to-speech technology also assisted her and other children who might benefit from this feature.

Finally, orchestrating equity in your classroom will mean thinking differently about linguistic diversity. Instead of viewing a non-English native language as a handicap, linguistic diversity suddenly becomes a valuable asset when you think about ways in which to utilize this talent as you communicate with classes around the world. Orlando's ability in Spanish became a special talent that was valued by all members of his class when Ms. Hammermill saw how it could be used effectively in her class. These opportunities gave Orlando a tremendous sense of self-worth as he became a central member of the classroom community. Moreover, Orlando acquired English much more rapidly as he translated messages and served as a conduit for communication with Spanish-speaking communities. While this was taking place, students in his class were also learning many new words in Spanish. Everyone gains when non-native speakers are included in classroom communities by teachers who know how to orchestrate equity.

E-Mail for You

```
From: Anne Nguyen (amnguyen@FREESIDE.SCSD.K12.NY.US)
      ESL Teacher
Subject: Supporting ESL students through e-mail

Hi!
     I'm sure it's obvious, but I had a wonderful experience with
some of my former students recently. I have 2 e-mail addresses—
one through my district that I had not used in 4 weeks because of
the summer holidays. Last week I went to school and checked my
district account. I had about 12 e-mail messages—all from my
students from last year. I pored over each and every one of the
messages and laughed in amazement. I was amazed at what they had
to say. Students seemed more willing to share personal informa-
tion with me in this format and asked readily for advice too.
     These are ESL students and I realized what a good method this
was not only to practice their writing skills, but also reading—
to read the replies they would receive. Those from teachers or
American students would most likely have correct grammar and
spelling—a good model! But I think the best thing is the ease
with which a teacher can touch base with ALL students.
     This experience has cemented an idea I have for my students
next year. I am going to make sure all my students get e-mail
addresses at the beginning of the year and are able to use them
to communicate with each other as well as with me.

     Anne Nguyen (amnguyen@FREESIDE.SCSD.K12.NY.US)
     ESL Teacher
     Syracuse City School District
     Syracuse, NY
```

Orchestrating Equity in Your Classroom

Chapter 4 described several strategies for orchestrating equity within Internet classrooms. Posting a schedule for all students to follow, rotating assigned computer times to avoid regular schedule conflicts, and rotating partners at the computer are all useful strategies. In addition, however, there are several important issues for you to consider. These will require you to make the subtle adjustments in your classroom that happen moment to moment as you seek to individualize learning experiences for each of your students.

Ms. Hammermill experienced one of these issues when she noticed that a group of children at the computer was excited about what they had discovered for the unit on diversity the class was studying. As enthusiastic as they were, Maya was losing important time on the computer because this group had forgotten their obligation to turn the computer over to the next person on the schedule. This is a common event in most classrooms and requires you to periodically monitor the computer schedule you establish for your class, reminding students when it is time to turn the computer over to the next person. You may also wish to bring this concern up during Internet Workshop and remind students why it is important to provide everyone with an equal amount of time on the Internet.

Another issue occurs when individual students fail to develop efficient navigation strategies for Internet use. Falling behind in this area prohibits students from acquiring as much useful information as other students who have become proficient at navigating the Internet. There are several techniques to help you to minimize this problem. First, observe carefully. Pay exceptionally close attention to the navigation strategies students develop or fail to develop as they work on the computer. Second, pair students who have not picked up important strategies with others who have acquired these strategies. Provide opportunities for these students to work together on the Internet. Many useful strategies can be acquired in this manner, but be certain to also provide individual time for students to practice new skills on their own; often, when you pair a proficient navigator with a less proficient one, the former dominates navigational decisions. Third, provide short tutorial sessions for students who are weak in navigation strategies. You may choose either a small group or an individual format. In either case, focus on a central strategy you have noticed that students lack. Finally, be certain to use discussions during Internet Workshop to both evaluate and teach navigation strategies. This is a perfect time to listen to students describe how they use the Internet and, at the same time, support students who have failed to acquire these skills.

It may also be the case that gender differences exist with respect to Internet use. While we have no hard data on this phenomenon, we have noticed that boys will sometimes dominate Internet use in a classroom and that some girls may express less interest in using this resource. You should watch for this in your class to see if it exists. Sometimes, communication experiences on the Internet are especially interesting to girls. You may wish to consider ways to exploit this interest by developing Internet Projects with communication opportunities between members of different classes. This may equalize any gender differences you see in your classroom.

Another issue to consider as you seek to support all students in your class is the unique potential of the Internet for supporting ESL students. Some districts are fortunate enough to have special bilingual programs or ESL programs for students. In addition, the Internet may provide you and your students with a very special opportunity. Just as Ms. Hammermill did, you may seek out opportunities where non-native English speakers can use their skills with their native language to support classroom learning. This reverses traditional attitudes about one's non-English linguistic background, turning it from a handicap into an advantage. Many good things will result from this change in perspective.

A final issue to consider is how to support challenged students in your class who have been formally identified with special learning requirements. In some cases, technology may be able to adapt to these students' needs, as was the situation with Tora in Ms. Hammermill's class. In all cases, there are resources on the Internet to provide useful information about accommodations you can make in your classroom to help each student reach his/her full potential.

Opportunities for ESL Students

The Internet provides several special opportunities for ESL students in your class. You have already seen the one adapted by Ms. Hammermill. Developing Internet Projects with schools who use the same language as an ESL student in your room is a wonderful method for supporting linguistic development. Having an ESL student assist with translations places that student in a valued role within the classroom's activities. If you have your student work with others on the translations, both native and non-native speakers will develop a better understanding of one another's language. To find a school with students who speak the language of ESL students in your class, you may wish to pay a visit to **Web66** (http://web66.coled.umn.edu/) and explore their **International Registry of K12 Schools on the Web** (http://web66.coled.umn.edu/schools.html). (See Figure 11-2.) Locate several possible schools and drop them an e-mail message with a list of projects you would be interested in completing together.

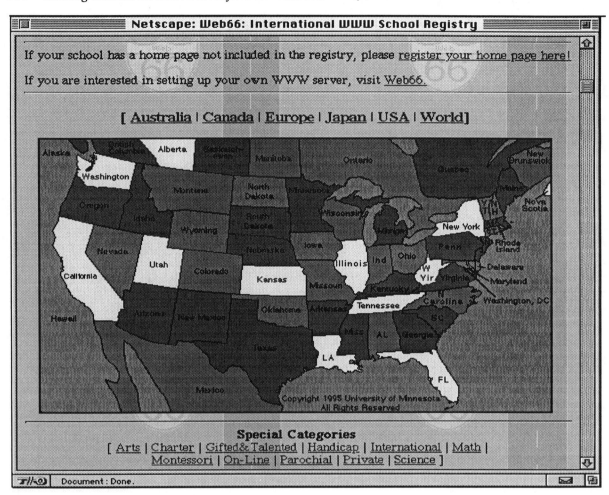

Figure 11-2.   International WWW School Registry: The Location in Web66 to Find Addresses for Schools Around the World (http://web66.coled.umn.edu/schools.html)

If you have an ESL student whose English ability is insufficient for this role, you may wish to try another approach. Pair the student with a native speaker in your class. Give them a regular Internet Activity assignment related to the country or culture from which the ESL student comes. To help you find Internet resources about this country or culture visit **The Virtual Tourist** (http://www.vtourist.com/webmap/) (See Figure 11-3.) and follow the maps to the country you wish to visit. An Internet Activity about the ESL student's country will engage both students in conversation about something familiar to the ESL student. This will motivate both students and make conversation easier for the ESL student. Be certain to include a writing activity as part of the Internet Activity to foster collaborative second language learning between the two students.

You may wish to direct the two students to develop their own Internet Activities. For the first week, for example, you may ask the two students to visit the sites in the student's country of origin and create a list of Internet Activities they want to complete. Then use this list to guide work during subsequent weeks. You might rotate partners every few weeks to allow the ESL student to meet and work with other members of your class. If you conduct Internet Workshop each week, you may wish to have the two students report the results of their assignment to the class. This provides a nice opportunity to support oral as well as written language development.

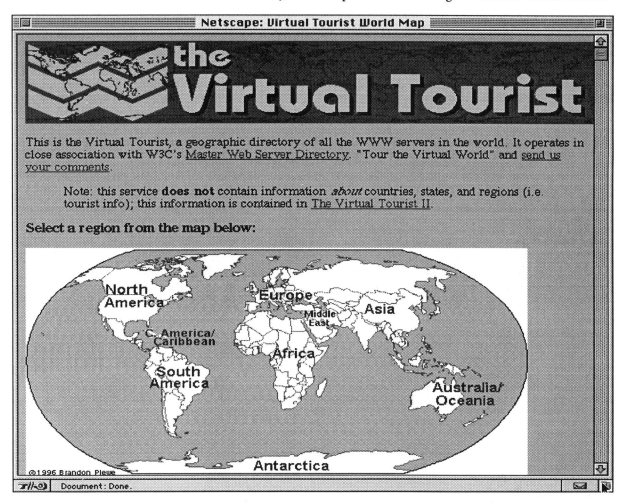

Figure 11-3.   Virtual Tourist, a useful location for finding WWW locations familiar to an ESL student
(http://www.vtourist.com/webmap/))

Other resources you may find useful on the WWW for supporting ESL students in your class include:

Useful Resources, Lesson Plans, and Teaching Materials—(http://www.ling.lancs.ac.uk/staff/visitors/kenji/teacher.htm

A central site with an extensive collection of ESL resources for teachers, including links to many web sites, listservs, journals, lesson plans, some bilingual education sources, and a few sites for students, too. Set a bookmark!

OPPtical Illusion...THEME-BASED PAGES—(http://darkwing.uoregon.edu/~leslieob/themes.html)

A series of links for instructional units and ideas for ESL students. Also a number of cross-cultural sources.

Dave's ESL Cafe—(http://www.pacificnet.net/~sperling/eslcafe.html)

This is a useful site for both teachers and students. It contains an idiom page, a quote page, a self-checking ESL Quiz Center, an ESL Help Center, a graffiti wall, student and teacher links, and an e-mail exchange. Set a bookmark!

Opportunities for Visually Impaired and Hearing Impaired Students

The Internet also provides special opportunities for including visually impaired and hearing impaired students in classroom lessons. For the visually impaired, a common problem is often a dependency on large print texts, texts which do not always coincide with the materials used in the classroom. Alternatively, large and bulky readers are sometimes used. Both are less than ideal solutions for many students.

Netscape and other browsers offer an opportunity to enlarge the print size appearing on the computer screen to nearly any size one wishes. This allows visually impaired children to access a wide range of information that might otherwise be inaccessible to them. To do this in Netscape, select the "Options" item from your menu bar and then select "General Preferences." Within "General Preferences," select the tab for "Fonts." You will see a window similar to Figure 11-4. Select the size you wish to use for both proportional and fixed fonts. You may select any size you wish. Note that one choice is "Other." This allows you to type in sizes larger that 24.

Enlarging the font size for visually impaired students works especially well on web pages that use a lot of text. It works less well at those sites with graphics, because graphics are not enlarged with this approach. In these situations, you may wish to add a control panel (for Macintosh) called CloseView. You may

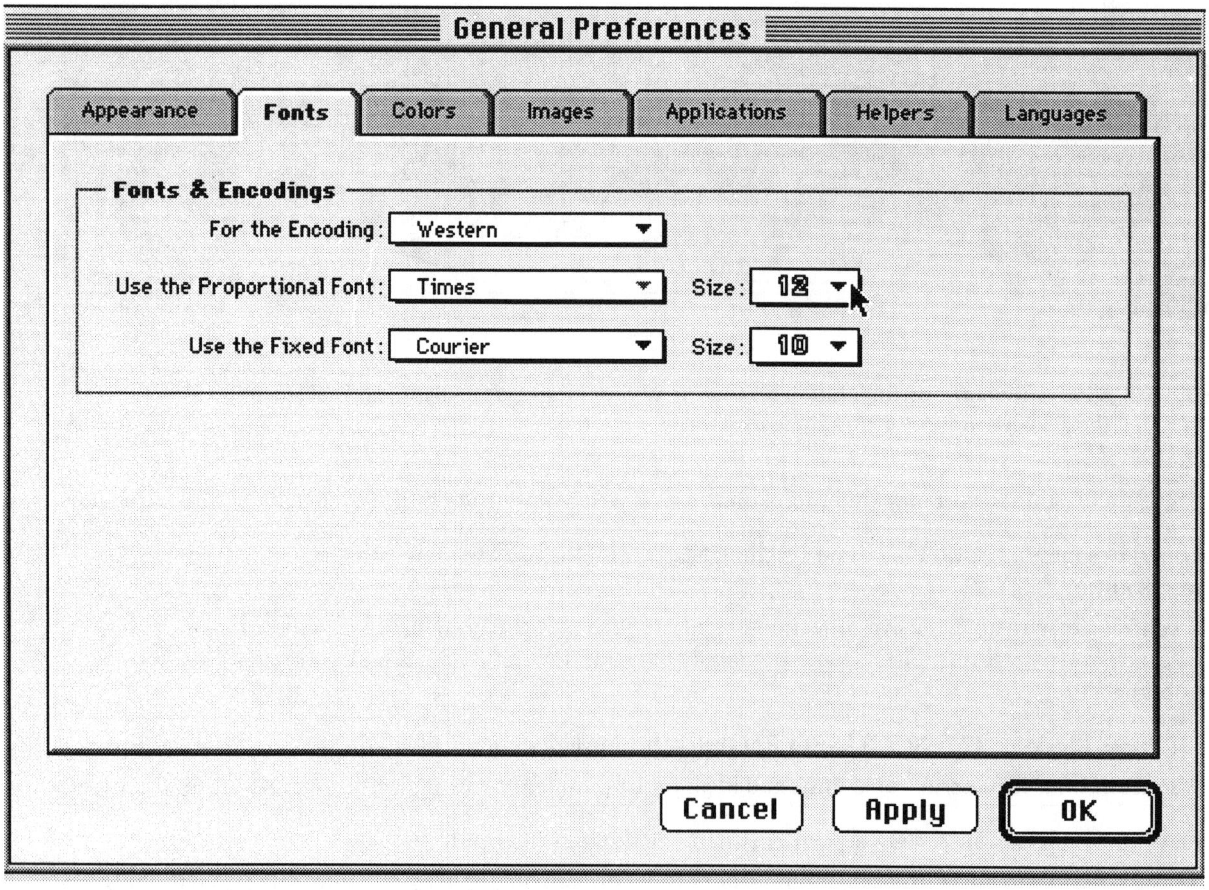

Figure 11-4.   The Fonts folder for Netscape. This is where you may change the size of the font used to display information on the WWW.

download this control panel at **Macintosh Access** (http://www2.apple.com/disability/macaccess.html). CloseView allows you to enlarge everything on your computer screen, not just the text.

A third alternative for visually impaired students is a new technology appearing on the web that converts text to speech on Macintosh computers. One of the more popular plug-ins for Netscape that permits your computer to read web pages is called **Talker** (http://www.mvpsolutions.com/PlugInSite/Talker.html). This location also contains directions for installing this software and an expanding set of links to sites that are designed to use it.

There are also locations on the web to support hearing impaired students. One very useful location is **Deaf CyberKids** (http://deafworldweb.org/dww/kids/), a part of the **Deaf World Web** (http://deafworldweb.org/dww/). This site supports e-mail communication for children who are hearing impaired.

Another location may be useful for all students in your classroom. **A Basic Dictionary of ASL Terms** (http://home.earthlink.net/~masterstek/ASLDict.html) provides an extensive signing dictionary. You may wish to make this site a regular part of your Internet Activities and begin to develop the ability to sign with your hearing students.

Opportunities for Other Students Who Are Challenged

Accommodating Internet experiences for other students in your class who have been formally identified as requiring special assistance does not differ substantially from the types of accommodations you make in other areas of your curriculum. Two ideas, though, may be useful as you seek to provide opportunities for each of your children to learn and grow.

First, our informal observations suggest that the Internet may provide special motivational opportunities for those children who have been less successful in previous academic tasks. We have seen this happen enough times in school classrooms to believe something important is happening. We do not know the reason for this phenomenon. It may be that multimedia resources provide multiple sources of information (graphics, animations, audio, video, etc.) so that students are not just dependent on a single, textual, source for information that has always given them difficulty. It may be that the interactive nature of this environment and the new types of strategic knowledge that are necessary advantage certain types of children over others, children who have not been previously advantaged in non-electronic environments. Or, it may be that the Internet kindles a new spark of interest among students who have lost interest in learning. In either case, it happens often enough that we should think about taking advantage of the phenomenon.

One way to do this is to sometimes share new information about navigation strategies with students who have been less successful in school learning tasks before you share it with others. Then, have these students teach others the new information. This quickly puts students who have been less successful into a privileged position, a position these students seldom experience in classroom learning tasks. The effects of this strategy can sometimes be quite dramatic as less successful students suddenly feel empowered and become more interested in learning. We encourage you to try this strategy.

A second idea is also useful. Spend time exploring sites on the WWW that can provide you with more information about your students who have been formally identified as requiring special assistance. There are many useful ideas for instruction and many other informative resources on the web. Exploring these sites will provide you with important assistance as you seek to include all students in your classroom activities. Sites we have found helpful include:

- **The Global School House Resources for Special Student Populations**—(http://www.gsn.org/gsn/gsn/special.html)
- **SERI: Special Education Resources on the Internet**—(http://www.hood.edu/seri/serihome.htm)
- **Internet Resources for Special Educators**—(http://www.interactive.net/~wader/sped.htm)
- **The Council for Exceptional Children**—(http://www.cec.sped.org/home.htm).

A Few Final Thoughts

As you plan instructional programming for children with special needs in your classroom, we hope you keep two ideas in mind. First, each of your students is, in fact, a child with special needs. Each and every child has unique needs that must be recognized as you make instructional decisions. You must always consider each student's background and abilities as you use the Internet in your classroom. Nothing is more important.

Second, legal and categorical designations used for legal and administrative purposes must never limit your instructional decisions regarding individual children or your expectations for their achievement. The use of labels has brought important benefits to students whose needs have too long been ignored, but we must ensure that those labels do not blind us to the individuality each of us expresses in our daily lives.

Instructional Resources on the Internet

Apple's The Disability Connection—(http://www2.apple.com/disability/disability_home.html)

Here is the location for getting in touch with all kinds of information about adaptive technologies provided by Apple Computer and other companies. This location also includes many free or shareware programs to use with your computer, links to disability related resources on the WWW, and opportunities to communicate with others about disabilities and teaching/learning issues. Set a bookmark!

Autism Resources—(http://web.syr.edu/~jmwobus/autism/)

A site with many links to resources related to autism and Asperger's Syndrome, including links to on-line discussions, mailing lists, news, treatment methods, research, and much more.

Scotter's Low Vision Land—(http://www.community.net/~byndsght/welcome.html)

A site developed by a person with low vision with many links useful to the visually impaired. Wonderfully designed.

Attention Deficit Disorder—(http://www.ns.net/~BrandiV/)

A location developed by an individual in California with much information and many links related to ADD and other learning problems. It contains a wide variety of resources to help you understand more about this condition.

Blindness Resource Center—(http://www.nyise.org/blind.htm)

A great location with extensive information about blindness and resources to inform teachers and assist students.

Family Village—(http://www.familyvillage.wisc.edu/)

One of the most extensive and best designed web sites with disability resources for parents, students, and teachers. This location contains a wealth of resources, including mailing lists for students and parents, information about many specific diagnoses, and much, much more. Set a bookmark!

Deafweb Washington's Kid Page—(http://www.wolfenet.com/~hydronut/kids.htm)

A location for deaf and hearing impaired children to post their stories, poetry, articles, and art.

Orton Dyslexia Society—(http://ods.org/)

The Orton Dyslexia Society (ODS) is an international, non-profit, scientific and educational organization dedicated to the study and treatment of dyslexia. This location provides access to its many resources related to this important learning disability.

Learning Disabilities Association of America—(http://205.164.116.200/LDA/index.html)

The home page for this organization with over 60,000 members. This location provides links and resources for individuals interested in learning more about learning disabilities.

Inclusion Resources—(http://www.hood.edu/seri/serihome.htm#inclusion_resources)

A nice collection of links related to inclusive education. The information at this location can provide useful background information to teachers new to inclusion.

The Family Village Inclusion Resources—(http://www.familyvillage.wisc.edu/edu_incl.htm)

Another nice location to provide resources for teachers interested in inclusive education. Contains links to locations to communicate with others, research, on-line newsletters, and web sites related to inclusion.

Listservs/Mailing Lists for Including all Students on the Internet

DEAFKIDS (listserv@sjuvm.stjohns.edu)

A discussion group for children who are deaf.

CHATBACK (listserv@sjuvm.stjohns.edu)

A discussion group on special education.

SPECED-L (speced-l@uga.cc.uga.edu)

A special education discussion list.

SPEDTECH-L (listproc@ukanaix.cc.ukans.edu)

A discussion group on technology and special education.

TESLK-12 (listserv@cunyvm.cuny.edu)

A discussion group on Teaching English as a Second Language in grades K–12.

Chapter 12
Developing a Home Page for Your Classroom

To: Our readers
From: djleu@sued.syr.edu (Don Leu),
        ddleu@syr.edu (Debbie Leu)

Re: Developing a Home Page Is an Important "Four-For"

   We are nearing the end of our journey together. You have
accomplished much in a short period of time. We hope you have
concluded that the Internet provides a host of benefits for you
and your students. There is one final topic we wanted to share
with you: developing a classroom home page on the WWW. This isn't
that hard to do. Really!
   Learning to develop a home page is what we call a "four-for,"
something that gives you *four* important results *for one* activity.
In a life where time is always a precious commodity, any "four-
for" should be treasured. Why is a home page so important?
   First, developing a home page helps your students. It provides a location for publishing student work and it allows you to
organize links to Internet locations so that your students can
easily access the information you want them to use. Second, developing a home page also helps other students. As you develop
instructional materials and links to information resources, you
can make these available so that others might also use them.
Third, developing a home page enables you to forge a tighter link
between home and school. As more computers enter the home, parents can use your home page to see what is taking place in your
classroom and communicate with you about their children. Finally,
developing a home page helps the teaching profession. As you
develop a home page for your class, it projects an important
image of professionalism to the public-teachers embracing new
technologies and using these in powerful ways to guide students'
learning. We hope you take the time to develop a home page for
your class. It will be useful for your students, other students,
parents, and our profession.

   Don and Debbie

It was 8:35 a.m. in Room 102.

"And I wanted to tell you that I have added a new link on our classroom home page called Virtual Tours. You may wish to visit **Virtual Tours** (http://www.dreamscape.com/frankvad/tours.html) when you are working on your Internet Inquiry projects. There are hundreds of tours of museums, cities, and government locations related to your work." Ms. Caudell was in the middle of the morning announcements to her class before the morning got underway.

"I also wanted to remind you that since this is Friday, you should be certain to write a short message to your parents or guardians about your work this week. Tell them about something special you have done this week. If they have an e-mail address, send it with my e-mail account and remind them to visit our classroom home page on the Internet. You can also type your message on Clarisworks and print it out to take home. I would like to check these before you leave today." Ms. Caudell made this assignment each Friday. She found that these little notes initiated important conversations at home about what was taking place at school and this helped her students.

"We have received three new messages from other schools that visited our home page yesterday. One was very impressed with the wildlife poems we did at the beginning of the year. Also, a student in Germany wanted to know if we could provide her with more information about the Battle of Lexington and Paul Revere's ride. Could you respond to this message, Katherine? You might want to send her a copy of your report. Please use my e-mail account. There was also a message from a teacher in Prince Rupert, Canada telling us how much he liked our home page. I posted a copy of each message on our "E-mail Around the World" board next to the computer. Read these new messages about the great work you are all doing in this class."

At the beginning of the year, Ms. Caudell had taken a workshop on developing a classroom home page on the Internet. She worked her way through **Writing HTML: A Tutorial for Creating WWW Pages** (http://www.mcli.dist.maricopa.edu/tut/index.html) (see Figure 12-1) and talked with others who knew about HTML (Hyper Text Markup Language). HTML is the programming language used on the WWW. She was especially surprised to see how easy it was to develop a home page. Somehow, she had thought that this required many years of experience and a lot of technical training. It only took her two hours in the workshop and then a few more hours on the weekend when she worked through the simple tutorial. As she told her colleagues, "If I can do this, anyone can." She had concluded that all someone needed was a few hours to work through one of many tutorials on the Internet and someone to help her load her home page onto the school's server. The workshop was nice, but not necessary.

Ms. Caudell had scanned in the school picture of her class and set up several sections on the classroom home page. One contained the wildlife poems they did earlier, another contained a set of links to locations on the web she used for Internet Activities, another displayed the research they had done on the Battle of Lexington during the Revolutionary War, and another contained photos and a description of the field trip they recently took to Bunker Hill. She also put her e-mail address on the home page so parents could get in touch with her or send messages to their children when they wanted to surprise them at school. Clicking on this address immediately opened an e-mail message window.

Lessons from the Classroom

The first few minutes in Ms. Caudell's class illustrates several important lessons about developing and using a classroom home page on the Internet. First, it shows that developing a home page is not all that complex if you are willing to spend a few hours working through one of several tutorials on the Internet. These are very easy to follow and take you step-by-step through the process of creating a classroom home page.

This episode also shows how a home page helps to organize Internet resources for classroom instruction. Ms. Caudell used her home page to organize the many links she used in each thematic unit. She simply created a page for each thematic unit during the year and added useful links she used for Internet Activities, Internet Projects, and Internet Inquiry. She saved these pages and updated them each year before she began each thematic unit. Setting up organized sets of links in this fashion also assisted her in

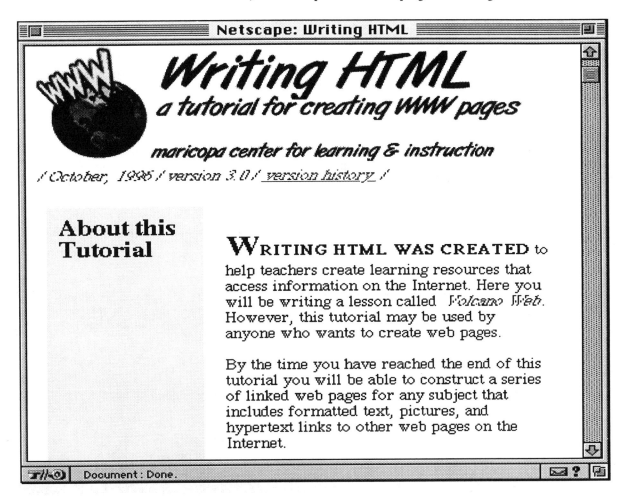

Figure 12-1. The home page of Writing HTML, one of the better tutorials for learning about HTML and creating classroom home pages. (http://www.mcli.dist.maricopa.edu/tut/index.html)

her child safety program. She always previewed the sites she included to be certain they would not lead her students off into areas of the web they should not be exploring.

Third, the episode shows how a home page may be used to publish the work that students complete in a classroom. Ms. Caudell always had a major writing project for each thematic unit. These major projects went through each phase of the writing process. In the final phase, students published their work on the classroom home page so that everyone in the class could read it and so that others around the world might also read it. The most avid readers, Ms. Caudell discovered, were the students themselves and their parents. Several times at the local library, she had found a student showing work to parents on the Internet computer located there. She also knew that parents viewed this work from home in the evening because several parents had left her messages.

Notice also how a home page for your class assists other students, outside your classroom, in their studies. Often, you will develop a thematic unit that other teachers may wish to use. Putting up the links for this thematic unit makes all of these web resources available to other teachers and their students. One of the more powerful aspects of the Internet in school classrooms is that it allows teachers to develop curriculum that is immediately available to others throughout the world. This potential will be exploited with increasing regularity in the future.

Home-school relationships are also strengthened when you develop a classroom home page. While not all families have immediate access to the Internet, this is rapidly changing as increasing numbers of families are coming on-line or using Internet connections in the local library. Having a home page allows your parents to see their children's work and all the fine work you are doing with them in the classroom. It also provides an opportunity for parents and guardians to drop you an e-mail message when they have a question. The Internet provides many new opportunities to work with the families of children in your class.

Finally, a home page for your classroom accomplishes another important goal: it projects an important image of teachers as professionals. Parents who see your classroom home page suddenly become aware of the many wonderful things you do to support their children's development. We are used to many members of the tax-paying public thinking that anybody can teach children. Putting up a home page, displaying your students' work, and inviting parents into your electronic classroom displays the many talents we all have as teachers. This is of central importance when school systems rely upon taxpayers to support their efforts, especially in a period when the teaching profession is sometimes criticized by individuals who are unfamiliar with what we do and what we know.

E-Mail for You

From: Doug Crosby (cherry@digisys.net)
Subject: Using the Internet in First Grade

Greetings!
Spring had finally arrived in Montana after a particularly long and cold winter. It was time to take our first grade field trip; this year we were off to a local biological station.

All year we had been publishing class books using a variety of media, but we wanted to make our field trip report something special. Our school had recently posted a home page on the Internet so we decided to publish our field trip report for all the world to see.

It was kind of a gray day with showers threatening but we had already postponed the trip once so off we went with our digital camera in hand. It turned out to be a wonderful day with a great variety of learning activities taking place. We snapped away with our camera; there were the aquatic insects, the stream, the microscopes, and of course the big log where we all sat to eat lunch!

After returning to school we all sat around the computer to view the photos and within a short time we had come up with a whole class report which was typed directly on the screen. It looked great once we posted it on our web page. We have had a lot of fun reading e-mail from people around the world who have come across our report (http://www.digisys.net/cherry/ Mr.Crosbyfield_trip.htm) and just dropped a note to say well done.

This has been a wonderful experience for my first graders in electronic publishing and a great introduction into the world of their future.

Doug Crosby, First grade teacher   Cherry Valley School
cherry@digisys.net   Polson, Montana
http://www.digisys.net/cherry

Examples of Classroom Home Pages

Before looking at strategies for learning how to develop a classroom home page, it might be useful to view several examples. Doug Crosby's classroom home page shows parents and others what has taken place in his class. (See Figure 12-2.) At the same time, it provides students with an opportunity to publish their work, knowing that people around the world will be able to view it. Projecting the classroom culture like this is important for the students who participate. It tells students that their work is valued as it prepares them for "the world of their future." Doug also has a location on his home pages for parents and others to contact him by e-mail. This enables him to stay more closely in contact with the parents of his students.

Tim Lauer at Buckman Elementary School in Portland, Oregon also publishes students' work on his classroom home page. (See Figure 12-3). What is nice about these publications is that they are often on issues and topics that other classrooms might also find useful in their own work. They include topics such as Bus Safety Rules, a Space Alphabet Book, and a timeline of the life and accomplishments of Martin Luther King, Jr. By posting this work, he invites other teachers to use these resources. This site is a rich one, sharing many other aspects of their classroom work. It provides a clear picture to parents of the many exciting things taking place in their child's classroom.

Figure 12-2.   One section of the classroom home page created by Doug Crosby describing their field trip.

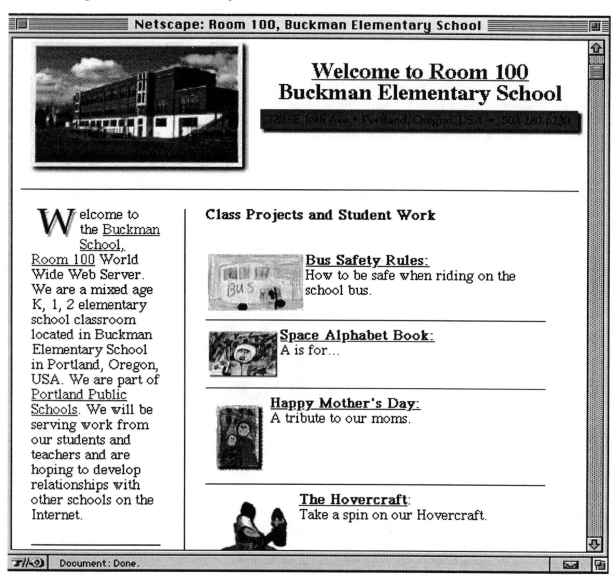

Figure 12-3.   Room 100 at Buckman Elementary School
            (http://buckman.pps.k12.or.us/room100/room100.html)

Mrs. Michaelsen's fourth grade class in Tempe, Arizona also publishes work on their classroom home page. You can see the hyperlinks to some of these publications in Figure 12-4. Mrs. Michaelsen also has her students write contributions to her classroom newspaper, *The Cobra Star News*. Reading these news contributions provides parents and others who visit the page with a wonderful look into what is taking place in this classroom. It also shares student opinions about issues important to this great group of fourth graders.

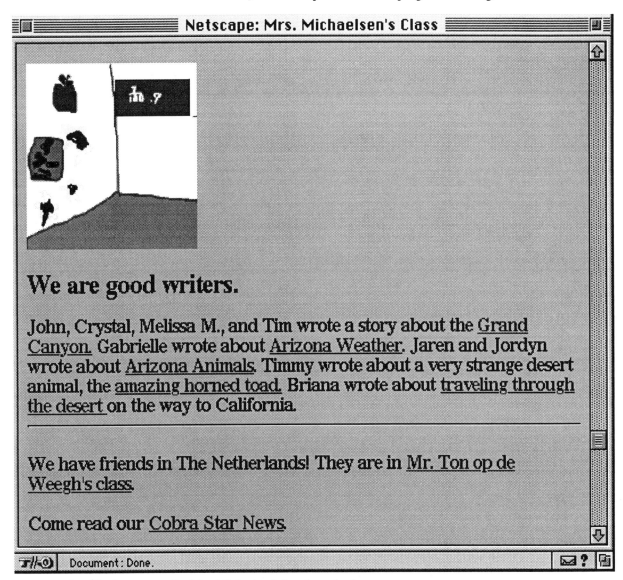

Figure 12-4.   The home page for Mrs. Michaelsen's fourth grade class
(http://seamonkey.ed.usa.ed/~hixson/jan/)

Learning How to Develop Your Own Classroom Home Page

Developing a home page may seem intimidating. After all, you need to use a programming language. Fortunately, though, this programming language is easy to learn. Moreover, there are a number of software tools that will automatically convert what you type into the programming language used on the web. So, all you really need to know is how to type with a word processor. If you also know how to copy and paste graphics, that is an added bonus.

The programming language used most often to design home pages on the WWW is called HTML, HyperText Mark-up Language. It looks like Figure 12-5.

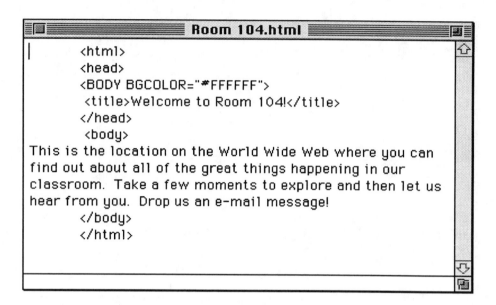

Figure 12-5.   An example of HTML (HyperText Mark-up Language)

When a browser such as Netscape reads a file in HTML, it converts it into what you see on your computer screen. So, if a browser read the HTML file in Figure 12-5, it would appear as in Figure 12-6. This is what happens each time you view a page on the WWW; your browser reads a file written in HTML and converts it into what you see on your computer screen. To demonstrate this, all you have to do is to open up any page on the WWW with your browser. Then, in the menu item called "View," select the item "document source." This will open up the HTML file used to create the page you were just viewing. You will see HTML code similar to what you find in Figure 12-5.

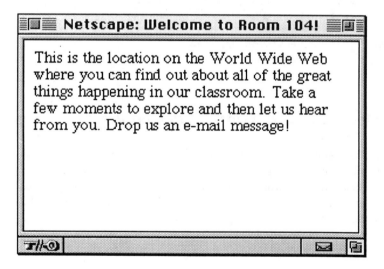

Figure 12-6.   What the information in Figure 12-5 looks like when it is read by a web browser such as Netscape.

There are two strategies for developing a classroom home page in HTML. One way is to obtain an HTML editor. This will allow you to develop your page using a regular word processor and then convert the pages that you type into HTML code. Thus, all you do is type up the page until it looks the way you wish it to appear, then select a converter program to convert your regular page into HTML. There are several fine programs that enable you to do this. You should begin by seeing if the word processor that you use has an HTML conversion program to go with it. Microsoft Word, for example, has an attachment called Word Internet Assistant that may be obtained for free (206-882-8080). Others are also available for free or for a nominal charge. Separate HTML editors, such as Adobe's PageMill (415-961-4400) or Rick Giles's HTML Editor (rick.giles@acadiau.ca) are also available. You may also wish to see if one of these programs is supported by your district. Perhaps copies are already available for teachers in your district to use.

A second approach for developing a classroom home page is to spend a little time going through one of several fine tutorials that exist on the Internet. These take you step-by-step through everything you need to know to develop a classroom home page. Most of these tutorials allow you to write information in HTML and then see immediately how it will look when someone accesses your page with a browser. They are very easy to follow and get you immediately into the world of HTML without assuming any prior knowledge. The best tutorial for teachers we have found is **Writing HTML: A Tutorial for Creating WWW Pages** (http://www.mcli.dist.maricopa.edu/tut/index.html). Others also exist, including:

- **A Beginner's Guide to HTML** (http://www.ncsa.uiuc.edu/General/Internet/WWW/ HTMLPrimer.html)
- **Introduction to HTML** (http://www.cwru.edu/help/introHTML/toc.html)
- **Web66: Classroom Internet Server Cookbook** (http://web66.coled.umn.edu/Cookbook/ contents.html)
- **Setting Up A Web Site For Your School: An On-Line Presentation** (http://www.fred.net/nhhs/ html2/present.htm)

If you decide to use an HTML editor, we still encourage you to work your way through one of these fine tutorials. Understanding the language of HTML will enable you to easily spot problems in your HTML code should these ever arise. It also permits you to individually modify elements in your home page in a way that might not be possible with an HTML editor.

Which Elements Should I Include in My Classroom Home Page?

The design elements you include in your classroom home page will inevitably reflect your teaching style and the culture of your classroom. You may, however, wish to consider elements such as a location where parents and others viewing your pages can send you and your class an e-mail message, a location where students may publish their work, a location where due dates for major assignments are posted, a location for organizing links to sites in various thematic units, and a location where students can publish a newspaper of classroom events and opinions.

It is important to think of your home page as a window through which the rest of the world may see your class. Part of this will involve providing an opportunity for others to communicate with you and your students. This is easily done on a home page. You can quickly make a link that will open up an e-mail message window containing your address. This makes it easy for parents and others to get in touch with you and your students.

You should also consider using your home page as a location where students may publish their work. This allows others to see what you are doing. It also makes material and information available for others to read and enjoy. Stories, poetry, descriptions of classroom events, responses to literature . . . . your home page will provide countless opportunities to allow your students to show off their best writing and art.

You might also wish to have a bulletin board listing due dates for major classroom assignments. Often, parents appreciate knowing when assignments are due. This is especially important in the older grades.

Another important function for your home page may be to organize links on the WWW for the various thematic units you cover during the year. You can save students much time by placing these at a single location where they are easy to access.

Finally, think about including a student newspaper in your home page. This can be a wonderful source of many writing activities. You may wish to appoint an editor for each two-week period and make that person responsible for soliciting articles and seeing that they are revised and edited to meet the standards of your home page. These provide students, parents, and others with a real understanding of all the great things that take place in your classroom.

E-Mail for You

```
From:     Mary Lou Balcom (mlbalcom@AOL.com)
Subject: Classroom Home Pages and Internet Use


    I've been exploring the WWW for a year and still feel awe-
struck by the wealth of information available. My classroom is
not currently wired for Internet access, so my journeys have been
at home. The WWW has provided me with current information on
topics I teach, actual lesson plans that I have used, great ideas
to try in my classroom and lots of interesting sites that don't
really relate to my curricula. As I think ahead to my eventual
use of the WWW, I am excited by the avenues that will be open to
my students. I feel that I will play the role of a facilitator as
I guide and structure my students' use of the WWW.

    I share the concerns of many colleagues regarding both the
appropriate use and optimal use of the WWW. I plan to include my
students in the development of appropriate use guidelines for the
WWW the same way that I have typically developed classroom rules.
My experience with class rules has been that students tradition-
ally include the basics that most teachers would incorporate, and
I think I could guide the process for Internet access in the same
fashion.

    My biggest concern is that students may waste the precious
little time they have access to the computer on pointless
meanderings around the WWW. One of the ways to avoid this is to
initially give very structured assignments to ensure that stu-
dents will have successful and meaningful experiences. It is also
beneficial to design your own home page that organizes the topics
you are studying. I recently took a class to learn how to design
a home page. At first I was overwhelmed by the process, but by
the end of the week had made a very simple page based on our
study of ancient Egypt. I would expect the page to evolve as my
students study Egypt and I would update the page. The page could
change to reflect the current topic of study.

    I think I'm ready to take on the challenge of using the WWW
in my classroom to enhance my students' learning. Now if I could
just get connected!


Mary Lou Balcom, Sixth grade teacher    Edward Smith Elementary School
mlbalcom@AOL.com                        Syracuse, NY
```

The End of Your Journey

No, this isn't the end of your journey. It is just the beginning as you discover new resources on the web, new friends around the world, and new sources of inspiration for the important work you do with the children in your classroom. We are firmly convinced that the world awaiting our students is one in which each of them has more potential to grow and to learn. We also believe that your role in this will be central to their success, especially with these new technologies. As we indicated in the first chapter, Internet resources will increase, not decrease, the central role you play in orchestrating learning experiences for your students. Each of us will be challenged to thoughtfully guide students' learning within information environments that are richer and more complex, presenting richer and more complex learning opportunities for both us and our students. We hope you have found the ideas we have to share useful in the important work you do to prepare children for their tomorrows. Best wishes!

Instructional Resources on the Internet

ColorCenter—(http://www.hidaho.com/colorcenter/)

Are you looking for a special color or background for your classroom home page? Here is the place. You can try out different text, color, and backgrounds by moving through the palette located here. A great resource. Set a bookmark!

Guides to HTML—(http://union.ncsa.uiuc.edu:80/HyperNews/get/www/html/guides.html)

A useful central site but only if you have some familiarity with HTML. An extensive set of resources.

How Do They Do That With HTML?—(http://www.nashville.net/~carl/htmlguide/)

Have you ever seen a great web page and wondered how they were able to use a special background pattern, animations, background sounds, or other tricks? Here is the page that explains everything and shows you how to include these and many other useful features in your classroom home page. Set a bookmark!

HTML Crash Course for Educators—(http://edweb.cnidr.org:90/htmlintro.html)

This is just what it says it is. A good place to begin your work and try out HTML programming.

Internet in the Classroom Tutorial—(http://www.indirect.com/www/dhixson/class.html)

See the section "Design and Post Your Classroom Home Page." This is a great place with useful ideas.

Resources for Icons, Images, and Graphics—(http://socsci.colorado.edu/~brumbaug/graphics.html)

Another nice location to obtain great visual elements for your classroom home page.

The Animated GIFs Library—(http://www.arosnet.se/agl/)

Once you have mastered the art of web page creation, you may want to include some animations to make your page really sing. Here is a place where you can get those animations.

The Art of HTML—(http://www.taoh.com/)

A very rich site designed to support individuals who are creating home pages on the WWW. Support ranges from information and resources for the very beginner to the very expert. One of the more comprehensive locations for information on designing home pages.

The Backgrounds Archive—(http://the-tech.mit.edu/KPT/bgs.html)

A great collection of visually appealing backgrounds for use on your classroom home page.

Web / HTML / Reference—(http://www.webreference.com/html/tutorials.html)

Here is a central site with links to an extensive set of tutorials and other resources for developing your own home page. One of the better collections on the web. Set a bookmark!

webreference.com—(http://www.webreference.com/)

This is a great site to learn about creating web sites. Information ranges from the very beginner to the expert.

Web66—(http://web66.coled.umn.edu/)

This is one of the best general sources of information and tools for developing a classroom home page. The section on technology contains step-by-step instructions for setting up a WWW server, HTML templates you may wish to copy for your use, and much more. Set a bookmark!

Listservs/Mailing Lists for Developing a Classroom Home Page

WEB66—(WebMaster@web66.coled.umn.edu)

A discussion group for teachers preparing web pages in schools.

About the Authors

Donald J. Leu, Jr. and Deborah Diadiun Leu first began teaching in the Peace Corps where they worked as elementary classroom teachers of English as a Second Language (ESL) in the Marshall Islands of Micronesia. Since then, both have worked to support language and literacy learning among many different populations using a wide variety of electronic media. Deborah has taught many types of ESL learners from engineers at the Bechtel Corporation in San Francisco to her current position where she teaches students in the English Language Institute at Syracuse University. She received her Masters degree from Syracuse University in Linguistics and English as a Second Language. Don worked as a classroom teacher and a reading specialist in California. He is currently Professor in the School of Education at Syracuse University and author of numerous books, articles, and software devoted to supporting teachers in literacy education and electronic learning environments. He received his Ed.M from Harvard and his Ph.D. in Language and Literacy from the University of California, Berkeley. Deborah enjoys her perenial flower garden while Don enjoys fly fishing. They both enjoy spending time together with their two daughters.

$\mathcal{I}$ndex

Text that appears in bold, are WWW sites.